RH

Susan Zaeske

University of Wisconsin
Department of Communication Arts
Vilas Communication Hall
821 University Avenue
Madison, Wisconsin 53706

THE
PROSPECT
OF
RHETORIC

CONTRIBUTORS

Karl R. Wallace
Samuel L. Becker
Richard McKeon
Lawrence W. Rosenfield
Henry W. Johnstone, Jr.
Wayne C. Booth
Chaim Perelman
Wayne Brockriede
Hugh Dalziel Duncan
Barnet Baskerville
Edward P.J. Corbett

Donald C. Bryant
Carroll C. Arnold
Lloyd F. Bitzer

Editors

LLOYD F. BITZER
EDWIN BLACK

University of Wisconsin

THE
PROSPECT
OF
RHETORIC

Report
of the National
Developmental Project

SPONSORED BY

*Speech
Communication
Association*

Prentice-Hall, Inc., Englewood Cliffs, New Jersey

PRENTICE-HALL SPEECH COMMUNICATION SERIES
Larry L. Barker
Robert J. Kibler
series editors

Library of Congress Catalog Card Number: 79-159415

Printed in the United States of America

13-731331-4

Current Printing (last digit):

10 9 8 7 6 5 4 3 2 1

PRENTICE-HALL INTERNATIONAL, INC., London
PRENTICE-HALL OF AUSTRALIA, PTY. LTD., Sydney
PRENTICE-HALL OF CANADA, LTD., Toronto
PRENTICE-HALL OF INDIA PRIVATE LIMITED, New Delhi
PRENTICE-HALL OF JAPAN, INC., Tokyo

FOREWORD

The essays, reports, and recommendations comprising this volume were prepared by some forty scholars involved in The National Developmental Project on Rhetoric. The Project was originated and sponsored by The Speech Communication Association (formerly The Speech Association of America) and was supported by a grant from the National Endowment for the Humanities. Additional support was provided by the Johnson Foundation, Racine, Wisconsin, and by the University of Wisconsin. The central objective of the Project was to outline and amplify a theory of rhetoric suitable to twentieth-century concepts and needs. At the Project's two major conferences, scholars from several fields considered rhetoric's past and future, identified the problems in contemporary life which require application of rhetorical concepts and methods, and recommended lines of research and educational programs needed to bring an effective rhetoric into relation to current and future needs.

WINGSPREAD CONFERENCE

The Wingspread Conference, the first of the Project's two meetings, was held January 25–27, 1970, at the Johnson Foundation's Wingspread Conference Center at Racine, Wisconsin. Twelve scholars were invited to prepare a major essay and take part in the conference. Half were asked to prepare position papers in response to the following: "What is the essential outline of a conception of rhetoric useful in the second half of the twentieth century? Further, amplify a portion of that outline." The others were asked to write critical essays in response to the position papers. The objective was to obtain well-conceived, stimulating essays on the future of rhetorical studies from able scholars in several academic disciplines. The essays were to serve both as background materials for the Wingspread Conference and as addresses to the academic world at large.

The position papers, Part One of this volume, were written by Samuel Becker, communication scientist, University of Iowa; Henry Johnstone, philosopher, Pennsylvania State University; Richard McKeon, philosopher, University of Chicago; Lawrence Rosenfield, rhetorician, University of Wisconsin; and Karl Wallace, rhetorician, University of Massachusetts. The critical response papers, Part Two, were prepared by Barnet Baskerville, rhetorician, University of Washington; Wayne C. Booth, literary critic, University of Chicago; Wayne Brockriede, rhetorician, University of Colorado; Edward P. J. Corbett, rhetorician and literary critic, Ohio State University; Hugh Duncan, sociologist and literary critic, Southern Illinois University; and Chaim Perelman, philosopher and rhetorician, University of Brussels. One scholar chosen to participate in the conference, David Berlo of Michigan State University, was unable to take part.

These men, who had written and exchanged the essays, met for two days of discussion at the Wingspread Conference Center. Their objective was to identify specific concepts, issues, lines of research, and practices which should receive priority attention by scholars, teachers, and administrators of rhetorical studies. They were asked to produce what was, in the broadest sense, an agenda for the next conference and a summary address to the world of humanistic and social-scientific scholarship. The two reports issued by this conference are presented as the concluding chapter of Part Two.

NATIONAL CONFERENCE ON RHETORIC

The Project's second major meeting, the National Conference on Rhetoric, was held at St. Charles, Illinois, May 10–15, 1970. Attending the meeting were twenty-three scholars selected from a field of nearly one hundred nominees. The general conception of the conference was that the participants, after reading essays and reports from the Wingspread Conference, would seek to refine, amplify, and translate Wingspread ideas into recommendations meeting specific needs and potentialities related to the humanistic study of rhetorical communication.

Participants were assigned to three committees.

Committee on the Advancement and Refinement of Rhetorical Criticism

Thomas O. Sloan (Chairman), University of Illinois
Richard B. Gregg, Pennsylvania State University
Thomas R. Nilsen, University of Washington
Irving J. Rein, Northwestern University
Herbert W. Simons, Temple University
Herman G. Stelzner, University of Massachusetts
Phillip K. Tompkins, Kent State University°
Donald W. Zacharias, University of Texas

°Professor Tompkins was unable to attend because of the tragic events on his campus immediately prior to the conference.

*Committee on the Scope of Rhetoric
and the Place of Rhetorical Studies in Higher Education*

Douglas Ehninger (Chairman), University of Iowa
Thomas W. Benson, University of California, Berkeley
Ernest E. Ettlich, Washington State University
Walter R. Fisher, University of Southern California
Harry P. Kerr, Harvard University
Richard L. Larson, University of Hawaii
Raymond E. Nadeau, Purdue University
Lyndrey A. Niles, Federal City College

Committee on the Nature of Rhetorical Invention

Robert L. Scott (Chairman), University of Minnesota
James R. Andrews, Columbia University
Howard H. Martin, University of Michigan
J. Richard McNally, State University of New York at Albany
William F. Nelson, University of Nebraska
Michael M. Osborn, Memphis State University
Arthur L. Smith, University of California at Los Angeles
Harold Zyskind, State University of New York at Stony Brook

Each committee had two assignments: first, to prepare and report to the whole conference a statement expressing the committee's aspirations for scholarship and practice in its area of concern, including an assessment of present scholarship and practice; second, to prepare and offer for adoption by the full conference specific resolutions—substantive as well as implemental, and addressed to scholars, teachers, administrators, and professional organizations in the field of speech communication and related disciplines—concerning (a) priorities in scholarly research, (b) graduate education for speech communication scholars and specialists in rhetoric, (c) undergraduate education for majors and non-majors, and (d) analysis and resolution of social conflict.

During the first three days of the conference week, the committees met for discussion and composition of reports and recommendations. During the last two days, committees presented their reports and recommendations in parliamentary sessions chaired by J. Jeffery Auer of Indiana University. Reports were received and filed by the conference automatically; but recommendations were moved as matters of formal deliberation. Thus, while the reports of the committees represent the judgment of the separate committees, the recommendations following each report represent the judgment of the conference.

The reports of the committees along with conference recommendations are presented in Part Three, Chapters 16, 17, and 18. On the first day of the conference, addresses were presented by Donald C. Bryant, President of the Speech Communication Association; by Carroll C. Arnold, member of the Rhetoric Project planning committee; and by Lloyd F. Bitzer, chairman of the planning committee. Their addresses comprise Chapters 13, 14, and 15.

ACKNOWLEDGMENTS

Thanks are due the National Endowment for the Humanities which awarded a generous grant (H-69-123) to the Speech Communication Association for the purpose of supporting the National Developmental Project on Rhetoric; to the Johnson Foundation, Racine, Wisconsin, which provided its Wingspread Conference Center as well as lodging and meals for personnel involved in the Wingspread Conference; to the University of Wisconsin which provided released time to the principal investigator and the project editor.

Several persons deserve notice here because of their tireless efforts in behalf of the Project. The members of the Project Planning Committee—Carroll C. Arnold, Pennsylvania State University, James J. Murphy, University of California at Davis, Gerald R. Miller, Michigan State University, William Work, Executive Secretary of the Speech Communication Association, and James E. Roever, Director of Research of the Speech Communication Association—met numerous times over a two-year period to prepare the grant proposal, plan the conferences, and oversee all phases of the Project. In his role as member of the Planning Committee and Director of Research, James Roever made invaluable contributions at every stage. To Donald C. Bryant, University of Iowa, we owe special gratitude—because he supplied the original sketch of a proposal for a national conference on rhetoric, and because as President of the Speech Communication Association during the term of this Project he provided the support of his office and took part in both conferences. Finally, we wish to thank Mary E. Anderson, Madison, Wisconsin, who expertly managed nearly all the secretarial work of the Project.

EDWIN BLACK, *Project Editor*

LLOYD F. BITZER, *Principal Investigator*

CONTENTS

THE
PROSPECT
OF
RHETORIC

PART ONE

WINGSPREAD:
POSITION PAPERS

1 / THE FUNDAMENTALS
OF RHETORIC

KARL R. WALLACE
University of Massachusetts

Whether one looks toward a modern theory of rhetoric or seeks merely to indicate the main lines of development rhetoric should take in the next decades, it is useful to have a working conception of rhetoric as an anchoring point. Rhetoric is, I think, primarily an art of discourse. It is an art because its principles and teachings are directed to two general ends or functions: the making or producing of utterances and the understanding and appraising of them. Rhetoric is, moreover, something more than a methodological art. Its principles reflect men's behavior in their conversing, discussing, and speech-making, when they are in practical settings rather than in specialized or professional ones. The principles and rules of its art refer to, and have relevance for, the subject matter or "content" of everyday discourse. They cover situations where men are acting as social creatures in their families, neighborhoods, communities, and political associations and are not speaking as experts to experts. This concern gives rhetoric its distinctive character among school and college subjects. Rhetoric is also a formal art. It deals with the patterns and structures of ideas men use in their reporting, explaining, arguing, judging, praising, and blaming. Rhetoric, then, appears whenever an individual must communicate, or chooses to communicate, by word, speech, and gesture in his customary dealings with others. The decision of a person to speak and the decision of an "audience" to participate imply that the parties involved believe they are capable of understanding the message and can profit from their engagement.[1]

Yet to think of rhetoric as the art of practical discourse is not to exclude its interest in science, particularly the scientific endeavor that yields the kind of knowledge and information an art finds relevant to its ends and wishes to bring into its corpus by adoption and assimilation. Some of the basic processes in speech and language communication today are investigated empirically under controlled conditions of observation and experiment, as for example, factors that influence speech intelligibility and verbal methods of influencing attitude and belief. The rhetorician must be aware of the linguist's scientific study of language structures, but he will be especially alert to implications for his own examination of rhetorical styles and delivery. The rhetorician must be concerned with the psychologist's study of human nature and personality, but in ways that may illuminate and lead to the study of men as communicators. Because the interests of rhetoric and communication overlap, some rhetoricians and some students of communication in practical situations often associate closely. Some rhetoricians focus their research on a particular aspect of the communication process, and some communication scientists in college and industrial settings teach courses in speechmaking, discussion and conference leadership. Every rhetorician is directly concerned with what goes on when men adjust to one another through their communications; he is concerned too with how communications work and how they can be made to work better.[2]

With a working conception of rhetoric before us, we can consider some of the problems that press upon rhetoricians today. In this paper I want to remark upon the basis for a theory of rhetoric and then concentrate on the subject matter of rhetoric and rhetorical discourse, proceeding later to deal briefly with the ethics and logic of discourse. I shall not try to outline a theory, although contemporary man doubtless needs a modern rhetoric. I simply want to suggest the starting points for theorizing. If these can be put clearly, my later observations should be perceived readily.

The ultimate data of the rhetorician are the speech and language men use when they believe they are communicating with one another. The obvious key concepts here are those of *speech* and its kin term, *speaking*. The first indicates a doing, a substantive act, and implies a temporal event; the second has implications and entailments that scientists often miss. In the history of their use, both words point to the producing of vocal sounds and the shaping of them in ways possible only to the human animal. Some of these events, but not all, are resolved into words. It is with words—the "parts" of speech, or as Caxton said, "the parts of reson"—and their combinations or "forms" that the lexicographer, the grammarian, and the traditional logician study more properly than the rhetorician. *Speech* and *speaking* are more than articulations and structures; they are concepts implying kinds of psychological activities that the Greeks called reasoning, imaging, and remembering. A man, they believed, had auditory images of what he said. These he could hold in his mind. These he could contemplate, divide, compose, and manipulate in ways that a rational animal would, that is, in ways that a discourser would. There were a *logos*, a logic, about this behavior and some rules. Hence *speaking*, for us as well as for the Greeks, consists of linguistic events that accompany or follow internal rational activity.[3]

The word *speech*, furthermore, implies events that are signs, sometimes symbols, of things and events not immediately present to the eyes and ears of speaker and listener. The signs can be used to refer to past and present things and events of mutual interest to communicators; they can be used to talk about, and sometimes to predict, future behavior. They can be used in this way because they are abstracted from objective reality and can be manipulated independently of their referents. Yet for all their apparent autonomy, linguistic signs elicit similar responses from the members of a language community possessing them. The signs, we say, are meaningful, and because they are communication is said to occur. The concept of speech, then, entails the notion of communication.

The raw data of the rhetorician, it is obvious, are men speaking to each other—speakers addressing audiences and audiences responding to speakers. (Written signs are but signs of speech signs.) It is less obvious that speaking and writing can be regarded as a kind of movement or motion. Uttering something or writing something is not the kind of continuous, interminable, submicroscopic motion in which the chemist, physicist, and physiologist are interested; the motion evident in speaking is marked by starts and stops of both physical and mental activity. The phenomena seems to be reducible to units. The units appear to be dominated by their symbolic function, that is, by meaning; indeed the occurrence of a unit and the occurrence of meaning are coterminous. Elsewhere I have called this unit the speech act or, what is the same thing, the unit of meaningful utterance.[4]

To regard what goes on in verbal communication as the linking together, producing, or making of meaningful acts is of great advantage to the rhetorical theorist. He finds that rhetorical acts do not differ essentially from speech acts and that the notion of act provides him with ways of analyzing the operations of rhetorical discourse that do not confine him to the precise quantifiables of laboratory experiment. These ways also encourage him to use the fundamental concepts belonging to the dynamics of the act more accurately and realistically than has been the case in the past century. The concepts are ancient ones as interpreted by modern scholars. They are the notions of end and its cousins, purpose, intent, motive, and goal; the material and substantial basis of action; form, structure, order, place, and position; the concepts of maker or artist, and of thing made or artifact. These concepts can be used to describe the essential features or conditions of an act of verbal communication, though they can be applied as well to any symbolic act in other media. These concepts are correlatives, having little significance without each other. Used together and applied to the verbal and gestural symbols entailed in speech and speaking, their significance is profound. They can help the theorist account for rhetorical action without reducing man to the point of inhumanity.

Such, then, are the basic materials and concepts of the rhetorical theorist. I wish now to consider certain emphases upon which rhetoricians ought to agree.

If men are to understand and use their discourse better, students and teachers of rhetoric in both school and university settings should focus on the materials and substance of popular discourse. There is a subject matter of rhetorical discourse and a theory of rhetoric must recognize it.[5] To continue placing emphasis on the forms, styles, and methods of speaking and writing is to miss the heart and much of the soul of communicating mankind.

A particular art or science is identified primarily by its point of view, purposes, and materials, and secondarily by its forms and methods. What is the point of view, the position, of rhetoric among the arts and sciences? The rhetorician is not looking at things or at experience with the eyes of the physicist, chemist, and biologist; he is not viewing human nature and experience in the way these are seen by the psychologist, sociologist, anthropologist, political scientist, and ethicist. The rhetorician looks at the things and experience that men share in common, at the interests and problems of society in general. He does not look at language behavior in ways that characterize the modern grammarian, phonetician, and semanticist; he is not directly concerned with describing speech and language behavior as such. Rather, he focuses upon that speech and language behavior that reflects the communal experience to which men become subject and to which men appeal in deliberating upon their mutual problems, in coming to decisions mutually acceptable to them, and in appraising their decisions and actions. This is not the focus of any other art or science.

The rhetorician's point of view has largely been lost sight of for the past eighty years. Students and teachers concerned with language have concentrated on the forms of linguistic behavior, its structures and style, and the principles and rules thereof. They have assumed that the child in acquiring speech has learned enough of communal experience or if he has not he will be supplied with the necessary materials of communication by the biological and social sciences. These assumptions are quite in contrast to those taken by scholars and teachers of poetic and dramatic discourse. Their materials are those reflected in comic and tragic experience, or put in another way their subject matter is seen in the imaginative use of experience, foreign to the sciences and practical arts, that only the poet, dramatist, and novelist can manage. The position and subject matter of the literary theorist, historian, and critic have so dominated the teaching of English that educators in the sciences as well as the humanities find it difficult to recognize and comprehend the position of the rhetorician.

The subject matter of popular discourse consists of the materials of experience that men become subject to in their public characters, that is, in the roles they take when they are not experts communicating with experts. The materials are to be found in problematic situations having three characteristics. The problems are of broad social and national concern. They extend beyond narrow parochial gossip and petty local disturbances. Respect for law and order, for example, though claiming prime attention at one moment in Middletown, is national in scope. The problems are not only wide ranging; they are important and significant. Evidence of their significance is their persistence from generation to generation and from century to century. Witness the problems created by the enduring aspirations of minority groups, racial or other. They reflect the ideals of social justice as men see them and apply them in real crises, not as the jurist and the ethicist contemplate them in theory. The general nature of such problems is ever present; it is the specific crisis, the decisions required, and the style of handling them that differ from time to time. The face is always familiar although the make-up is new. Finally, the subjects of rhetorical discourse, because they reflect problematic situations, always present alternative possibilities. Confronted with them, men must weigh and choose unless they run away from their obligation to think and act. Their decisions depend upon materials drawn from the "common subjects of deliberation," as Aristotle truly saw, and on the information, values, definitions, and explanations relevant to them. Even in ancient times the common subjects can be recognized: the advantageous or useful, the virtuous, the just, the beautiful, as relevant and applicable in any given case.

The nature of such persistent subject matter, at least in current American life, can be readily illustrated by reference to two paperbacks, *Issues of the Sixties*, and *American Issues*. Drawing upon a variety of books, articles, and speeches, their editors have assembled materials designed to point up some of our more important and significant problems. Some of their headings indicate subjects about which educated persons should be able to sustain discussion:

> The temper of American society: the individual and the group, ghetto and suburbia.
> Civil rights, social justice, and minority groups.
> Freedom of speech and its limits.

Television and its influence on taste, opinion, and morals.
Advertising: credibility and responsibility.
The impact of science and technology on the human spirit.
Educational reform in the sciences and humanities.
The affluent society and the struggle for power: management and labor, public control and private enterprise.
War and peace: aid for emergent nations, the conflict in Viet Nam, communism and coexistence, nuclear strategy and disarmament.
Rebellion in the arts: self-expression or communication?
The church and public and private morality.

Such topics hint at our problems. From them emerge scores of specific issues that require deliberative thought and bring to bear all the resources of human experience. The issues are aired, influence exerted, and decisions taken through discussion by the many, not merely through expert fact and opinion.

There are other ways of recognizing the materials of public discourse. One approach would be through philosophers of education. The materials would emerge from their responses to a query like this: What common stock of knowledge and what experience in using that knowledge should be at the command of the high school graduate? Of the college graduate? Philosophers of education I take to be experts in judging what knowledge and experience are mandatory for membership in the national social, political, and cultural community. They should be capable of saying what learning benefits all members of the society and holds promise for the well-being and happiness of the individual. Another approach would be to confront the college professors of established departments and fields of study, and inquire: What in your field is worth knowing by the student who does not major or specialize in your subject? One would ask the professor of economics, for example: What should the nonmajor know about economic society and know well enough to draw on it at appropriate moments in conversation and discussion?

Still another way of getting at the subject matter of public affairs is to ask rhetoricians to describe it. What do people speak about and discuss when they are not specialists talking to specialists? What are the parameters of nonspecialized discussion in a wide variety of settings and situations? What are they in the family, for example? In the school and college, particularly in extra-classroom discourse? In community affairs, societies, and campaigns? In television and the public press? The task of classifying the contents of nonspecialized discourse is not impossible. Aristotle showed the way, and the modern rhetorician should be as capable of inventing modes of classification to suit his purpose as Aristotle was to suit his.

He need not be dismayed by what the structural linguist declares to be the uniqueness of every "sentence" or utterance. Doubtless no two utterances are identical either in their production, function, or meaning. But this fact does not mean that speech and language behavior are chaotic in their public dimensions. Every individual is unique, so it is believed, but this conviction has never deterred humanistic psychologists from classifying human behavior in ways that permit generalizations and theories. One can locate the subject matter of rhetorical communications by looking for the kinds, varieties, and subvarieties of occasions. And rhetorical occasions are simply those sets of circumstances to which men have become sufficiently subjected to call forth speech or its offspring, written language. It may be that in the modern world rhetorical occasions exceed in number and complexity those categorized by classical rhetoricians. If this be true, the difficulty might be more than offset by programming utterances for machine analysis. The reward of classification would of course be a set, or sets, of modern rhetorical *torpoi.*[6]

Doubtless it has occurred to some readers that the nature of public discourse is virtually the same as the nature of what used to be called liberal education or general education. It is indeed.[7] To focus on the materials of public discourse is to focus on the substantive equipment of the liberally educated person. Some rhetoricians understand this, and in their basic courses think of themselves as engaging in the education of youth through oral and written communication. Few educators, however, have seen the large overlapping territories of things rhetorical and things liberal. Some, in thoughtless moments, speak of mere rhetoric or mere speech or mere language as if communication could occur without a material and substantive basis. Or they think that rhetoric is limited to forms and styles of writing and speech and that the content and ideas of discourse belong entirely to scientific fields of study and are derived primarily from them. Or in their devotion to individualism, they value more highly the private life of the individual than his public life. If there are educators who still think well of that which is liberal or general, or that which is not the servant of a technology, a science, or a profession, they might make their goals intelligible to the modern student, and their means viable and relevant, by recognizing the subject matters of public life and the arts of verbal communication. I suggest that rhetoricians in the next decades can make their greatest contribution to the general welfare of the free and open society by acting in part as educators essential to the development of the public self of the individual.

Anyone concerned with the social welfare of men as well as with the arts of rhetoric and communication is appalled at the separation of rhetorical discourse from its subject matter. Such an attitude began as early as the sixteenth century, and resulted in the denigration and distrust of popular knowledge and was accompanied by the growth of prestige and confidence in scientific knowledge. The change was marked by disrespect for opinion and respect for fact. In the process, popular knowledge became as good as lost to the worlds of scholarship and higher education, except perhaps to the British in the nineteenth century. In the process, too, rhetoric—perhaps like the arts generally—was persuaded that it had no proper responsibility for the materials, substance, and content of discourse and devoted its attention to the forms, structures, style, and expression of language as written and spoken.

The causes of such a state of affairs, although still obscure and inviting much scholarly investigation, are beginning to be apparent. The parts of rhetorical doctrine called invention and disposition were taken over by dialectic, later known as logic. The movement was given impetus by Peter Ramus and his followers and was accelerated by Francis Bacon's interest in methods of scientific discovery and the activities of the Royal Society. This trend was probably stamped with its essential character for over 200 years (roughly 1660–1890) by the Port Royalist tradition in logic, led at first by Antoine Arnauld. Logic was held to be the art of thinking, and it had as its province knowledge of all mental powers. As the movement developed logicians lost interest in practical reasoning and contingent truth, and concentrated on the conditions and formal rules of judgments productive of scientific Truth. Arnauld avowed that logic was the servant of the sciences. If ideas were clear and trustworthy, they must correspond to fact. Words were encumbrances to rigorous thought. Creative insights and new ideas were the inventions of men of science; seminal insights Bacon attributed chiefly to accident. Logic had no business with the springs of invention; rather, its function was to steady men's thinking about their insights and discoveries, to discipline their thought and symbols, to criticize inferences, and to expunge error. So Logic, for centuries as interested as Rhetoric in producing *topoi* that were intended to help man systematize his experience, prompt his memory, and stimulate himself to produce ideas for his reasonings, abandoned responsibility for the content and materials of thought to other disciplines. It ceased to care for ideas which at one time it held to be the "units" of thinking; it cared only for the management of precise relationships among ideas. It became a formal, a methodological art.[8]

The result of assigning the materials of discourse to the sciences is all too evident. Although repudiating the ideal of achieving certainty of truth, science set its sights on the attainment of truths having only the highest probability. Why, then, should a science bother with either the forms or materials of men's ordinary discourse where reasoning was rife with uncertainties, unreliability, and low-level probabilities? So science, striving to become as "pure" as possible, lost interest in popular knowledge. It neglected what it had claimed from the formal and methodological arts.

And what of rhetoric during this massive change? Rhetoricians appear to have acknowledged the claims of logic and science, despite the respect that a few lecturers—notably Joseph Priestley in England and John Quincy Adams in America—had for what their classical forebears said about invention and disposition. George Campbell adapted to the new scheme of things by offering through his rhetorical philosophy "a tolerable sketch of the human mind." He thus steered rhetoric in the direction of psychology. The outcome has been that psychology and rhetoric today have a common interest in the nature of the human being and in speech and language behavior. This mutual interest, perceived more clearly by rhetoricians than by psychologists, has brought strength to rhetoric. Yet rhetoric has not recovered from the grievous loss it suffered when it surrendered responsibility for the content of public discourse. The surrender meant the complete loss of contact with political science and ethics, for the relationship with these fields of study is through the materials and subject matters of discourse, not through forms, methodology, or style. Kinship is through mutual concern with public situations that require deliberation and appraisal: deliberation over what can be reasonably predicted and done in a particular case, adjudication for him who has transgressed the law, and in general, justification of what merits praise or censure for him whose action (whether of speech or conduct) may be, or may not be, in keeping with sanctioned rules, practices, and conventions of a civilization and national culture. It is clear, then, that the great task of rhetoricians in the generation ahead is to reinstate the study of the materials of public argument. It is these that are to be learned, to be stored in experience as the property of the young. If rhetoricians do not undertake the task, no one will. Political science and ethics in their special studies and research are no longer centrally interested in the discourse of citizens at large. Linguists, phoneticians, speech and communication scientists, and grammarians, all have their eyes on structures and forms of speech and language behavior; they have neglected and disavowed the subject matters of public discourse. In the ancient trivium, rhetoric was the substantive art; it should become so again.

Both rhetoricians and educators should be alive to the values that can attend the subject matters encountered in public discourse. I shall mention but two values here. The study of rhetoric provides the modern undergraduate, beset by the pressures and confusions of specialized curricula, his only opportunity of seeing, as he nears maturity, what unity there may still be among the studies of his higher education. If he has come to rhetoric early in his education, he perceives that the subject mat-

ters of rhetorical discourse connect directly with the materials and concepts he encounters in the social sciences, the arts and literature, ethics,
semantics and aesthetics. Two examples must suffice. If he argues for, or
observes others arguing for, justice and rights for the Negro, he discovers
that these concepts have a long history in political science and ethics. If
he becomes interested in the characteristics of speakers and audiences,
writers and readers, he finds that ethics and psychological studies extend
his knowledge of the sources, agencies, and parties to communication.
The student who learns to think rhetorically can hardly miss the relevance
of his formal studies. He sees that rhetoric constitutes a general introduction to the subject matters, ideas, values, and rational operations that specialized studies extend and refine. In the manner that the general points
to the special and the individual is distinguished from the special and
general, he finds the integrity of his education and his own integrity as
well. The student who orders his college years around rhetoric is bound
to acquire a liberating point of view toward human problems and human
nature.

The second value to be mentioned is one that has hardly been recognized among graduate schools. It should win respect in the future. A
philosophically oriented doctorate program in rhetoric could yield teachers and scholars who possess insights helpful to other disciplines. They
might be members of departments of rhetoric, communications, or speech
as is customary now, but in appropriate circumstances they might have
faculty status in other departments. Historical and political events often
have components that the rhetorician is best equipped to evaluate. In all
the arts that will admit to having a communicative and persuasive function, there are rhetorical qualities. The point of view of the rhetorician
provides ideal perspectives for empirically grounded studies in the speech
sciences and communication processes. The rhetorician's view of practical
deliberation in discussion contexts can complement the ethicist's theoretical treatment of deliberation as it is revealed in moral contexts. The ad-
visor and counsellor, the psychiatrist and the physician can profit from
the rhetorician's art. Whenever, wherever, and however men communicate there is likely to be a marked rhetorical ingredient, and in the understanding and evaluation of the artifacts of communication rhetoricians
are likely to be useful.

If there have been confusion and uncertainty in years past over the
subject matter of public communications and doubt whether rhetorical
theorists, not to mention educators, should cope with it, there has also
been uncertainty whether rhetoric as an art is properly concerned with
the ethics and morality of discourse, speakers, and listeners. Without
touching on the position of the Greek and Roman rhetoricians on this
matter, I shall say simply that the modern rhetorician is beginning to see

that speech and language behavior are *of* the man, not separate from him. It is said loosely that man uses language as an instrument to do so-and-so for such-and-such purposes. But speech is not a lifeless thing, external to a speaker or instrumental like a hammer. Speaking is man's distinctive mode of acting, reflecting every dimension of his being. So what is properly meant by the use or using of language is man's use of himself. The fact that speech becomes an integral part of the human being—even if one denies that its appearance in the child is due in any degree to heredity and believes it to be entirely the product of learning—explains in large measure why language is not neutral. Language reveals every facet of the cognitive, conative, and affective aspects of personality, particularly when the media are speech, voice, and gesture. Indeed, speech is an action and tells as much about the speaker as writing a check, going fishing, or bowing to a lady.

Rhetorical action is no less a product of a communicator, of a communication source, than is a speech act. Its material and subject matter are of the nature we have been describing. The purpose of a rhetorical action, the dominance of that purpose in functioning to select and form the materials of the act to the point of substantiality, the entire relationship of means to purpose, the communicator (or rhetor) and the communicatee (or listener) as persons engaged in the acting—all these entail and require choices in the doing of a rhetorical act. And it is the factor of choice that introduces inextricably into the act an ethical dimension.

It is acknowledged in academic communities that the field of ethics and its neighbor, politics or political science, are populated by teachers and scholars who are experts on the nature of choices and the proper ways of appraising and justifying them. The ethicist, concentrating on private actions and the private self, and the political scientist, focusing on public actions and the public or social self, find that choices are always evident when men encounter two fundamental kinds of situations: What shall be done or believed? What ought to be done or believed? The situations bring practical reason into play, and this kind of activity exhibits three modes: deliberation, justification, and explanation. These modes of rational behavior directly or indirectly reflect men's values, and value-concepts constitute the guides and criteria we use in making our choices. Value-concepts of the greatest generality are familiar to all of us: good and evil, pleasant and unpleasant, right and wrong, altruism and the general welfare, duty, obligation, self-interest, truth-telling, promise-keeping, honesty, fairness, courage, law observance, utility, and the like. These concepts, of course, typically appear in general statements called rules of conduct, regulations, laws, codes, principles, and moral maxims.[9]

Although rhetoricians are not ethicists, they should think about rhetorical acts in the way that students of ethics and politics think about the justification of social actions. Ethicists and rhetoricians should share the same concern for the quality of actions about which they are expert. Whether they be teachers, critics, or researchers, rhetoricians who recognize the province and integrity of their art must also recognize the morality of their art. Some of them now see, and all ought to understand, that ethical concepts are working in the choices men make when they argue, persuade, explain, and so forth. In speeches and writings, choices and their justifications are indicated or implied in statement form as reasons, warrants, premises, laws, principles, and beliefs. As they operate in the preparatory stages of utterance, ethical criteria govern the communicator's consideration and choice of purposes, the selection of material from the subject matter available, the kind of ethos to be revealed, and finally the degree of respect for conventional forms of presentation. As applied in the appraisals of communications by audience and critics, ethical guides function in much the same way as they do for the communicator, although the critic is more likely in his final analysis to consider what the speaker or writer ought to have done.

What is needed in the years ahead is concerted study directed to questions like these: What considerations apply to the rhetor's choice

Of purposes, intentions, goals, motives?
Of means, methods, strategies, and tactics for the realization of purposes?
Of special ingredients in self-portraiture?
Of linguistic, vocal, and gestural styles?

Rhetoricians may find it difficult to agree on the ethical criteria of public utterances that range from discussion (including some kinds of conversation) at one end of a continuum to presidential addresses at the other. Probably there is no neat, concise collection of commandments to be found and perhaps no code is less broad, more precise, or more sanctionable than the rules that apply to advertising, television, and the law. Yet the essential conditions of the rhetorical act—purpose, material, form, and rhetor—function not only to explain an act; they also imply the basis of its justification. In fact, the conditions of the act point to the kernel queries:

Why do people talk when they do?
Why don't people talk when the situation invites talk from them?
How do people account for and justify their talk?

To undertake such study is probably more urgent today than ever before. Has any prior age been subjected to the number and complexity of communications that our age has? Has confidence in political communications, in advertising, or in the phenomena of "public relations" generally ever been so low? It is not the business of rhetoricians to consider the ethics of communication in the technologies and professions. It is not their business to monitor the politician talking to politician, the publisher to publisher, the TV network owner to TV network owner, but it is the obligation of rhetoricians to appraise the ethics of the public discourse about which they are supposed to be experts. These include the politician's speeches and reports to his public, the publisher's magazine and newspaper communications, the verbal persuasions emanating from public relations sources, and the rhetorical messages purveyed through television.

The logic of public discourse has always bothered rhetoricians probably because they have been torn between the ideal of rationality as pursued by the sciences and the reality of rational behavior as observed in argument. In centuries past when dialectic and rhetoric were closely allied, speakers felt their reasoning ought to meet the tests of strict deductive and inductive inference. The feeling persists in modern textbooks on rhetoric. It now appears to be mistaken and outmoded. Two considerations support this judgment.

If rhetoric be an autonomous art, the discourse its theory reflects is not like that of any of the special sciences. Rhetorical discourse, as has been seen, has its own materials and subject matter, and this circumstance in part gives to the study of rhetoric its distinctive character and independence among the arts and sciences. In part, of course, the ends of rhetoric testify to its autonomy, these being simply to understand the kind of discourse we have described and to work toward making it better. It seems self-evident that an autonomous art, though it may derive help and comfort from other arts, ought to study not only its own materials but the ways they are used. Rhetoricians have talked much about "logical" proof, its modes, and its standards. But they have done so from the point of the logician and they have employed his categories. Perhaps Richard Whately was the last rhetorician to undertake sustained study of rhetorical reasonings, though he did it in the light of his *Logic*.

The second consideration that suggests a new look at the logic of public discourse is the direction indicated by the work of Stephen Toulmin, Chaim Perelman, and Gidon Gottlieb. Toulmin has pointed out that in the field of law-court argument, lawyers and judges have developed their own patterns and rules of rational activity, for which the field of reference is their own field of practice. The law has found that acceptable and workable standards of rational proof exist without being syllogistically proper and inductively perfect. Justice is believed to be served. Taking a few hints from Toulmin, Gottlieb has examined the concepts of rule and rationality as they apply to legal and moral reasoning. He reminds us that reasoning occurs in any context in which there is an end-means relationship. Hence there is a logic other than that of an analytical-formal nature and other than that based on the model of scientific reasoning. Gottlieb suggests, too, that the field in which reasoning takes place generates its rules. These guide a reasoner in choosing his purposes, means, and methods and in judging the consistency of his inferences. Perhaps enough has been said to suggest at least the possibility of a rhetorical logic.[10]

I want to go a bit farther and suggest the probability that rhetoricians can work out a substantive logic. It would serve two functions: it would guide speakers in making their choices during moments of preparation—the moment or the hours prior to final commitment as utterance; it would reflect the speaker's arguments and would to a considerable extent constitute the justification of the speech. Such a logic would be quite in line with the four causes or conditions of rhetorical action: the rhetor and his audience, his purpose, his materials, and the form of his act. Gottlieb refers to his logic as the logic of choice. We might call ours the logic of rhetorical action.

One is almost bound to construct rules of rhetorical action by looking in these directions: (1) What guides can be formulated that help a rhetor to choose the purpose of his speech? Related questions are these: What are the factual conditions bringing speaker and audience together? What values (including motives, desires, feelings, commitments, etc.) are explicit and implicit in the circumstances? For the speaker? For the audience? Are there rules that would help a speaker to resolve competing and conflicting values? If the purpose of communication were to be achieved, what are the consequences likely to be? What is the relationship of the speech at hand to the speaker's more remote ends or goals? Out of such problems, rules and principles should emerge, perhaps to be treated first as hypotheses. Let me try stating two rules for the sake of illustration. The purpose, or purposes, of communication in a given case ought to be consistent with the nameable values present, and the value dimensions of the circumstances should be consistent with the factual circumstances. (2) In seeking to achieve his purpose, what means are available to the speaker and which are sanctionable? What materials and resources are at hand? Which are to be searched for? What information is trustworthy? What information is to be preferred, if time or other constraints require limitation? Of the materials residing in the value systems of the speaker and audience, what ones can be used? What ones cannot? What, then, are the rules of speaker ethos and of audience ethos? Among the traditional methods and techniques of treating information and of making explanations, arguments, and persuasions, what ones are allowable? What are the rules that guide speaker and audience in judging what strategies and tactics are sanctionable and appropriate? Let me offer two illustrative rules: Revealing factual materials creates trust in a speaker, suppressing them produces distrust. Communicators ought not to distort their utterances to suit their purposes or the values of their audiences. (3) As for the forms of rhetorical action, are there rules of style, of gesture, of vocal and articulatory production? Are there guides for the choice of words and word combinations? Are there public unutterables in the culture or in the circumstances of the communication? These are technical problems, and the more technical the problem the more clearly the rhetorician is distinguished from the communication scientist and linguistician. The rhetorician must make value judgments; the scientist tries to avoid them. The rhetorician must have preferences about what is better or worse; the scientist need not.

Rhetoricians need not fear that the rules of a rhetorical logic—the rules of rhetorical reasoning—will have the rigidity of mathematical rules. They will, of course, be prescriptive, and often binding. Rules of the kind we envision are guides, not inflexible laws of nature or axioms of geometry. They monitor a communicator's decisions and provide criteria of consistency. They can neither command nor demand; they direct a communicator to be reasonable and intelligible rather than arbitrary and irrational. Nevertheless, upon occasion a set of rules may be considered acceptable by all parties to the communication; the set then becomes binding, and operates and functions as an objective frame of rational reference, giving the speaker confidence in his decisions and constituting his ultimate basis of appeal if he needs to justify his arguments.

As observed by a speaker, the rules of rhetorical action will constitute his ethos. That this may turn out to be so should hardly be surprising, for as someone has remarked, logic as a concept overlaps those of ethics and knowledge, participating in both. If rhetoricians take seriously the logic of public discourse, they will be busy for some time to come.

If rhetoricians—and for that matter, educators—once again see that public discourse has distinctive materials and subject matters, if they see that public communications as acts must have an ethic and a logic, if they acknowledge the fundamentals of their art, they will find that many of their other problems will acquire an illuminating perspective. What of rhetorical criticism, its ends and methods? It seems to be generally agreed among rhetoricians that one of their signal failures in the last 70 years is the failure to produce in any significant numbers practicing critics of public discourse. What of the concept of appropriateness? Is it uniquely a rhetorical concept? If it is central to and guides every decision of a rhetor, can it be fruitfully defined and rendered in some ways empirically manageable? What of style and delivery? Especially, what is the communicative force of certain kinds and dimensions of vocal behavior, of bodily behavior and gesture? These matters of symbol and form, now the object of serious study by some psycholinguists, have been too long neglected by rhetoricians. Bodily gestures, facial expression, and vocal behavior of all kinds are obvious sources of nuances and textures of meaning as well as of information about speaker and listener, and rhetoricians should abandon any pathological fears about such matters that they may have acquired from the excesses of nineteenth century elocution.

FOOTNOTES

1. Some views of rhetoric are to be seen in three articles by Donald C. Bryant: "Aspects of the Rhetorical Tradition: The Intellectual Foundation," *Quarterly Journal of Speech*, 36 (April, 1950), 169–76; "Emotion, Style, and Literary Association," *ibid.* (October, 1950), 326–32; and "Rhetoric: Its Function and Scope," *ibid.* 39 (December, 1953), 401–24. See also Kenneth Burke, *A Grammar of Motives* (New York: Prentice-Hall, 1945) and *A Rhetoric of Motives* (New York: Prentice-Hall, 1950); Robert M. Gorrell, "Very Like a Whale—A Report on Rhetoric," *College Composition and Communication*, 16 (October, 1965), 138–43; Daniel Fogarty, S. J., *Roots for a New Rhetoric* (New York: Teachers College Series in Education, Columbia University, 1959); James J. Murphy, "The Four Faces of Rhetoric: A Progress Report," *College Composition and Communication*, 17 (May, 1966), 55–59; Marie Hochmuth Nichols, *Rhetoric and Criticism* (Baton Rouge: Louisiana State University Press, 1963); Richard Ohman, "In Lieu of a New Rhetoric," *College English*, 26 (October, 1964), 17–22; I. A. Richards, *The Philosophy of Rhetoric* (New York: Oxford University Press, 1936); Joseph Swartz and John A. Rycenga, *The Province of Rhetoric* (New York: The Ronald Press, 1965); Richard Weaver, *The Ethics of Rhetoric* (Chicago: Henry Regnery, 1953), and W. Ross Winterowd, *Rhetoric: A Synthesis* (New York: Holt, Rinehart and Winston, 1968).
2. Models of the communication process are legion. One of the more recent ones is rich in implications for both the rhetorician and the communication scientist. See J. Edward Hulett, Jr., "A Symbolic Interactionist Model of Human Communication. Part One: The General Model of Social Behavior: The Message-Generating Process," *AV Communication Review*, 14 (Spring, 1966), 5–33.
3. The meanings of *speech* and its forms are many, even if the student had to stop with those listed by OED. They all imply or entail the essential rationality of the human species. Or, put in another way, the human animal is constituted by his learning to speak. His humanness is extended and refined to the degree that his speech and language behavior are extended and refined. J. L. Austin bolsters the confidence of the humanist by pointing out that the wisdom of the race resides in its speech. *Philosophical Papers* (Oxford: The Clarendon Press, 1961), p. 130.
4. *Understanding Discourse: The Speech Act and Rhetorical Action.* Baton Rouge: Louisiana State University Press, 1970.
5. This position seems to have been first taken by Aristotle in the *Rhetoric* whose first two books constitute the earliest presentation of rhetorical topics. See especially the *Rhetoric* 1355 b 26–36 and 1356 a 31–34 (Rhys Roberts' or Friese's translations) for Aristotle's allusion to the subject matter of persuasive dis-

course. The position has been echoed, more or less clearly, by every major rhetorical theorist who believed that one of the parts of the art was *inventio*.

6. The possibility of a modern set of *topoi* appropriate to rhetorical discourse remains intriguing. Interest has been evident by those rhetoricians who recognize that substance is the primary feature of saying something. Carroll Arnold offers some basic topical categories in collaboration with John F. Wilson, *Public Speaking as a Liberal Art*, 2nd ed. (Boston: Allyn and Bacon, 1968), pp. 105–20, and Edward Corbett has reexamined the classical system of topics with a view to their use in rhetoric classes: *Classical Rhetoric for the Modern Student* (New York: Oxford University Press, 1965), pp. 94–142. Suggestive also are Otto Bird's "The Re-discovery of the Topics," *Mind*, 70 (July, 1961), 534–39, and Richard L. Larson's "Discovery Through Questioning: A Plan for Teaching Rhetorical Invention," *College English*, 70 (November, 1968), 126–34. Mortimer Adler and associates constructed a syntopicon that is intended to help readers organize the essential ideas of the Great Books. Chaim Perelman's discussion of *loci* as the ultimate bases of argument is intriguing: *The New Rhetoric: A Treatise on Argumentation*, by Ch. Perelman and L. Olbrechts-Tyteca, trans. John Wilkinson and Purcell Weaver (Notre Dame: University of Notre Dame Press, 1969), especially pp. 65–114.

The possibility of finding a set of modern *topoi* should not be dismissed without at least asking whether there are real questions for research. Are (and were) *topoi* aids to learning? To learning what? For what purposes? Do the topics that aid learning also aid "inventiveness," that is, the sort of creativity and insight that is evident in making a communicative utterance, or in the locating of an issue, or in creating particular kinds of utterances, say kinds of arguments and figures of speech? Perhaps one gets to the same questions from another direction: How does one index a book? What does an index do?

7. From time to time in the pages of the *Quarterly Journal of Speech*, Everett Hunt has identified the content of general education courses with the subject matter of public discourse: 2 (July, 1916), 252–63; 35 (October, 1949), 275–79, (December, 1949), 419–26; 41 (April, 1955), 114–17. Hunt's point of view is expressed in this passage:

> If we can keep as basic our conception that the humanities embrace whatever contributes to the making of free and enlightened choices, whether it be knowledge scientific, sociological, or poetic, and that in addition to adequate knowledge of all the alternatives there must be imagination to envision all the possibilities and sympathy to make some of the options appeal to the emotions and powers of the will, we can see that rhetoric is an essential instrument for the enterprises of the human spirit.
>
> A familiarity with the history of its theory and practice cannot but have a liberalizing effect in the midst of technical specialties.
>
> *The Rhetorical Idiom*, ed. Donald C. Bryant (Ithaca: Cornell University Press, 1958), p. 4.

8. Professor David Vancil, University of Wisconsin, is completing a dissertation whose aim is to account for the disappearance of *inventio* from the books on rhetoric, 1550–1850. I am indebted to him for some of the materials on which the line of thought in this paragraph is based.

9. Among the theoretical ethicists, Richard Brandt has perhaps had the most direct influence on me, especially his *Ethical Theory: The Problems of Normative*

and Critical Ethics (Englewood Cliffs, N. J.: Prentice-Hall, Inc., 1959). Among the ethicists who have their eyes on practical discourse are Kurt Baier, *The Moral Point of View* (Ithaca: Cornell University Press, 1958), Paul Edwards, *The Logic of Moral Discourse* (Glencoe, Illinois: The Free Press, 1955), and Bernard Diggs, "Persuasion and Ethics," *Quarterly Journal of Speech*, 50 (December, 1964), 359–73. Particularly interesting are J. O. Urmson's notion of good as a grading concept: "On Grading," *Mind*, 59 (1950), 145–69, R. M. Hare's *The Language of Morals* (Oxford: The Clarendon Press, 1952), and Abraham Maslow's work on value hierarchies, *Motivation and Personality* (New York: Harper and Row, 1954), particularly Chapter 5. Among rhetoricians, interest in the ethics of discourse is seen most recently in Thomas R. Nilsen, *Ethics of Speech Communication* (Indianapolis: Bobbs-Merrill, 1966), and the collection of readings edited by Richard L. Johannesen, *Ethics and Persuasion* (Random House Studies in Speech, New York and Toronto, 1967).

10.   Gidon Gottlieb's book is *The Logic of Choice* (London: George Allen and Unwin, 1968). Perelman, *op. cit.*, has taken a fresh look at a substantive logic and also at one of the concepts entering often into argument in *The Idea of Justice and the Problem of Argument* (translated from the French by John Petrie, New York: The Humanities Press, 1963). Helpful is Ray D. Dearin, "The Philosophy of Chaim Perelman's Theory of Rhetoric," *Quarterly Journal of Speech*, 55 (October, 1969), 213–24.

2 / RHETORICAL STUDIES FOR THE CONTEMPORARY WORLD

SAMUEL L. BECKER
University of Iowa

Douglas Ehninger has described the ways in which our conceptions of rhetoric have altered at various periods through history to adjust to the needs of the times.[1] A rhetorical system, he tells us, "cannot be merely good or bad; it must be good or bad for something."[2] It is appropriate that we meet in 1970 to consider the sort of alterations called for by *our* time. It is appropriate that we be concerned with the needs of our time and the conception or conceptions of rhetoric which will be "good" for serving those needs. Ours is the age which has been characterized bombastically as undergoing a "knowledge explosion" and a "communication revolution." We have a plethora of communication or communication-related problems—problems of communication between husband and wife, between young and old, among students, faculty, and administrators, between white and black, between and within countries. We have the problem of the individual who must cope with the many and varied messages with which he is constantly bombarded; we have the problem of the society which must "reach" the individual through that morass of other messages. It is for these needs, for these times, that new conceptions of rhetoric are needed.

I have no such new conception to offer; I wish that I did. I do have some questions to raise, and some suggestions which I hope can make a contribution to the development of these conceptions.

21

During the course of this conference, I hope that we will not be too concerned with the trivial question of what is or is not "rhetoric," or what is or is not a "rhetorical theory." I hope, rather, that we will concentrate upon the problems of human communication with which scholars in our field should be concerned. I hope that we will concentrate specifically upon the major sorts of problems which people in our field who call themselves rhetoricians or public address scholars can do much to illumine and the ways in which they can do so.

I assume that the rhetorical theorist and public address scholar have three major functions:

1. To identify and describe the various phenomena we label communication in terms of commonly understood and useful sets of categories or concepts.
2. To describe the relationships which exist among these concepts as precisely as possible.
3. To identify the factors in various communication processes which can be altered with predictable results on other factors in these processes.

In the terminology of the philosophers of the social sciences, a "conceptual scheme" can fulfill the first function; an "analytic system" is needed to fulfill the second; and a "theory" is necessary for the third. A major concern for every contemporary rhetorical theorist or public address scholar is to be confident that his work is contributing to the development of systems and theories. We need rhetorical systems and theories which do more than provide category systems for messages or communication situations or elements within them. We need systems and theories which explain the complex web of interactions among ideas, messages, and men, and which are *testable* in some fashion. Even more, at this point in time, we need criticism or public address studies which depart more sharply from literary criticism or internal criticism where the major purpose is to "explain" the way in which a message "works." We need public address studies which have a closer relationship to some of the contemporary rhetorical theories and which provide precise data on all elements of contemporary communication situations, the sorts of data which can be used for the development of better rhetorical theories and for the testing of such theories.

One of the first and essential steps toward such studies and such theories is the determination of what to count as a datum. There are two aspects to this problem: one is the question of specificity and level of abstraction, the other is the question of scope—of what to include as part of a communication situation or a communication process. We need unambiguous criteria for identifying and delimiting the data with which we are concerned. In most of the physical sciences, this problem has been fairly well resolved; the kinds of abstractions acceptable and necessary for each science are beyond question. No physicist worries about whether Isaac Newton's apple was red, rotten, tasty—or even whether it was, in fact, an apple. The essential fact for the physicist is that it was a body of a certain mass moving with a certain acceleration relative to other bodies.[3] In many of the social sciences and, even more, in most of the humanities, we seem unable to agree on what is and is not a relevant datum. To be more specific, we can not agree on the level of abstraction which we will use. Thus, in rhetorical studies, we have no clear guide to what is and is not relevant detail in a message or in the "rhetorical situation." In many instances, we appear to be shying away from any abstraction; we too often treat rhetorical situations and messages as though they were unique objects and we can do no more than attempt to describe them—neglecting to note that description itself is an abstraction. This failure to abstract sufficiently and to agree as a field upon the kinds of abstractions which are acceptable and necessary are among the important roadblocks to a meaningful level of generalizations about communication and to the development of more sophisticated and more useful rhetorical theories.

Some agreement on levels of abstraction would help us also to resolve the problem of the units of analysis to use for various sorts of problems. It would help us to determine whether a message, for example, a speech, is to be a unit, or whether an argument or proof within a message is to be the unit, or whether it will be the word. Clearly, we need to decide by what *criteria* such decisions are to be made.

Turning to the question of scope, I believe that, in too many of our studies of public address to date, we have taken too narrow a view of the functions which communication serves; our historical and critical studies which have not been primarily biographical have tended to be built almost exclusively upon an influence or persuasion model. Yet, persuasion is only one of the many important functions of communication. We need more historical and critical studies which provide data on that communication which operates to prevent rather than bring about change.[4] We probably need additional studies which provide data on communication which serves an ego-defense function, or a value-expressive function, or a knowledge function—which serves the needs of individuals to give structure to their universe.[5] I would suggest that more scholars of public address take a cue from some of the current mass media studies and theorizing and have their analyses be guided by an equilibrium model, rather than an influence model. With such a model, one would not ask how a communicator influenced, but rather how he helped the system to maintain equilibrium. For this equilibrium model of communication, one might draw an analogy with some of our major industries. When General Motors shifts from a production person to a marketing person in its top management position, generally we can see a shift in policy. The new manager, however, did not bring the shift about so much as the shift, or need for the shift, brought him about. Thus, we might look at Senator Ted Kennedy's speech on television explaining his behavior the night of the Kopechne incident in different and, possibly, more fruitful ways if we think of the speech as an effort to restore equilibrium, rather than as an effort to influence. The rhetorical situation, to use Lloyd Bitzer's term, made a speech of this sort imperative.[6]

More than any other need in our rhetorical studies, though, is the need to take a far broader view of what constitutes a relevant datum in the study of a particular communication situation. For example, what stimuli will be considered part of a message? What will be the defining characteristics of a message? What is and is not to be included in our systems and theories? Two of the three contemporary trends in public persuasion noted by Franklin Haiman are "body rhetoric" and "civil disobedience."[7] Are we to include these? Clearly we must consider the possibility, just as the Supreme Court is considering the question of "symbolic speech." Is it fruitful to include civil disobedience under the rubric of rhetoric? What about billboards and traffic lights? Perhaps we need to ask what is to be excluded?

There may be a close analogy between the reasons that rhetorical theory—and even more, rhetorical criticism and the history of public address—have not contributed more to understanding of communication processes as they generally occur in our society—in the "real world"—and the reasons that the bulk of experimental studies of communication in the laboratory have not done so.

1. Both the critic and the experimental researcher tend to define the message as something which is concentrated and which has an internal organization. In most important communication situations, the message is scattered and unorganized.

2. Neither the critic nor the experimental researcher generally studies a situation or that part of a communication process in which there is much repetition of a message or parts of a message; yet, in most important communication processes, those involved tend to be exposed to parts of the message many times.

3. The critic and the experimental researcher tend to act as though those who are exposed to a message are exposed equally. In fact, there is tremendous heterogeneity among almost any group of persons in amount of exposure to an important message.

4. Similarly, in the laboratory study, for any given experimental condition, all subjects are generally exposed to precisely the same message. Critics seem to assume this same homogeneity. In most important

communication processes, though, it follows from my first two points above that there is great variance in the "message" to which subjects are exposed.

Both the critic and the experimental or behavioral scholar must be constantly aware of these distinctions. More of them must begin to take into account the total communication environment and the heterogeneous ways in which people are exposed to messages, and the heterogeneous messages to which they are exposed.[8]

I believe that some critics of public address have erred in these ways because they have focused too exclusively upon major speakers and writers, the nature of their messages, and the relatively direct impact of these messages. They have ignored the fact that the output of these speakers and writers is only a minute part of the communication environment, and the increasingly abundant evidence that any one communication encounter, or even a series of encounters by a single speaker or writer, accounts for only a small portion of the variance in human behavior. This is true especially where the message deals with an important issue, for on these issues there is greater likelihood of the relevant behaviors being well set in the members of the audience and for even a series of messages or encounters to comprise only a minute fraction of the total set of relevant influences. Only in rather rare cases do we have a *single* source of relevant information. We learn from a great number and variety of media and from a great number and variety of people. All of these need to be taken into account if we are to get at all of the important processes of communication. When we focus almost exclusively on major speakers and writers, we tend to overlook the *processes* by which public discourse affects and is affected by the society in which it occurs. We can only get at these processes if we examine more systematically and intensively all of the links (or lines or branches) through which information passes, up to and through the point at which it affects the behaviors of or is used by a meaningful set of the critical audience or society. We must examine these communication processes as they extend over periods of time so that we can understand precisely the long-range effects—the cumulative impact—on the public's views of the world and their behaviors which are related to those views. This is not to say that we must always be concerned with the general public as the end point. The critical audience, at times, may be a much smaller group which has the power to act for all.[9] We must also be concerned with the complementary functions of different channels in the diffusion process, since there is fairly good evidence that different media are generally most appropriate for different tasks.

Evidence for the importance of studying the diffusion of messages over *space* and *time* comes from many sources. One especially clear example is the finding from a study of the communication of birth control messages in Taiwan that three out of four acceptors of the advocated method of birth control had had no contact with the official communicators (or field workers) and, by the end of the year in which the campaign occurred, a fourth of the acceptors came from areas not even being reached directly by the formal campaign.[10] If our rhetorical studies and theories are to be of maximum use today, they need to shed some light on the lines and linkages in this sort of communication or diffusion process. They need to be concerned not only with the public speech and the published writing, but also with the mundane sorts of communication encounters in the home, the office, and the cocktail party—the communication encounters that are key links in the diffusion of information and influence.

In gathering data and developing theories of rhetoric for the twentieth and twenty-first centuries, we must take into account the sort of communication environment in which any man in a modern or highly industrialized society lives. This man lives in a veritable pressure cooker of communication; everyone and everything is pushing him. The media are pushing him to buy a car and cigarettes and to stop smoking; to use deodorants and to wear an auto seat belt and to vote for the party of his choice and to support our most recent war effort and to parade against war. His children are pushing him to play with them or to give them money for the movies or to buy them a car. And his wife is telling him to mow the lawn and take it easy and fix his tie. And those above him at the plant or office are pushing him to work harder, and those below him are pushing him to stop making *them* work so hard. And all of this pushing is done through communication. He is pushed by his television set and radios and newspapers and magazines and billboards and handbills and memoranda and even the old-fashioned open mouth which is often so uncomfortably close to his ear. He is pushed not only through verbal communication, but through non-verbal. He is attacked not only at the supraliminal levels, but at the barely liminal and even at the sub-liminal. He cannot escape this barrage of communication, and his wife wonders why he is not more communicative in the evening when she demands, "Talk to me. Why don't you ever talk to me?"

Even this list does not exhaust the complexities of this communication environment. We are constantly getting new media of communication which have far-reaching effects. These changes wrought by new developments in communication technology are fairly easy to see when viewed from a distance of time or space. They are more difficult to see when one is closely involved in the change process itself. I wonder how many of us are cognizant of some of the changes occurring as a result of the development of something as simple as the xerox machine?

The xerox is only one of many examples which we could cite of the ways in which messages are processed and diffused. Rhetorical critics have been concerned with message processing—but, to too large an extent, with only that processing done by a single speaker or writer. They have examined the sources of his ideas and other influences on his writing or speaking. They have not been concerned, as they must be, with processing in longer chains. For such studies and theorizing, we can learn much from and contribute much to the body of existing research and theory on the way in which information is diffused and the factors which regulate its flow, its shape, and its uses.

One of the developments which have made us more aware of the importance of diffusion in the last decade or two is the potential rapidity of such diffusion. For example, President Kennedy was shot at 12:30 p.m. (C.S.T.) on November 22, 1963. The doctors announced his death thirty minutes later. By that time, over two-thirds of the adults in the United States had heard the news. By the time another hour had passed, over nine-tenths of the adults in the country knew. Four hours later—five and a half hours after the event—virtually everyone in the country (99.8 per cent) was aware of it.[11] Especially important for those of us concerned with communication processes is the fact that less than half these people got their initial information from the mass media; most people first heard about the event from other people.[12] Nor was the diffusion of information about this event restricted by national boundaries. Within twenty-four hours of the assassination, a Gallup survey in Greece showed that ninety-nine per cent of Athenians knew of the event.[13]

The assassination of President Kennedy was obviously an unusual event, but this potential speed of diffusion clearly must be taken into account in some of our rhetorical theories if they are to shed light on contemporary communication processes. One major implication of this fact for the public address scholar is that he can not wait in hopes of increasing "objectivity" until twenty-five or fifty or a hundred or more years after a communication event before he studies it; he must also study the communication that is going on now. This means that he must be prepared to go to at least the sort of lengths some social scientists went to following the John Kennedy killing in order to study associated events. Immediately after the assassination, at least one social scientist was sensitive and sensible enough to contact a group of scholars who gathered in Washington just two days after the assassination to plan a nationwide study.[14] Still other scholars were gathering data within hours of the assassination. It was this immediate and concerted effort that made possible the fine collection of studies, edited by Bradley Greenberg and Edwin Parker, on communication processes following and associated with that event. It was the same sort of effort that made possible the first collection of studies of this sort, the volume on the Kennedy-Nixon debates edited by Sidney Kraus.[15]

Not only must we be prepared to act quickly and in concert when an unexpected event occurs, we must also have the foresight to plan such large scale or cooperative studies of communication situations which can provide important data even before they occur. The University of Leicester Institute for Mass Communication Research carried out such a study in October 1968 (the report of which should be published soon). When it became known that there was to be a very large anti-Vietnam demonstration at the University of London, they quickly gathered a large group of scholars and planned a detailed and systematic study of the event and the communication about it. Observations of the national papers and the news departments of the two networks began two weeks *before* the demonstrations. Not only was the news output carefully studied, but observers were placed within the news organizations to obtain as complete and accurate data as possible on the relevant decision-making processes. During the demonstration itself, they had a large group of policemen, a large group of students, and a large group of "neutrals" watching the television coverage (the three groups were kept separate) and later discussing it. Careful analyses were made of all broadcasting and newspaper coverage of the demonstration. This was checked against the reports of forty observers who viewed the demonstration from the ground at the University and from helicopters above. The director of the study is quick to admit that this is not the perfect study, nor do I cite it as a model for such research. However, it is a model of an attempt to collect important data on an important communication situation as it is in process.

A rhetorical theory for today, or a critic of contemporary communication or public address, must consider the factors that shape messages as they are diffused among various publics. If we are to understand the way communication operates in a modern society, we need to include some consideration of the ways in which a speech gets out "over the heads" of its immediate audience to the larger audience or audiences. We need to consider what happens to it on its way—the ways in which it is shaped and the reasons for that shaping. For example, a scholar studying the speaking of a public figure on the topic of education would do well to take into account some of George Gerbner's findings from his study of newspaper reporters who cover educational news.[16] His generalizations about the institutional pressures upon reporters which result in certain shaping of educational news is highly relevant to rhetorical studies. The finding from another study that newsmen are often more influenced by what they believe to be the attitudes toward the job of their fellow newsmen then they are by the sources of the news or the perceived audience[17] also is relevant to a meaningful rhetorical theory for today. A related factor which shapes the messages which appear in the media—and, hence, the data which become involved in our communication processes—is the pressure to beat the competition. William Rivers documents some of the ways in which the efforts of newspapers to get more details than their competitors, coupled with the competition to broadcast or publish it first, have resulted in a flood of erroneous "facts."[18] This is not to say that attempts are not made by newsmen to be accurate. This is to say that there are many factors in the media situation which affect the definition of accuracy and departures from it. These factors must be understood and considered if we are to develop adequate theories of public discourse for our time.

Some scholars have hypothesized that, in some situations, broadcasters themselves become the central message, rather than the messages or events which they are presumably conveying. This issue has been raised especially in connection with network coverage of election events such as the political conventions in this country and the General Election campaigns in Great Britain.[19] If the aim of our rhetorical scholarship is to explain the functions of discourse in our society and the effects of that discourse, it may be even more important to analyze broadcasting and newspaper treatment of the speeches and writing of public figures than to analyze the original discourse. In this era, when the broadcast account of a speech, for example, may have far more impact than the speech itself, it is terribly important that our rhetorical studies at least take media processes into account. One of the many possible ways of doing that is exemplified in a study by Elizabeth Kyes. She studied the ways in which certain newspaper variables influenced the coverage of John Kennedy's televised press conferences. She was not especially concerned with analysis of the conferences themselves. She was more concerned with the interaction of the conferences, the practices of various types of newspapers, and the effects of this interaction on information received by the public.[20] One of the questions with which rhetorical scholars might well be concerned is the extent to which any given source or type of source controls its saturation with a particular message set. For example, the degrees of freedom the television networks had in choosing what to cover or not cover of the police-demonstrator melee on the streets and of the speeches in Convention Hall during the 1968 Democratic National Convention in Chicago is a question that seems to me to be quite relevant for the rhetorical theorist and critic.

Another important set of questions concerns the relationship of messages transmitted via the media to those transmitted via interpersonal communication. The idea of the "two-step flow of communication,"[21] which posits the flow of information from the mass media to opinion leaders who, in turn, pass it on to other people, and the idea of the "multistep flow" developed by a number of communication scholars, which posits a series of such steps are useful for some types of cases. They are not adequate to describe all of the kinds of communication flow which exist. For example, for certain kinds of information—those which are not especially important to either the bulk of the population or a specialized minority—the information flow seems to be almost exclusively from media to people. Those kinds of information have been characterized as being "consumed." On the other hand, for relatively complex and abstract matters such as world affairs, interpersonal communication is important, but the flow from media to opinion leaders to others does not seem to exist; the flow appears to be rather from media to so-called "knowledgeables" who, in turn, pass on and discuss the information with other knowledgeables. If there is a flow downward at all, it occurs over a long period of time and in more complex ways than those described by the two-step and multi-step flow conceptions.[22] What these ways are is one of the questions which those of us concerned with contemporary rhetoric ought to be discovering.

As scholars of rhetoric and public address, we also need to give more serious thought and study to the impact of the corporate communicator or source on the communication environment. The concept of *a* source—*a* speaker or *a* writer—is not very meaningful for a contemporary study or theory of rhetoric. Not only is the validity of this concept thrown into question by the idea of processes described by Berlo and others, and the widespread use of speech writers or ghost writers, but even more by the fact that mass media messages are corporate efforts. As one extreme example, by the evening of the day President Kennedy was killed, the *New York Times* had at least thirty-two correspondents working on the story.[23] The ABC network had every member of its news department and many members of other departments working on this story almost constantly for most of four days.[24] And these were just one of the three major networks and one of many major newspapers.

Another of the increasingly important developments in communication with which we need to be concerned is so-called "symbolic speech." This phenomenon too has been influenced by the media, especially television. Since the norms of those who work in television favor the showing of an act over the transmission of a word, one has a greater chance of being "heard" if he *does* something than if he *says* something. Thus, when the agitators in Chicago during the Democratic National Convention of 1968 wanted to communicate their "message" about oppression in the American system, the best chance of getting their message diffused across the country was to goad the police of Chicago into responding brutally—oppressively—to demonstrations.[25] This visual manifestation of the society's oppression was carried by all of the major mass media, few if any of which would have bothered with speeches on the topic by the leaders of the dissenting groups. This lesson has been learned so well by those without a strong political power base in this country that it has become an important factor in our contemporary communication environment and, hence, must be an important factor in our theoretical conceptions. Wilmer Young, founder of two Quaker pacifist groups, has told of the chief probation officer in Omaha who asked him why the Quakers didn't

> do educational work in the usual way, write books and articles for magazines, give lectures, use the radio [rather than demonstrate]? This would not make people angry and excited, and they could think more clearly. I assured him that we had been trying to do these things for 25 years and here he didn't even know about it. . . . I reminded him that one could not get the radio or any of the mass media to accept and use what we were offering. I told him that the very fact that he knew nothing about the writing and lecturing on peace that had been going on for years was a clear indication that other methods were needed.[26]

The major point in all that I have said so far, the major conclusion that I believe must be drawn, is that our traditional concept of the message has severely limited usefulness for understanding contemporary communication. The emphasis of rhetorical studies should probably remain upon the message, but we must define message in a more fruitful way, in a way that is more descriptive of what man as receiver is exposed to, rather than what man as source creates. If we begin with the general finding I noted earlier that any single communication encounter accounts for only a small portion of the variance in human behavior and begin to explore why, the answer—or at least a partial answer—is immediately obvious. There are important differences between a "message" prepared by a source (i.e., a newspaper story, speech, television program, etc.) and the "message" to which almost any receiver tends to be exposed. Consider, for example, the message of the Vietnam war. The Vietnam message prepared by a source is relatively free of redundancy; it is organized; it is short. The message to which a receiver is exposed is scattered through time and space, disorganized, has large gaps; he is exposed to parts of it again and again; and there is great variance with the message to which other receivers are exposed.[27]

Many of the new arts provide a paradigm of the contemporary message. If we consider the mixed-media presentation or the most avant-garde theatre, we may begin to get some insights into contemporary communication. The traditional director in the theatre has been much like the traditional critic or theorist of rhetoric. In studying a script for ideas on its direction, he looks for "through lines of action"—for an organizing principle—so that his conception and direction are relatively linear, a "meaningful" succession of images. In the new theatre, directors arrange random multiple images and whatever meaningful organization is given to these images is given by the individual member of the audience.[28] Thus it is with the Vietnam message and the rest of our communication environment. Despite the efforts of individual sources, we do not get our information in neatly organized fashion; each person gets a different experience, a different set of multiple images and, from these, abstracts some sort of relatively organized story.

If we could reconstruct and compare the ways in which each of us got and continues to get the message of Eugene McCarthy, or of the Ted Kennedy-Mary Jo Kopechne accident, or of the student demonstrations at Berkeley or Columbia University, we would begin to get some sense of the variations in the message which each of us has experienced. To illustrate this conception of message that I am proposing, I have tried to reconstruct as accurately and completely as possible the way in which I was exposed to the message of the murder of Martin Luther King during the forty-eight hour period following the event. I first heard of the assassination from a Chicago cab driver as we were coming into the LaSalle hotel for the Central States Speech Convention. He wondered (aloud of course) whether President Johnson was going on television that night. My query about whether something new had occurred regarding the Vietnam peace feelers brought the information about King. In rather quick but scattered succession over the next two days I heard snatches of conversation about these events in the hallways and lobby and meeting rooms of the hotel; I heard an assortment of newscasters and interviews with Negro and white leaders; I saw film footage of the burning and looting; I heard Whitney Young of the Urban League declaring that it was time for us self-styled white liberals to stop talking and start doing; I read stories in the Chicago papers about the events; I saw the store window across from the hotel broken by one of a group of Negro youngsters who marched by; I heard an impassioned speech in a hotel room by a close friend justifying the burning and looting being done by Negroes in many parts of the country; I saw the hotel employees locking all of the entrances to the hotel but one; and I engaged in discussion with my friends and colleagues about whether it was safe to go out of the hotel for dinner. And these were only a small portion of the relevant bits of the message to which I was exposed during that two day period. Not only was I exposed to bits of the message, I was forced to respond to many—to create my own bits and, in the process, to develop points of view about the events. Many of these communication transactions were redundant. I saw some of the films on television innumerable times; I heard and read some of the same stories; I even heard myself responding to various individuals with the same phrases. In other words, there were two kinds of processes at work: there was an ever-increasing number and variety of pieces and sources of information and, at the same time, there was a certain amount of repetitiveness, of going through the same or similar transactions again and again.

Though the way in which these events dominated our communication channels for that forty-eight hour period may be atypical (though not unique), given the fact that these communication transactions normally occur at less rapid intervals, I believe that this set is an accurate and useful paradigm of the sets of communication transactions in which we are involved for a large portion of the important events and ideas of our lives.

These various message sets are, in effect, overlayed to form the large and complex communication environment or "mosaic" in which each of us exists. This mosaic consists of an immense number of fragments or bits of information on an immense number of topics. As I suggested earlier, these bits are scattered over time and space and modes of communication. Each individual must grasp from this mosaic those bits which serve his needs, must group them into message sets which are relevant for him at any given time, and within each message set must organize the bits and close the gaps between them in order to arrive at a coherent picture of the world to which he can respond. Individuals vary widely in their pictures of the world for there is a great deal of variation in their needs and backgrounds and the order in which they are exposed to the bits, the media which facilitate exposure to each bit, and the gaps between the bits. These gaps between message bits are also of various sorts. Some are spatial gaps between message bits which are sensed simultaneously. Some, on the other hand, are temporal gaps between message bits. There are what we might call source gaps between bits which are sensed from different media or through different modes of communication or from different writers or speakers, and of course, there are information gaps, for no individuals are probably ever exposed to all possible information about a topic. Evidence that we have from studies of ordinal position effect, perception, and learning indicate that these differences among types of gaps make a difference. A message whose bits one has sensed simultaneously has a different effect from a message with comparable bits sensed at various points in time, and that each has a different effect from a message with bits whose substance appears comparable but which are sensed through different sources.

I have developed a visual representation of this mosaic analogue which I find fruitful for stimulating ideas for the kinds of communication studies which most interest me; the visual representation suggests some ways to get from the general conception to data gathering and perhaps some hypothesis testing. This is certainly not the only way to visualize this conception, and it may not be the most fruitful representation for all of the varied approaches to the study of communication which we find in our field. Perhaps, though, some suggestions for other ways to represent the basic idea may come from this conference. I have been thinking of the communication mosaic largely in terms of a constantly changing cube through which a receiver is constantly moving. The cube is made up of an almost infinite number of minute cells.

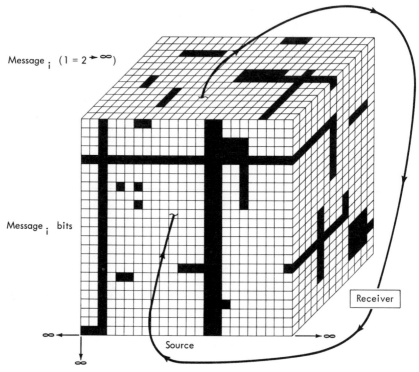

The Message$_1$ set—the front slice of the cube—might be the set of message bits about the Martin Luther King murder. The ordinate represents all of the possible bits in that message set; the abscissa represents all possible sources. The darkened cells indicate that, at that point in time, those particular message bits are not available from those sources. Some bits are probably unavailable from *any* source at some points in time. An entire message set may be unavailable from some sources sometimes, perhaps even unavailable from certain sources any time. In addition, the message sets and bits available change more rapidly for some sources than others. With the print media, the change is quite slow; with the electronic media it is very rapid; with people it varies a good bit, though we find some who seem to perseverate a good while on some bits of information. Thus, the front layer of the cube represents the message bits about

King which can be found at one point in time from each possible source.

The other slices of the cube represent other message sets—the Arab-Israeli conflict, the student power movement, the field of speech, and so forth.

We could conceive of the receiver as moving through the cube in continuous loops, or of the mosaic cube moving past or changing as the receiver remains stationary. Both kinds of movement occur much of the time for most of us. However, I believe that it is more fruitful to visualize the receiver moving through the constantly changing cube. This emphasizes the restricted and sequential nature of exposure and the phenomenon of contextual cues. We also need to include in this conception the element of randomness. Whether I overhear a conversation or happen to be listening to the radio just when a particular bit of the message about the King affair is available from that source is in large part chance. In addition, the people with whom I converse or whose conversation I overhear, the radio station to which I am listening, or whether I am listening to any radio station or talking with any people at a particular point in time is in large part chance. On the other hand, not all of it is chance. Many studies of how news is diffused, for example, show that when people are exposed to information which they believe is important, they will generally turn to additional sources to verify or supplement what they got from the original source.[29] As one would expect, evidence also indicates that people communicate about major news events with their friends primarily, with relatives somewhat less, with mere acquaintances still less, and with strangers least, though within the first ten hours of the shooting of President Kennedy, it was found that four per cent of the sample in one study reported talking with strangers about the event, and within the first ten hours after the shooting of Oswald five per cent of the sample reported doing so.[30] Additional evidence that the exposure of individuals to certain message set-source combinations is non-random can be found in some of the studies of media usage. One study of the audience for information on world affairs, for example, which categorized people as part of the "mass majority," the "peripheral mass," the "non-elite educated," and the "educated elite," found a good bit of relevant evidence. The educated elite, comprising about a quarter of one per cent of the population, is defined as that group of professors, journalists, social commentators, business leaders, and political party influentials who account for almost all of the relevant foreign affairs "activity" in the United States. The non-elite educated, comprising ten to twenty-five per cent of the population, are mainly college graduates with the background to absorb information about foreign affairs but without the interest or expertise to question much of it. The peripheral mass, comprising between twenty and forty per cent of the population, are generally the high school graduates or

those with some college who are relatively free of economic worries. They
have been characterized as "tolerators" of international news; that is to
say, they are aware of some of it, but do little to seek it. The fourth group
is the mass majority, estimated to comprise fifty to sixty per cent of the
population. These are mainly individuals with less than a high school education and a minimal interest in world affairs. Their major concern is
"getting by." Few would say that news programs are among their favor-
ites on television; more than any of the other groups, they are likely to
want less, rather than more, newspaper space devoted to foreign news. If
we look at the media usage for each of these groups, we can get some basis for setting probabilities of exposure to certain messages in certain
media:

APPROXIMATE MEDIA USAGE FOR EACH OF FOUR AUDIENCE GROUPS[31]

	Mass Majority	Peripheral Mass	College Grads	Elites
Read any non-fiction books in the last year	5%	15%	30%	50%
Read one issue a month of *Harpers, Nat'l Review*, etc.	½	2	10	25
Read an issue a month of *Time, Newsweek, or US News*	5	10	45	70
Read one issue a month of *Look, Life,* or *Post*	25	50	65	30
Read a daily newspaper	70	80	90	95
Read *New York Times*	⅕	½	5	50
Read nat'l or internat'l news first in paper	10	20	30	50
Want more foreign news in paper	10	20	30	50
Listen to radio daily	60	70	85	No info.
Hear radio news daily	50	60	65	No info.
Use television daily	80	75	65	?
TV news	45	45	45	?
TV is favorite news medium	60	35	20	?
News is favorite TV show	5	15	30	50

An individual's sex is another factor which affects his probabilities of exposure to various sources and, hence, the probabilities of his exposure to
certain message bits. It has been found that women tended to hear about
the John Kennedy assassination sooner than men did and were more likely
to hear about it first from television or to turn to television immediately
for details. Men depended more upon other people—primarily co-workers
—for the first news of the event and were more likely to turn to radio for
confirmation. In general, men talked more with other people about these

events during the weekend than women did; women saw much more of the television coverage.[32] Clearly there is an interaction between sex and time of day or day of the week which affects the opportunities for people to talk with other people or to read, listen, or view the mass media. A negative correlation between age and amount of reliance on other people as sources has also been found.[33] There appears to be an interesting interaction between economic level and race which affects diffusion patterns also. It has been found that poor people—whether black or white—use and trust the electronic media more than people with average or high incomes do, but that poor blacks depend upon their friends and acquaintances for information (rather than upon newspapers or other media) far more than whites (poor or otherwise) do.[34] Clearly these variations in probability of exposure to different sources affect the part of any given message set to which one is likely to be exposed and his response to that exposure. Many contemporary communication scholars are explaining the phenomenon of selective exposure in terms of prior attitudes of receivers. It seems apparent to me from the evidence that, in addition to—or as part of—the variables I noted above, what we might call an individual's "life style" is a much more important determinant. In "life style" I include such things as one's social and intellectual pursuits, standard of living, geographic location, and occupation.

Not only do classes of individuals vary in the relative attention they give to various media, they vary in the total amount of time and attention devoted to what we would normally categorize as communication. In other words, in terms of our mosaic, there is great variation among receivers in the frequency of their loops through the cube. Some receivers expose themselves to many more kinds of information and to more of each kind than other receivers do.

Another important point which this analogue makes salient is that there is not only a relationship between sources and bits of one message to which a receiver is exposed, but also a relationship between these and the bits of other messages against which they are sensed. Thus, two individuals may be listening to the same report of the Martin Luther King funeral on the radio but, at the same time, one is reading the newspaper about the gallantry of black soldiers in Vietnam while the other is looking at a photograph of young blacks looting a liquor store. The effect of this sort of contextual cue is quite obvious. Less obvious is the effect of contextual cues which we might label irrelevant or even distracting. There is increasing evidence that the pressure within individuals to make sense of their environment results in their seeing relationships among quite independent stimuli, thus changing to some extent the meaning of both. In one study at the University of Iowa, for example, subjects were exposed to a videotape in which the sound track was a speech denouncing fraternities. The visual track for half the subjects was a film showing the journey of a locomotive across the lovely French countryside. The visual track seen by the other subjects was a film showing the pollution of our environment through burning refuse, dumping matter into our streams, and inadequate disposal of garbage. Typical of this film was the closeup shot of maggots crawling through old coffee grounds. In neither videotape was an effort made to coordinate the sound and visual tracks. The intent was, rather, to have the visual track distract the audience from the sound track. Thus, the investigators wanted them to be unrelated. They found, though, that the subjects were *not* distracted because they *perceived* a relationship; they found support for the verbal message in every scene of each film. They decided that the reason for showing a film of a steam engine was that fraternities, like steam engines, were antiquated. They decided that the shots of garbage were shown to indicate that fraternities accept only the social elite and discard—like garbage—everyone else.[35]

An even more obvious example of the probable effect of contextual cues—cues in sequence this time, rather than simultaneous—is the television coverage in the summer of 1968 of the Democratic National Convention in Chicago. The perception of the convention by most television viewers would have been quite different if the message bits which they saw from Convention Hall had not been interspersed with bits from the message set about police and demonstrators in the streets. These constant reminders placed the convention in a context which was grotesque, and it too became grotesque for many viewers.

The context against which a message bit is sensed is obviously in large part a chance matter. It is probably not completely so though. We need some studies which give us a basis for predicting the probabilities of various sorts of message bits being in the mosaic simultaneously. For example, when the probability is high of hearing about the Ted Kennedy-Mary Jo Kopechne accident, is the probability of hearing about Jackie Onassis increased? When there is a major student uprising on a college campus, do sources tend to give greater play to messages about drugs?

There is still another kind of variation, not apparent in the diagram, which is important. This is the variation of the message sets themselves over time; they increase and decrease in prominence and the nature of some changes. Consider, for example, the change over time in the nature of the message set about the Vietnam war or about Lyndon Johnson. The shape and nature of the message sets also change as one moves through space or, in some cases, educational or social level of receivers. Such changes may mislead us into believing that a message set no longer exists and so the communication scholar stops observing. Here again, we must become sensitive to this sort of audience variable.

Long ago, mass media scholars recognized the fallacy of the conception of a "mass audience"—a large, homogeneous blob. Yet, it seems to me that many other communication scholars still conceive of the audience in this way—still fail to make some estimate of the variety of audiences involved in some communication situations. We must begin to categorize audiences in terms of the context in which a particular message set is sensed, and in all of the other ways which may be relevant. In one sense, I am suggesting here that the rhetorician take a cue from the statistician and become more concerned with variances than with means—more concerned with the nature, extent and relevance of differences among segments of the audience and less concerned with their central tendency, with describing the "average" audience member. In another sense, I am suggesting that we take a cue from some of the contemporary artists who describe their collages as "accumulations." Conceptualizing the human communication experience—the rather wild assortment and juxtaposition of message bits—as an "accumulation" may suggest some of the kinds of stimulus-response relationships for which we should be looking.

Rhetorical theorists also have a responsibility to generate ways for us to handle these various sorts of interaction I have described; they must provide some handles with which to grab and turn and analyze these phenomena. One set of these handles is the set of critical abstractions or key concepts which we use to talk about and generalize about communication processes. As I noted at the beginning of this paper, much more original thought needs to be given to this aspect of our work than we have been giving in the recent past; we need to develop the kind of critical abstractions which will help us to describe and understand the sorts of contemporary communication processes I have discussed here. We need to develop the kind of abstractions which not only will help us to understand and describe an event in the past, but enable us to generalize in a more meaningful way from past to present and future events.

We also need to examine the abstractions which we are now using more critically—such abstractions as credibility or ethos, motive appeals, attention, attitude, persuasive message, and informative message. Are these useful abstractions for helping us to describe and understand important communication processes as *precisely as possible*? It may even be useful to raise the question of the *criteria* we use for determining the fruitfulness of a concept.

A major part of this development and testing of the fruitfulness of concepts is the determination of the most fruitful unit and level of analysis for different sorts of problems. We must be concerned about whether the most useful unit of analysis for messages is some part or bit of individual messages, whether it is the total objects we now call a message—such as a speech, whether it is some sort of message set, or whether it is some group of message sets. Similarly, we must give serious attention to our unit of analysis for studying those involved in communication processes. For example, when studying the communication involved in the spread or adoption of some particular idea, we must consider whether our unit of analysis will be the adopting group—a school, a school system, a city council, a corporation—or whether it will be the individual within the group. How are we going to conceptualize those involved? To what extent are we going to focus on properties of the group? To what extent are we going to conceptualize the group as some composite of the individuals within it? I am convinced that both our rhetorical and communication theories have tended to conceive of the relationships among those involved in a communication situation in far too simple ways. We have tended to talk of degree of ethos or source credibility or, in somewhat more sophisticated fashion, have considered various dimensions of source credibility, such as trustworthiness and competence. Surely there are other dimensions of the relationships among people which affect the communication processes which occur. What about simply probability of encounter? Type or degree of familiarity? What about the degree to which those involved in a communication situation are alike or different on various dimensions? How are we going to conceptualize types of communication topics, time, situations, and kinds of responses in our contemporary rhetorical theories and research?

In developing these conceptions, we must have as a major goal the understanding of the way human beings attempt to make sense out of their environment, the ways which they find to organize the fragmentary and disparate bits of messages to which they are exposed. In other words, I am calling for a message-audience centered rhetoric, as opposed to the source-message one which has dominated our field to too great an extent in the past. I am also calling for a substantially altered conception of message from that which we find in most of our research and theorizing about rhetoric and public address.

Related to these shifts, and perhaps even more important, I am suggesting that we devote at least as much serious, sophisticated, scholarly work to contemporary communication phenomena as we have to that which occurred in the past. Too many scholars of rhetoric and public address have been concerned only with the discourse of the past—discourse on which one can, presumably, gain a more "objective" perspective. Whatever perspective and objectivity is gained is more than overbalanced, however, by the loss of sources of data through time. We are too often satisfied with a relatively accurate manuscript of a speech, or a recording. We are overjoyed if we have a film or television kinescope. However, we are generally unconcerned with the problem of accurate data on the rhetorical situation—all of the kinds of data I have been discussing which affect the many and varied processes of communication preceding and following the formal speech. We can only get these kinds of data—we can only probe the kinds of questions which I have been proposing here—if we turn more of our attention to today.[36]

Last, but most important, since we can not study everything, a major criterion in our choice of what to study should be its probable theoretical significance. We must be prepared to argue that our "research topic" will probably contribute something to the explanatory-predictive mosaic that we are building together.

FOOTNOTES

1. Douglas Ehninger, "On Systems of Rhetoric," *Philosophy and Rhetoric*, I (1968), 131–44.
2. *Ibid.*, p. 140.
3. Example from Tim Moore, *Claude Levi-Strauss and the Cultural Sciences*, Occasional Papers No. 4 (Birmingham, England: Centre for Contemporary Cultural Studies, Birmingham University, n.d.).
4. See, for example, some of the many studies by McGuire and others on the inoculation of audiences against counter-persuasion. One report of this research is William McGuire, "Resistance to Persuasion Conferred by Active and Passive Prior Refutation of the Same and Alternative Counterarguments," *J. Abnormal and Social Psychology*, LXIII (1961), 326–32.
5. Daniel Katz, "The Functional Approach to the Study of Attitudes," *Public Opinion Quarterly*, XXIV (1960), 170.
6. Lloyd F. Bitzer, "The Rhetorical Situation," *Philosophy and Rhetoric*, I (1968), 1–14. Bitzer's analysis of the rhetorical situation is similar to what systems theory would describe as an imbalance in the system, calling for emergency steps to restore balance. Systems theory goes further though in adding the additional process of restoring normal functioning around the new balance.
7. Franklyn S. Haiman, "The Rhetoric of the Streets: Some Legal and Ethical Considerations," *Quarterly Journal of Speech*, LIII (1967), 99–114. As Haiman notes, the term "body rhetoric" was probably originated by Leland Griffin in "The Rhetorical Structure of the 'New Left' Movement: Part I," *Quarterly Journal of Speech*, L (1964), 113–35.
8. Herbert Zettl, in "The Paradox of Educational Television and the Educational Process," *Western Speech*, XXXI (1967), 224–31, has pleaded for this sort of thing in the research on instructional broadcasting. He says that "simple tests designed to find out whether a student can remember a sentence better when it is written on a blackboard or shown on the television screen will tell us little about the actual potential effectiveness of television as an educational method within a total educational context. Once I am obliged to pass a course, it matters little to me whether I print my notes carefully on high-grade parchment or scribble them on the back of an old envelope, as long as I can read them. Any test that seeks to determine solely whether I learn better from the parchment or the envelope is bound to result in the all-too-familiar 'no significant difference.' What I want to point out here is that simple, conventional experimental studies that isolate the educational context from television communication no longer

seem adequate in measuring and assessing the effectiveness of television in education. . . . Research designs must be constructed as to take into full consideration the educational context within which specific phenomena are measured; that is, the research approaches should be geared to the *inclusion* rather than *exclusion* of complex group variables. For example, we might as well admit that the easy access of the home viewer to the refrigerator or the bathroom is an important factor in viewing behavior which we simply cannot afford to omit in our studies on home viewing."

9. For example, in the late 1950's and early in 1960, the critical audience for the message about integrating public schools in Dallas, Texas, was not the total population of Dallas, nor even the total adult population; it was a group of 250 men who call themselves the Dallas Citizens Council. These are the owners or executive heads of some of the major corporations in Dallas. When this group "got" and accepted the message that Dallas should integrate, the action was as good as done. See William R. Carmack and Theodore Freedman, *Factors Affecting School Desegregation* (New York: Anti-Defamation League of B'nai B'rith, n.d.)

10. Bernard Berelson, "National Family Planning Programs: Where We Stand," Paper prepared for the University of Michigan Sesquicentennial Celebration, November, 1967, pp. 15–16. (Mimeographed.)

11. Paul B. Sheatsley and Jacob J. Feldman, "A National Survey on Public Reactions and Behavior," in *The Kennedy Assassination and the American Public*, ed. Bradley S. Greenberg and Edwin B. Parker (Stanford: Stanford University Press, 1965), pp. 152–53.

12. Wilbur Schramm, "Communication in Crisis," in Greenberg and Parker, p. 16.

13. Sheatsley and Feldman, p. 153.

14. *Ibid.*, pp. 150–52.

15. Greenberg and Parker, *op cit.* Sidney Kraus (ed.), *The Great Debates* (Bloomington: Indiana University Press, 1962).

16. George Gerbner, "Institutional Pressures Upon Mass Communicators," *The Sociological Review Monograph*, No. 13 (Keele [U.K.]: University of Keele, January, 1969), pp. 205–48.

17. Walter Sieber, "Two Communicators of the News: A Study of the Roles of Sources and Reporters," *Social Forces*, XXXIX (1962), 76–83.

18. William L. Rivers, "The Press and the Assassination," in Greenberg and Parker, pp. 51–60.

19. See, for example, Herbert Waltzer, "In the Magic Lantern: Television Coverage of the 1964 National Conventions," *Public Opinion Quarterly*, XXX (1966), 33–53; and Martin Harrison, "Television and Radio," in *The British General Election of 1966*, ed. D. E. Butler and Anthony King (London: Macmillan, 1966), pp. 125–48.

20. Elizabeth Ann Kyes, "President Kennedy's Press Conferences as 'Shapers' of the News" (unpublished Ph.D. dissertation, University of Iowa, 1968).

21. Elihu Katz and Paul F. Lazarsfeld, *Personal Influence* (Glencoe, Illinois: The Free Press, 1955).

22. John P. Robinson and James W. Swinehart, "World Affairs and the TV Audience," *Television Quarterly*, VII (Spring 1968), 54.

23. Harrison, E. Salisbury, "The Editor's View in New York," in Greenberg and Parker, p. 38.

24. Elmer Lower, "A Television Network Gathers the News," in Greenberg and Parker, p. 67.

25. Example from unpublished paper by John Waite Bowers, "Confrontation and Control: Chicago, August 1968" (Iowa City: University of Iowa, Department of Speech and Dramatic Art, Communication Research Laboratory, n.d.).

26. Wilmer J. Young, *Visible Witness: A Testimony for Radical Peace Action* (Wallingford, Pa.: Pendle Hill Pamphlet, 1961), p. 29, quoted by Robert J. Gwyn, "Some Reflections on Television and Symbolic Speech," *Television Quarterly*, VIII (Spring 1969), p. 62.

27. I began the development of this idea in an earlier paper, "Toward an Appropriate Theory for Contemporary Speech-Communication," in *What Rhetoric (Communication Theory) is Appropriate for Contemporary Speech Communication?* ed. David H. Smith (Minneapolis: University of Minnesota, 1969), pp. 9–25.

28. The notion of multiple images in the new theatre was suggested by Richard Schechner in "Comment," *Tulane Drama Review*, X (Spring 1966), 23.

29. See, for example, Otto N. Larsen and Richard J. Hill, "Mass Media and Interpersonal Communication in the Diffusion of a News Event," *American Sociological Review*, XIX (1954), 426–33; Wayne Danielson, "Eisenhower's February Decision: A Study in News Impact," *Journalism Quarterly*, XXXIII (1956), 433–41; Paul J. Deutschmann and Wayne A. Danielson, "Diffusion of Knowledge of the Major News Story," *Journalism Quarterly*, XXXVII (1960), 345–55; Stephan P. and Nancy S. Spitzer, "Diffusion of News of Kennedy and Oswald Deaths," in Greenberg and Parker, pp. 99–111.

30. Spitzer and Spitzer, p. 110.

31. Robinson and Swinehart, p. 47.

32. Bradley S. Greenberg, "Diffusion of News about the Kennedy Assassination," Greenberg and Parker, pp. 95–96.

33. *Ibid.*, p. 96.

34. See, for example, Bradley Greenberg and Brenda Dervin, "Mass Communication Among the Urban Poor" (unpublished paper, Department of Communication, Michigan State University, n.d.). (Mimeographed.)

35. William G. Freeman and Daniel J. Perkins, "Persuasion in Situations of Pleasant and Unpleasant Distraction" (unpublished study, Communication Research Laboratory, Department of Speech and Dramatic Art, University of Iowa, n.d.). (Mimeographed.)

36. This is obviously not an original thought. Among the foremost rhetorical scholars advocating more intensive study of the contemporary scene are Douglas Ehninger and Wayne E. Brockriede. See, for example, Brockriede's eloquent statement, "Toward a Contemporary Aristotelian Theory of Rhetoric," *Quarterly Journal of Speech*, LII (1966), 33–40.

3 / THE USES OF RHETORIC IN A TECHNOLOGICAL AGE: ARCHITECTONIC PRODUCTIVE ARTS

RICHARD McKEON
University of Chicago

I. CONTINUITIES AND REVOLUTIONS
IN THE DEVELOPMENT OF RHETORIC

Rhetoric has had a long and variegated history. It has been influential in the development of theory, practice, and art, and methods to produce and use the products of knowledge, action, and production. It has been influenced by truths of sciences, circumstances of times and communities, and analogies of arts; and it has been expounded in propositions of theory, in rules of practice, and in maxims of art. Its history has been a continuous one, because basic terms, distinctions, and schemata reappear and are put to new uses. It has been an ambiguous history, because continuing terms assume new meanings in their new applications, and the innovations are seldom guided by knowledge of how renewed terms were used in earlier traditions. Histories of rhetoric, which throw little light on the principles or purposes by which present methods and uses of rhetoric might be evaluated or changed, tend to be pedantic explorations of traditions of rhetoric as an art of persuasion and belief, of deception and proof, of image-making and communication, which follow through the consequences of pejorative or positive judgments posited as premises. Discussions of rhetoric in the past and in the present and projections of rhetoric in the future reflect estimations of its nature and operation. Apparently it has been practiced widely as an art of deception, public relations, alienation, and self-interest, and it has been one of the factors contributing to the degradation of knowledge, morality, and culture. Apparently it has also been practiced as an art of revolution and renaissance, and it has been one of the factors contributing to innovation and growth in theory, practice, and production.

Rhetoric is an instrument of continuity and of change, of tradition and of revolution. The history of rhetoric is the history of a continuing art undergoing revolutionary changes. It has played an important part at some points in the formation of culture in the West, notably during the Roman Republic and the Renaissance. In both periods it was enlarged in its operation, using an extended form of the rhetorical device of "amplification," to become a productive or poetic art, an art of making in all phases of human activity. It was systematized in its organization, using a comprehensive form of the rhetorical device of "schematization," to become an architectonic art, an art of structuring all principles and products of knowing, doing, and making. If rhetoric is to be used to contribute to the formation of the culture of the modern world, it should function productively in the resolution of new problems and architectonically in the formation of new inclusive communities. Rhetoric can be used to produce a new rhetoric constructed as a productive art and schematized as an architectonic art. At a second stage the new rhetoric can be used to reorganize the subject-matter and arts of education and life. What rhetoric should be and to what conditions it is adapted are not separate theoretic questions but the single practical question of producing schemata to guide the use of the productive arts in transforming circumstances.

The nature and methods of an architectonic productive art and the technical languages in which arts and sciences are classified, like many of the processes of inquiry and analysis and much of the technical language of distinction and systematization in the West, can be clarified by going back to beginnings made in the distinctions and analyses of Aristotle. He gave a technical meaning to the ordinary Greek expression *architecton*— "architectonic artist" or "master craftsman"—and used it in his schema of the organization of the sciences. In that organization he gave a technical meaning to the Greek expression *poiesis*—"production" or "poetry" or "making"—and used it to name one of his three sciences "poetic science" or "productive science." Later thinkers, doers, and makers have revolted against Aristotle's metaphysics and poetics more frequently than they have used them. Nevertheless they have constructed like devices for making principles and relations, and the ambiguous history of architectonic productive arts affords some guidance in understanding and changing the uses of the productive arts in an age of technology.

Aristotle distinguished between the art of the user, who knows the form, and that of the master-craftsman, who knows the matter and makes the product, although the art of a user, such as a helmsman, has architectonic functions in determining the form in which the product, the helm, is to be made (*Physics* i. 2. 194^{b}1–7). In the transition from things better known to us by sensation to things better known in nature by science the sequence runs from sensation to experience, to art, to architectonic art, to productive sciences, to theoretic sciences (*Metaphysics* i. 1. 981^{b}25–35). The architectonic arts are themselves principles (*ibid.* v. 1. 1013^{a}1–14), and wisdom (or as it was later to be called, metaphysics) is the science of first causes or principles. Metaphysics functions as an authoritative or architectonic art by organizing the sciences according to principles, subject-matters, and methods into the theoretic, practical, and productive sciences —the sciences of knowing, doing, and making.

An architectonic art is an art of doing. Architectonic arts treat ends which order the ends of subordinate arts (*Nicomachean* Ethics i. 1. 1094^{a}1–17). The architectonic art is the most authoritative art. The practical science, politics, which has as its end action, not knowledge, is such an art, "for it ordains which of the sciences are to be pursued in a state, and what branches of knowledge each of the classes of citizens is to learn, and up to what point, and even the most esteemed capacities fall under it, such as strategy, domestic economy, and oratory" (*ibid.* i. 2. 1094^{a}27–^{b}5). The moral virtues are the sources of actions in accordance with the rule of right reason. The rule of right reason is put into effect by prudence, which is a calculative intellectual virtue, engaged in ordering and interpreting the variables of action, and it is in turn under the guidance of wisdom. Prudence and wisdom make use of architectonic arts to guide subordinate arts of doing (*ibid.* book vi., esp. chapter 8. 1141^{b}22–28).

The second calculative intellectual virtue, art, likewise makes use of an architectonic art. Prudence is architectonic with respect to doing (and its sphere of doing includes sciences, actions, institutions, and arts). Art is architectonic with respect to making, and the architectonic art of making is rhetoric, in so far as rhetoric is an art of thought. Diction and thought are two of the six parts of tragedy which Aristotle distinguishes in the *Poetics*. Poetic diction is treated in the *Poetics*, and it is distinguished from elocution or the architectonic art of speech, which includes not only propositions, which are treated in logic, but statements in general, in aspects which do not bear directly on their truth or falsity—commands, prayers, threats, questions, answers, and other modes of simple and connected discourse. Thought is not treated in the *Poetics*; in the *Rhetoric* to which Aristotle refers in the *Poetics* for the treatment of thought, account is taken not only of cognitive processes of proof and disproof, but also of noncognitive devices of amplifying and restricting, that is, enlarging and diminishing, maximizing and minimizing (*Poetics* 19. 1456ª32–ᵇ19).

Later ages continued to use the vocabulary of these distinctions; and the overall characteristics and problems of ages may be stated by determining the architectonic productive arts by which theoretic, practical, and productive arts are organized and related to each other in production, and by which products of the arts and sciences are set up and justified in experience. Aristotle formulated rhetoric as a "universal art," limited to no one subject-matter but applicable to all. For Aristotle rhetoric is not a "science," because each science has a particular "method" suited to its particular subject-matter and operative according to its proper principles. One of the sciences, politics, is an architectonic art, for it is a science of doing, and it is architectonic of actions, individual and communal, including actions which bear on the cultivation of sciences and arts. But the architectonic art of politics is to be distinguished from rhetoric. The vocabulary of the distinctions between architectonic and subordinate arts, and between practical and theoretical arts and sciences, continues to be used, but the distinctions are shuffled and the meanings and applications of the terms are altered: all the basic terms and relations undergo this transformation and transportation—art and method; theoretic, practical, and productive; being, thought, action, and statement.

Cicero enlarged rhetoric into a universal productive art, an *ars disserendi*, and applied it to resolve what he conceived to be the basic problem of Roman culture, the separation of wisdom and eloquence, of philosophy and rhetoric. The diremption between wisdom and eloquence had been a consequence of Socrates' great achievements in philosophy: earlier Greek philosophers and statesmen had practiced both arts, but after the development of the philosophical arts by Socrates, those who learned to analyze problems were unlearned in the arts of speech, while those who acquired eloquence were ignorant of what they talked about. Socrates had also been the first to bring philosophy down from the heavens to find its subject-matter in the homes and cities of men. Cicero therefore made use of Hellenistic readjustments of the earlier Greek philosophic distinctions and vocabulary to reformulate the practical subject-matter and methods of a philosophy rejoined to rhetoric. He based his method on questions or issues, the *constitutiones* of rhetoric operating as a productive art to construct or constitute the matter of problems or cases and of conclusions or judgments. The four constitutions are practical transformations of Aristotle's four scientific questions. Aristotle distinguished the methods of the sciences, which are applicable to particular fields, from the universal arts, which are applicable to all subject-matters. Both "methods" and "arts" are presented problematically, however, and in terms of the questions for which they provide means of inquiry. Aristotle enumerates four scientific questions—ways of discovering and establishing facts and causes in subject-matters—(1) is it? (2) what is it? (3) what properties does it have? and (4) why? (*Posterior Analytics* ii. 1. 89ᵇ21–31). These are transformed from theoretic methodological questions into practical operational questions in Cicero's use of rhetoric as a productive architectonic science—(1) the conjectural constitution for the establishment of fact, (2) the definitive constitution for the definition of name, (3) the general or qualitative constitution for the justification of qualifications or evaluations, and (4) the translative constitution for the choice of proper or competent judges. Aristotle's questions provide principles for the methods of particular sciences which explore the structure of fact and cause within the subject-matters of those sciences. Cicero's questions construct issues for the arts of rhetoric which establish the facts and resolve the "causes" by relating facts, words, values, and judgments; they are not adapted to a pre-existent particular subject-matter but are used to constitute or produce a determined subject-matter.

Since differences of subject-matter are produced by discovering and justifying answers to questions, the arts and the sciences will not be organized according to differences in the subject-matter which they treat, but according to differences of question, action, statement, valuation, and judgment. Aristotle divided the sciences into theoretic, practical, and productive on the basis of differences of subject, method, and purpose or principle. He also divided rhetoric into three kinds on the basis of differences of audience, speaker, and subject, and he treated dialectic as a universal art and a counterpart of rhetoric. A productive architectonic art produces subject-matters and organizes them in relation to each other and to the problems to be solved. The changes in the names of the kinds of rhetoric are signs of the transformations they underwent when they became fields of action, production, or knowledge. Aristotle's "forensic" rhetoric, which is concerned with accusation and defense, with past actions, and with justice and injustice, became "judicial." His "political" rhetoric, which is concerned with exhortation and dehortation, with future actions, and with expediency and inexpediency, with utility and inutility, became "deliberative." His "epideictic" rhetoric, which is concerned with praise and blame, with present persons, their characters and actions, and with honor and dishonor, became "demonstrative." The difference between rhetoric and dialectic became the difference between eloquence and wisdom and is found in the difference between particular and universal questions.

Cicero's use of rhetoric as a productive architectonic art laid down the structure of a program of education and culture designed to reunite eloquence and wisdom in action. The great architectonic achievement of the Romans was the organization of Roman Law. But with the institution of the Roman Empire, political deliberative rhetoric ceased to play an important part in political deliberation and action, and the old dichotomy reappeared between eloquence and wisdom, between language and action, words and deeds. Justice, prudence, and wisdom were determined by the actions of the emperor, not by deliberation. Judicial and demonstrative rhetoric became verbal arts, the one an art of disputation, debate, and controversy in Roman Jurisprudence, the other an art of verbal construction and exhibition in the Second Sophistic. In the Empire two branches of rhetoric were cultivated, judicial or legal and demonstrative or sophistic. Judicial rhetoric exercised a productive architectonic function in the formation and organization of law by the jurisconsults, both the civil law of Rome and the *jus gentium* which universalized law to all peoples. It exercised a productive architectonic function in ordering the actions of men toward universal peace and justice in the *Pax Romana*. Sophistic rhetoric exercised a productive architectonic function in the formation of a literature of consolation, instruction, pleasure, and sublimity, of adroitly differentiated styles and intricately elaborated figures, of tales and histories, prose, poetry, and the merging of the two in *satura*, of drama, satire, philosophy, and the history of philosophy and of sophistry. With the spread of Christianity the dichotomy of eloquence and wisdom continued. Honor and dishonor, merit and sin, good and evil were determined by interpretation of revealed truths and by action of the church, not by *deliberative* rhetoric. The art of disputation developed in *judicial* rhetoric was used in canon law to establish the concordance of discordant canons and was adapted to education and to theology in the development of the scholastic method. Political or deliberative rhetoric was dichotomized in its productive architectonic function between the city of God and terrestrial cities, divine laws and human laws, and *demonstrative* or artistic rhetoric became one of the verbal arts of the trivium, and in the development the arts of words and the arts of things became technical, abstract, and empty of content and subject-matter.

Renaissance philosophers and rhetoricians sought to rejoin eloquence and wisdom and developed within the new rhetoric they constructed a new universal subject-matter. They sought to make rhetoric a productive architectonic art of all arts and of all products rather than a productive technical art of language and persuasion. To make that transformation they transformed the architectonic functions of rhetoric from the practical or legal organization of actions in virtues and institutions to the productive or poetic organization of constructions in art objects and cultures. They made use of Cicero in this rebirth and innovation, as Medieval rhetoricians and philosophers had used the schemata of Ciceronian rhetoric to build a unified religion and tradition. Indeed, Renaissance rhetoricians invented the "Middle Ages" first by revolting against "middle Latinity" to return to the Latin of Cicero, and they continued the task by discovering in that middle period, which separated them from ancient Latin and Greek wisdom further dichotomies of language and content to be removed by rejoining rhetoric and wisdom. Instead of distinguishing divine and human letters, they edited and interpreted Greek and Latin authors and applied the philology and hermeneutics of the study of literature to interpret Moses and the prophets, Paul and the evangelists, as poets. Instead of distinguishing divine and human law, they constructed history and political theory from the study of the history of ancient institutions and of the problems of the new nation states and international relations. Instead of distinguishing knowledge of universal laws of nature from empirical experience of natural occurrences, they constructed heuristic devices of discovery in which they borrowed from the common and proper places of rhetorical invention. Nizolius, in *On the True Principles and True Method [Ratio] of Philosophizing against the Pseudophilosophers* (which was later edited by Leibniz under the title *The Philosophical Anti-barbarus*), placed among the five general principles of philosophizing, (a) knowledge of the science of precepts and documents developed by the grammarians and the rhetoricians, and (b) assiduous reading of approved Greek and Latin authors and understanding of language of authors and people. Francis Bacon made use of the Topics in the formulation of his New Organon for scientific discovery. Ramus exposed the errors of the rhetoric of Aristotle, Cicero, and Quintilian (Cicero adds to the errors of Aristotle, and Quintilian to the errors of both), and reformulated the disciplines of the liberal arts using materials from ancient literature, oratory, and history. A long line of commentators on Aristotle's *Poetics* make part of their interpretation the adjustment of Aristotle's *Poetics* to the rhetorical criteria employed in Horace's *Ars Poetica*.

The Renaissance use of rhetoric as a productive architectonic art laid down the structure of a program of education and culture designed to reunite eloquence and wisdom in art. The great architectonic achievement of the Renaissance was the discovery and organization of the beautiful arts and the beautiful letters, for which the names *beaux arts* and *belles lettres* had to be invented. But with the accelerating progress of science, poetic demonstrative rhetoric ceased to play an important part in poetic insight and construction, and the old dichotomy between eloquence and wisdom reappeared, not in its practical form as a distinction between words and actions, but in its poetic form as a distinction between art and nature. This was to develop into a distinction between values and facts, and then between the humanities and the sciences. Philosophers, philologists, and historians began to imitate the methods of the sciences in the seventeenth century. They found and used methods of proof, not methods of discovery, although seventeenth century scientists worked to develop a heuristic method. By the nineteenth century, scientific method was conceived as a method of proof, and even philosophers like Mill and Whewell who disputed concerning the processes of scientific discovery, agreed that there was no "method" of discovery. The architectonic processes initiated in the Renaissance to rejoin the poles of medieval dichotomies have been conceived as phases of a process of "secularization" in which arts and sciences have been turned from the contemplation of another heavenly world to the production of this secular world for secular men. The productive processes have produced new subject-matters—literature, history, philosophy, and science, each with its proper methods or arts, and the continuation of these processes have been conceived as phases of the "fragmentation" of knowledge, community, and communication. Rhetoric ceased to operate as the productive architectonic art initiating and guiding these processes. It was replaced by the numerous arts of making and disposing which prepared for and produced a technological age, and rhetoric itself became technical: it turned from applications in other subject-matters, even *belles lettres*, except as they could be treated as instances of the proper subject-matter of rhetoric conceived as the art of speech. The fragmentation of knowledge is diagnosed and treated by juxtaposing subject-matters in "interdisciplinary" inquiry and study, and the rival productive arts of the associated fields compete for the role of architectonic art in relating and organizing the parts.

At each stage of the evolution of the arts and sciences since the Renaissance, an architectonic art was sought and used. Seventeenth century philosophers sought to apply the methods of the physical sciences or the mathematical sciences to human thought and action and to construct a "universal mechanics" or a "universal mathesis." The revolt of Kant against theoretic or speculative or dogmatic metaphysics was a revolt against that architectonic art. His Copernican revolution consisted in turning from the search for an architectonic science in the principles of being to seek it in the analysis of the forms of pure reason. "Human reason," he says, "is by nature architectonic. That is to say, it regards all our knowledge as belonging to a possible system, and therefore allows only such principles as do not at any rate make it impossible for any knowledge that we may attain to combine into a system with other knowledge" (*Critique of Pure Reason*, I, Part II, Division II, chapter 2, section 3, p. B. 502). An architectonic is an art of constructing systems, and the final chapters of the "Transcendental Doctrine of Method," with which the *Critique of Pure Reason* closes, are a chapter on the "Architectonic of Pure Reason" and one on the "History of Pure Reason." The architectonic science against which Kant revolted was theoretic metaphysics or ontology; his critical epistemology was to provide an architectonic basis for treating the problems of

Theology, Cosmology, and Psychology, the parts of the old metaphysics. It provided in fact a beginning to the controversies of the nineteenth century concerning theology and science (which have been conceived as phases of a warfare of science and religion), concerning the "methodologies" of the sciences (which have been conceived as phases of the developing opposition between materialism and idealism), and concerning the concepts and methods of sciences of facts and sciences of values, *Naturwissenschaft* as contrasted first to *Geisteswissenschaft* and then to *Kulturwissenschaft*, the natural sciences as contrasted to the human sciences or humanities and the social sciences (and the contrast has been conceived as an opposition and separation of two cultures based respectively on knowledge of universal, necessary laws and awareness of concrete, contingent facts). The twentieth century began with a series of revolts against metaphysics which were revolts against the methodologies of idealism and materialism rather than simple repetitions of Kant's revolt against the ontologies of empiricism and rationalism. Feuerbach placed the beginnings of modern philosophy in the "critique" of Hegel; G. E. Moore used critique of idealism and of utilitarianism as a propaedeutic to common sense.

As we enter into the final decades of this century, we boast of a vast increase of output in all arts, and we are puzzled by the absence of interdisciplinary connection and by the breakdown of interpersonal, intergroup, and intercultural communication. We need a new architectonic productive art. Rhetoric exercised such functions in the Roman republic and in the Renaissance. Rhetoric provides the devices by which to determine the characteristics and problems of our times and to form the art by which to guide actions for the solution of our problems and the improvement of our circumstances. The history of the development of culture in the West sketched in the preceding paragraphs is an application of the methods of rhetoric to the discovery of ourselves and our times. It is in opposition and refutation of many accepted or advocated interpretations, but more important than its use in adversary opposition, it opens up possible methods of directing and relating knowledge, action, and production, by instituting an architectonic productive art of improving and increasing both the production of utilities and goods (*utilia* and *honesta*) and the use and enjoyment (*uti* and *frui*) of the products. The guidelines for both tasks are found in the continuing use of basic distinctions made in the fundamental vocabulary of rhetoric, and the mark of the validity and relevance of those distinctions is found in the fact that the common vocabulary in which we discuss the problems of our times is already structured on those distinctions and that facts are as much determined by orientations as orientations are determined by facts.

The architectonic productive art in an age of "technology" is obviously technology itself given a rhetorical transformation. The architectonic productive art of the Romans was rhetoric with a practical orientation. In the Renaissance it was rhetoric with a poetic orientation. There is every reason to think that the art we seek is rhetoric with a theoretic orientation, and a rhetorical sign that this is the case is seen in the fact that, whereas the orientation of the seventeenth century, at the beginning of the modern period, found expression in "ontology," and that of the nineteenth century in "methodology," contemporary culture makes use of "technology," which combines a main stem meaning "art" with a suffix meaning "science," suggesting that it would be well to elaborate a "science of art." The subject-matter determined as the field of such problems and the methods to be instituted to treat them are foreshadowed in structure and direction, as they have been found in other innovations, by following the lead of rhetorical constitutions for questions and methods and the lead of rhetorical kinds for subject-matters and fields of activity.

II. THE NEW RHETORIC, ITS METHODS AND ITS PROBLEMS

Determination of the problems of our times, and action to resolve them, stand in need of an architectonic productive art. The problem of constituting such an art and applying it once constituted is one of rejoining eloquence and wisdom, rhetoric and philosophy. The continuing vocabulary and schemata, of words and of things, afford guidance in the constitution of such an art. The initial exploratory applications of devices borrowed from older rhetorics is facilitated by the fact that the data of experience are labelled and classified in common language using the same vocabulary and schemata. The new architectonic productive art should become a universal art, an art of producing things and arts, and not merely one of producing words and arguments; but the first step in constituting and using an enlarged objective rhetoric should be the reformulation of the structure and program of verbal rhetoric and its subject-matter. Roman rhetoricians and philosophers made rhetoric an architectonic art which related all things by means of law and the actions of men. Renaissance rhetoricians and philosophers made rhetoric an architectonic art which related all things by means of art and the constructions of men. Rhetoricians and philosophers today might make rhetoric an architectonic art which relates all things by means of science and the experiences of men. Rhetoric in all its applications is focused on the particular, not the universal—particular questions or constitutions in law, particular works or compositions in art, or particular facts or data in experience and existence.

In an age of technology the diremption to be removed is the separation of theory and practice by the constitution of a technology which is theory applied, the *logos* of *techne*. We seek to produce it in concrete experience and existence by rejoining reason and sense, cognition and emotion, universal law and concrete occurrence. A first step can be taken by sketching the methods and the fields of rhetoric on the analogy of revolutions in rhetoric in earlier periods.

A. THE METHODS AND PRINCIPLES OF RHETORIC

Aristotle distinguished between productive *sciences*, like Poetics (which have particular *subject-matters*, kinds of things made or produced, genres of artificial objects or objects of art) and architectonic *arts*, like Rhetoric (which direct and organize thought concerning any *subject-matter*). The sciences have become, more and more, sources of production, of new matters and new forms, in need of organizing methods and principles. We have seen how Aristotle's four scientific questions concerning objective causes were transformed into four rhetorical questions concerning verbal issues. In the latter form, they have been enlarged from time to time to become universal in their scope and productive in their operation. The traces of such past distinctions and structures are present in our search today for inclusive methods, by which to understand our situation and problems, and operative principles, by which to reorient and open up actions. The echoes take on meaning when placed in their rhetorical contexts and suggest directions of inquiry and construction which might be followed to transform the methods of rhetoric and make them applicable to new problems.

(1) CREATIVITY AND INVENTION

Creativity has taken a conspicuous place in modern discussions of the objectives and methods of education, action, art, and inquiry. "Creativity" usually has no meaning and provides no guiding criterion for learning or doing other than those implicit in "innovation," in the sense of setting and following a course different from those pursued by others in the past or the present. There is no method or standard of creation, discovery, or innovation. "Invention" has always been an important part of rhetoric. During the nineteenth century, under the influence of the dichotomy of language and wisdom, it was questioned whether invention is essentially the same as, or fundamentally different from, discovery. This is one of the dichotomies which the new architectonic rhetoric must eradicate. Invention can be joined to discovery in an art which is productive of things and arts or skills rather than of words and arguments or beliefs. When a productive inventive art deals with content as well as form, it is an art of active modification—rather than of passive reception—of the data of existence.

The art by which the orator discovered or created arguments in the midst of debate and controversy was based on the topics, the places or seats of argument. From the beginning, on the testimony of Quintilian, commonplaces have commonly been degraded from instruments for discovery of new ideas or arguments to repertories for repetition of old devices or adages. Existence as well as documents is approached and illuminated by places which guide discovery, and experience is limited and obscured by commonplaces of existence which are often borrowed from commonplaces of literature and speech. We need a new art of invention and discovery in which places are used as means by which to light up modes and meanings of works of art and natural occurrences and to open up aspects and connections in existence and possibility. The data and qualifications of existence are made by attention and interest; and discoveries made in a book or a work of art should provide places by which to perceive creatively what might otherwise not be experienced in the existent world we constitute. It is a long time since topics have been used as an art of invention in rhetoric. Ancient and Renaissance treatises on invention can be used to rediscover the art of invention in the use of words, which can be applied to discovering invention in reading and to using the art of invention in one's own constructions from the elements of discourse and from the data of experience. A reconstituted verbal art of invention, adapted to our circumstances and arts, might be used to shadow forth the methods and principles of an architectonic productive art generalized from invention in language to discovery in existence.

(2) FACT AND JUDGMENT

Recent revolts against metaphysics have been motivated by distrust and distaste for *a priori* methods and universal principles. We seek to apply our methods to concrete facts, to what is happening in the world here and now, and we find our principles operative in concrete occurrences and processes. Older rhetorics had methods by which to determine what is the case, and these methods of judgment or definition by which facts were characterized in answer to the question, what is it? or what did he do? were distinguished from, and related to, the methods of invention by which data were discovered in answer to the question, is it? or did he do it? Cicero makes the difference between a conjectural issue and a definitional issue a difference between the determination of what the fact is and the determination of what word should be used to describe it. The dichotomy of words and things has been subject to question in our times, and the methods of rhetoric suggest that invention of words and symbols contributes to discovery of things and that things are delimited in the definition of words.

Judgment of the issue concerning what the fact is and how it is defined and named starts from hypotheses advanced for consideration and transforms one of the hypotheses entertained into a sentence or a true proposition. A sentence or a true proposition makes or states a truth or a fact. We need a new art of judgment to relate experience to existence, an art of recovery or recognition of facts to be used with the art of discovery or apperception of data to provide instrumentalities for our contemporary respect for concrete facts of experience and for our determination to adhere to them and use them in the formation of knowledge and attitudes, in the constitution of science, experience, and expression. A beginning can be made by reexamining rhetorical methods of interpretation of the facts and artifacts of past times which are subjected to reinterpretation in the perspectives of one's own age. A reconstituted verbal art of judgment, adapted to the recovery and reinterpretation of past circumstances and arts in their present significances and relevances, might be used as a step in the development of the methods and principles of an architectonic productive art generalized from judgment of motivations and acts in narratives and histories to judgment of hypotheses and facts in experience.

(3) Sequences and consequences
in discourse and in fact

Facts are questioned, and are defended when questioned, by argument. The adversary oppositions of court-room trials set the basic form of Roman rhetorical argumentation. Argument as debate continued in the concordance and systematization of medieval canon-law. In the scholastic method it was supplemented by methods of dialectical dialogue and of logical refutation and proof. Renaissance rhetoric took into account arguments of dramas, tales, and histories, and in the eighteenth century rhetoric was applied systematically to the judgment and criticism of *belles lettres*, as in the *Lectures on Rhetoric and Belles Lettres* of Hugh Blair. This enlargement of the construction of sequences and consequences from pleading or persuasion to proof, question-answer, plot, action, motivation-action-reaction, cause-effect, experiment has never been brought together in schematic organization or by productive methods. They can be related to each other as answers to the third rhetorical question, the qualitative constitution: How is the fact or occurrence qualified or characterized? Approached in that perspective the arts of making connections can be related to the arts of invention and the arts of judgment. A universalized verbal art of making, and modifying, connections could be used to relate the separated fields of the arts and sciences and to trace themes as they move in variations from field to field; and a reconstituted verbal art of connections could prepare the way for moving from formulating the consequences of discourse to tracing the sequences of processes and actions and events in a generalized architectonic productive art of structures.

(4) OBJECTIVITY AND
INTERSUBJECTIVITY IN
COMMUNICATION AND KNOWLEDGE

Metaphysicians and ontologists sought principles in the causes of things. Epistemologists and methodologists sought principles in the forms of thought and in the consensus of experts. We are suspicious of causes and concepts, and when the suspicion becomes doubt, we posit principles in postulates and theses. Yet the function of "principles" remains the same: they provide beginning points of verbal discourse and discursive thought which we can defend as beginning points of sequences of occurrences, facts, and objective relations. Theses are posited to account for positions, and positions are consequences derived from theses. We are suspicious of systems of being and of knowledge, but we organize and systematize information and raise questions and draw consequences from schematized data, facts, and relations. The arts of objective designation and intersubjective communication are practiced in new forms by machines and men in decision-making and mass-communication. A reexamination of the verbal arts of reference and systematization, of validification and justification, could be made a first step to the constitution of a generalized architectonic art of objectification and systematization in forming, and exploring the operations of, compositions of things, constitutions of communities, and constructs of communications.

B. THE FIELDS AND PROBLEMS OF RHETORIC

Our concern with the "fragmentation" of knowledge and our "interdisciplinary" innovations to constitute new fields more relevant to the problems we encounter, and more viable to processes of inquiry and action, are indications that we do not find subject-matters ready made nor do we encounter problems distributed precisely in fields. We make subject-matters to fit the examination and resolution of problems, and the solution of problems brings to our attention further, consequent problems, which frequently require the setting up and examination of new fields. Rhetoric has replaced metaphysics as an architectonic art, in the past, when the organization and application of the arts and sciences was based, not on supposed natures of things or perceived forms of thought, but on recognition of the consequences of what men say and do. Cicero did not make use of Aristotle's classification of kinds of sciences according to subject-matter and method to provide subject-matter and data for the issues and decisions of rhetoric. He did make use of the Aristotelian differentiation of kinds of rhetoric and of dialectic according to speaker, audience, and subject, according to method, time, and objective, to constitute the fields and the subject-matters under discussion and adjudication. He did not adjust rhetoric to a subject-matter, but used the four kinds of issues or constitutions to develop the three kinds of oratory, that is, he used rhetorical methods to constitute relevant fields. We may well follow his example. Having examined the methods and principles of invention, judgment, disposition, and systematization, we can abandon the rigidities of accepted classifications of knowledge—institutionalized under headings like theoretical, practical, and productive; physics, logic, and ethics; science, poetry, and history; natural sciences, social sciences, and humanities —and return to rhetoric for hints concerning how to construct new interdisciplinary substantive fields by the use of the methods and principles formed for the resolution of problems for which new fields are needed. As in the case of our inquiry into methods and principles, we shall find signs of the relevance of the enterprise, and criteria by which to plan and judge steps to be taken in it, by the remnants of the terms of the art of rhetoric—"demonstrative," "judicial," "deliberative," and "dialectical"— which are found scattered in contemporary analyses and discussions of fields and problems.

(1) DEMONSTRATIVE RHETORIC AND THE DATA OF EXISTENCE

"Demonstration" is a term which has wrapped up—in the meanings which we attach to it consciously as well as those which come to our attention unexpectedly, and in the applications which we make of it intentionally as well as those which extend the scope of "demonstration" unexpectedly—a rich variegated history of human thought, action, and production. Aristotle had two Greek words, *apodeiktikos* and *epideiktikos*, to apply to processes of presentation and manifestation: they are constructed from the same verb and, therefore, both mean "exhibit," "show forth," "make known," modified by prepositional prefixes which make "apodeictic" also mean "prove," that is, show forth "from" or "by," and "epideictic" also mean "display," that is, show forth "on" or "for." For Aristotle apodeictic proof was scientific proof, and epideictic oratory was display oratory. When "epideictic" became "demonstrative" oratory in the writings of Cicero, the certainties and necessities of proof were merged with the estimations and necessities of action. Aristotle distinguished three kinds of necessity, one absolute and two hypothetical, which are used in the apodeictic proofs of the three theoretical sciences. He argued that praise and honor are not reliable guides in the practical sciences, although praise and blame are the proper functions of epideictic oratory. For Cicero praise and blame are the functions of demonstrative discourse and action, in which he distinguished simple or absolute necessity from three necessities which govern actions taken to avoid or gain something: the necessity of the honorable (*honestas*), the necessity of security (*incolumitas*), and the necessity of convenience (*commoditas*) (*De Inventione* ii. 57. 170–58. 175). Our most recent revolt against metaphysics has been a revolt against, or an adjustment of, the apodeictic certainties of nineteenth century idealism and materialism. Yet we seem to be surprised that "demonstrations" have become exhibitions, presentations, manifestations rather than inferences, inductions, proofs.

The architectonic productive arts are not adapted to pre-existent subject-matters for the solution of recognized problems. The transformation of demonstration from proof to manifestation is not an error to be corrected by returning from agitation to evidence: it is a phenomenon of our times to be recognized as a datum to be studied and an instrumentality to be reduced to art. We have had enough experience of demonstrations to recognize not only the problems they "presented" as demonstrations but also the problems they "presented" in the insufficiencies of our conceptions of subject-matters and problems and the need for an architectonic productive art to change them. (1) Verbal demonstrative rhetoric is discourse for praise or blame. Recent demonstrations have not exhibited virtues and accomplishments for praise, but wrongs, injustices, and evils for blame. They have been effective as methods of discovery, of bringing to attention neglected data, but they have also made some use of the methods of judgment, disposition, and systematization. (2) Demonstrative rhetoric is designed to be productive of action as well as of words, that is, to arouse others to action and to accept a common opinion, to form groups that share that opinion, and to initiate participation in action based on that opinion. (3) The scope of demonstrative rhetoric is not limited to specific social, legal, and moral questions: it extends, even in application to those initial problems, to the whole field of human activity and knowledge, to all arts, sciences, and institutions. (4) Demonstration uncovers data, that is, "makes" them since data depend on the perspective in which they are "given." An assertion or demonstration by any one constitutes a datum, and affects the processes of judgment, disposition, and systematization. We need to constitute the field of demonstration in which such data can be treated without the distortions we feel justified in introducing by appeal to the assertions or demonstrations of experts. (5) The modality of demonstrative statements and actions is different from the necessities, contingencies, and possibilities of judicial, deliberative, and dialectical discourse. Epideictic oratory and modern demonstrations are about the present, and the statements they employ are assertoric. Judicial rhetoric is about the past, and judgments about the past can be necessary; deliberative rhetoric is about the future, and its proposals are contingent. (6) The field of demonstrative rhetoric is epideictic not apodeictic: it is not fenced off from, but fenced off for. In the nineteenth century when philosophers were seeking apodeictic certainties they explored the limits of concepts and of reason. The field of demonstrative rhetoric should provide the grounds for discovery and invention, going beyond the bounds of what is already known and the fields of that knowledge. The field of demonstrative rhetoric, set forth in assertions and explored by the art of invention or discovery, is a field of "topics" in the two senses which the term has acquired: subject-matters for consideration and places for invention.

(2) JUDICIAL RHETORIC AND THE
FACTS OF EXPERIENCE

"Judgment" is a term which has been employed in action, art, and knowledge. Judgments are decisions or "sentences" in law-courts concerning past actions; they are appreciations or "criticisms" of works of art; they are conclusions or "propositions" which are true or false. After "forensic" rhetoric became "judicial" rhetoric in the vocabulary of Cicero, the interrelations among judgments as "sentences," "evaluations," and "propositions" have been uncovered at each turn of development. The methods of accusation and defense have been enlarged to become the methods of verification and falsification, and their field has been universalized from past actions to be judged to facts and values to be determined and to general truths and laws to be established. "Cause" shares the productive ambiguity of "judgment": "causes" are discovered in things, pleaded before judges, pushed against established powers, and won in the progressive solution of problems. Judgments are a central theme in Kant's three Critiques, and the *Critique of Judgment* forms a connecting link between theoretical and practical reason by analyzing aesthetic judgments and purposiveness. We have revolted against the separation of facts and values, and we have turned to actions and circumstances to rejoin them. This reformulation of our problems makes it necessary to constitute and explore the field of judgment in which the facts and values of experience are related to each other and to the data of existence uncovered in the newly constituted field of demonstration.

The growing interest in the new hermeneutics is further sign of the need to establish a working domain of judgments of knowledge and action. In that enlarged field the controversial opposition of verification and falsification is not resolved by victory or defeat of a protagonist but by the establishment or refutation of a hypothesis. Since the art of interpretation and judgment applies to known truths and values, the field of judgment includes all recorded literature, which is the subject of hermeneutics or semantics, but it includes the facts as well as the records of experience. It is in this field that hypotheses can become facts and the elements of invention and discovery can be joined in a statement or apperception of fact. One of the important tasks to be accomplished by the new architectonic productive art of rhetoric is to clarify the topology of the relation of the field of invention to the field of judgment. This will make it possible once more for the semantics of known facts and values to contribute to the discovery of new truths and the production of new accomplishments, and for places and elements to be used heuristically in the establishment of ideas and arguments, facts and values.

(3) DELIBERATIVE RHETORIC
AND THE STRUCTURE OF CONNECTIONS

"Deliberation" and its companion terms "choice" and "decision" have already been universalized in our common language of diagnosis and action. They were terms in the practical science of ethics for Aristotle: they were limited to actions within our power; with respect to such actions we can deliberate and choose means, but not ends. The subject-matter of political rhetoric was future actions. When "political" oratory became "deliberative" oratory after Cicero, the terms of art, of ethics, politics, and rhetoric merged, and deliberation could be applied not only to ends as well as means, but to theoretic and productive as well as practical problems. We deliberate not only about the expedient and the inexpedient, but also about the good and the bad, the true and the false, the pleasurable and the distasteful. Decision-making and methods-analysis require a universal field, and our universal methods could be used more effectively if that field could be subjected to positive definition rather than only the negative limitations provided by lack of limits, infinity, or indefiniteness. When the verbal rhetoric was universalized, it included all discursive sequences—inference, narrative, plot, lyric, history, aphorism, paradox—with related forms and methods. We have become accustomed to statements of the relations among their arts—that poetry presents truths, that mathematics expresses beauties, that history sets forth universal laws—but we have not constructed the subject-matter which provides the content for the operation and interrelation of these arts. As we proceeded with its constitution we would give substantive meaning to the "structures" which appear so frequently in our discussion of problems of education and action and which need grounding if the formal precision derived from mathematics is to be translated into concrete processes of operation determined by context and subject-matter. A beginning can be made by using the fields of invention and of judgment for data and facts to be related in structured sequences and intelligible consequences. This is the field of "arts" and "methods," in which themes are continued and undergo variations which reflect changing arts and constitute changing regions of the structure of connections which constitute the field of deliberation.

(4) DIALECTIC AND THE
PRINCIPLES OF OBJECTIVITY
AND COMMUNICATION

Aristotle treated dialectic as a counterpart of rhetoric. The differences between them were in part consequences of the difference between the particular audiences of rhetoric and the universal audience of dialectic. Arguments can be adapted to the predilections of groups or communities of men. They can also be framed by art so that anyone who uses art or intelligence can follow them and appreciate them. The difference between dialectic and rhetoric became for Cicero a difference between universal questions of philosophy and science and particular questions concerning particular actions of particular men at particular times and places. The growth of science and communication, the increase of knowledge and the formation of world community, have begun to lay out the field of systematic organization both as a system of communication for a universal audience, mankind, and as a system of operation of an ongoing development and inquiry, technology. It is a field which provides grounding for the intersubjectivity of communications of persons and groups and for the objectivity of conclusions of inquiry and action. It is within this field that the possible worlds, which are discussed in plans and policy, are constructed, and theses which are posited are stabilized into principles. Theses and principles have a history which carries back in tradition to principles that were called eternal and universal but were also derived from theses which posit being in the context of an agent, his environment, and his subject. It is the field of reflexivity and responsibility, which must be explored in rational action concerning rights and justice, laws and conventions, sanctions and obligations, utilities and values, and opinions and truths. The field of the new dialectical rhetoric, of debate and dialogue, is being travelled and cultivated by chance and by art. An architectonic-productive survey of the field of these activities could make its beginning by orienting rhetoric from the oppositions of the past to the understanding and projection of the new processes and needs of the present.

Verbal rhetoric is productive of arguments and architectonic of attitudes. It provides the principle, in both the sense of beginning-point and of guide-line, for the construction of an architectonic productive art of rhetoric and philosophy which can be used to create a method productive of the arts and a subject-matter substantive to the problems of an age of technology. It should be a rhetoric which relates form to matter, instrumentality to product, presentation to content, agent to audience, intention to reason. It should not make technology the operation of a machine, in which the message is a massage; it should not take its form from its medium and it should not be adapted to use to communicate established judgments (which are jostled commonplaces) or revolutionary convictions (which are repeated dogmas) on the supposition and intimation that they might be related to traditional ends or novel objectives and that they are somehow means to those ends. It should be adapted to inquiry into what is the case rather than to semantic analysis of what somebody else has said. It should be positive in the creation, not passive in the reception, of data, facts, consequences, and objective organization. It should be an art in which what any one says to be the case, judges to be good or evil, connects in relations, and establishes with some show of system and principles, is relevant as subject-matter, content, and product. In a technological age all men should have an art of creativity, of judgment, of disposition, and of organization. This should be adapted to their individual development and to their contribution to forming a common field in which the subject of inquiry is not how to devise means to achieve accepted ends arranged in hierarchies but the calculation of uses and applications that might be made of the vastly increased available means in order to devise new ends and to eliminate oppositions and segregations based on past competitions for scarce means.

4 / AN AUTOPSY OF THE RHETORICAL TRADITION

LAWRENCE W. ROSENFIELD
University of Wisconsin

The predicament facing modern rhetoric is not one of redefinition, nor even obsolescent rhetorical theories. It is symptomatic of a disturbance threatening all humanistic inquiry. Theology and political theory, for example, are today in disrepute in the academic world, passed on from teacher to student under the drumfire of behaviorism in a manner reminiscent of Christians transmitting the faith in the Roman catacombs.[1] Philosophy has for the most part reduced itself to two unsatisfying alternatives, the history of metaphysics and linguistic analysis. Rhetoric's survival is menaced by such Manichaean competitors as attitude change research and psycholinguistics.

Tradition itself has in our time been called into question, if not decisively rejected. The line of influential literature stretching back to Plato and the Bible has become merely quotable. No longer is the authority of the past a legitimate guide to institutions. This is not to argue that the past lacks wisdom for the present, but only that we are no longer willing to piously submit to tradition's authority.[2] Hence, the task of modern rhetorical scholarship is broader than simple renovation; it is part of a more general effort to regenerate historico-critical thought. And no conception of rhetoric will be fully adequate which does not account for how our link to tradition has come to be broken at this time.

Consequently, I shall take as my present objective the question:

what intellectual factors have caused orthodox commentaries on rhetoric to become unsatisfactory for contemporary thought?[3] I shall argue that in its initial formulation the classical Greek notion of rhetoric depended upon a presumed correlation between the philosophical experience and the political experience. I shall further contend that the dominant response of Western thought has been to gradually realign these dual experiences of Man Thinking and Man Acting, coming increasingly to isolate them and put them at odds with each other.[4]

The reverberations of this estrangement are today being felt in almost all humanistically oriented disciplines,[5] but nowhere perhaps so clearly as in the systematic elision of rhetorical theory to which two thousand years have been witness.

Without pausing to make finer distinctions among particular thinkers, we can characterize the pre-Socratic legacy to Western habits of thought by its emphasis on common sense, distance, and curiosity. This constellation of terms confirms the fundamental theme of Greek civilization, that man is a social animal who achieves a unique dignity in the act of speech.[6] If we ransack the archives of antiquity, the full import of this theme and its supporting terms emerges with emphatic clarity.

Common Sense—It has often seemed to me unfortunate that the Greek term *doxa* which looms so large in ancient rhetorical theory is usually translated as "opinion," with all of the connotations of being in dispute and distrusting one's senses which modern man attaches to that abused word. For *dokeimoi*, from which *doxa* is drawn, translates as well in the form "it seems to me," with "seems" taking on the special sense of "appears." In other words, *doxa* would mean for a people who trusted their own senses "that which appears to anyone who has a certain perspective appears also to me." In this sense, *doxa* becomes that aspect of the whole of reality which the individual recognizes and shares with others[7].

It was precisely because a degree of "common-sense" was presumed at least among members of the *polis* that the arts of discourse (rhetoric, poetic, dialectic) became possible. Dialectic, for example, was for the pre-Socratics a form of critical activity practiced in association with others.[8] It, like its counterpart rhetoric, thus opened directly into the public (and hence the political) realm of human activity.[9] We have it on the word of Xenophon that:

> The very word *dialegesthai*, according to [Socrates], owes its name to the practice of meeting together for common deliberation [dialegein, sorting, discussing things after their kind]: and therefore one should be ready and prepared for this and be zealous for it; for it makes for excellence, leadership, and skill in discussion.[10]

It is no wonder then that the first great thinkers of Greece were renowned as political figures more often than as mere thinkers (think of Solon, Pericles, Empedocles, and that pre-eminently public man, although lacking in power, Socrates).

Being and appearance were fundamentally related, and this gave rise to a "common-sense" feature of reality which could be disclosed to all those who shared comparable experiences. Thus was a common foundation for a public endeavor established, and thus more importantly for our purposes was thought conceived to be inseparable from its public expression.[11] Rhetoric perhaps more than dialectic relied upon this common sense presumption, for what is more fugitive than thought if not political activity? And if dialectic and rhetoric differed mainly in the audiences the two arts addressed, then rhetoric, which addressed the entire membership of the *polis*, was that much more dependent upon this common sense precondition for public activity.

Distance—There was for the Greeks no body of revered doctrine, no accumulation of obligatory philosophical propositions to which men need adhere. Our notion of "faith" or dogmatic belief seems quite alien to the classical spirit.[12] Such flexibility in personal commitment permitted the thinker to achieve a "critical detachment" from the object of his contemplation, a distance signified by *theorain*, the direct apprehension of reality as it is given to the mind through the senses.[13] Now *theorain* (whose root is *theo*, spectacle, and which gave us our term "theory") was a seeing of a special sort, the kind of beholding characterized by the spectator at a religious festival. Lacking in its meaning was the certainty of vision typified by science or demonstration.[14] The stress instead lay on a steady, impartial recognition of the order inherent in phenomena. There was implicit in such a theoretical stance a tranquility, an objectivity, quite distinguishable from indifference and irrelevant to modern perception theory's emphases on sheer organic sensation.[15] The ancient theorist was denied the modern's ultimate function to "change" reality in any form by the working of experiments.[16] But by the same token, this form of objectivity (which is crucial to ancient rhetorical theory) affords an impartiality to the spectator-as-witness which enables him to interpret, indeed, to evaluate, the reality given to his reason in a manner which modern theorists try in vain to achieve.[17] Where rhetoric as an activity sprang from the political grounds of common sense, it attained its theoretical character from the possibility of distance which was afforded consciousness in the Greek mind.

Curiosity—Common sense and theoretical perspective combined to fulfill for the pre-Socratic thinker a rather remarkable impulse. In a most revealing passage, Aristotle marked the beginning of all philosophy in child-like delight:

> For it is owing to their wonder that men both now begin and at first began to philosophize; they wondered originally at the obvious difficulties, then advanced little by little and stated difficulties about greater matters . . . And a man who is puzzled and wonders thinks himself ignorant . . .[18]

The key term here is *thaumadzein*, confirming wonder, the kind of chortling exhilaration one might feel if he were to by chance encounter a lovely maiden in the forest. It is this *thaumadzein*, this wonder at everything that is as it is, this essentially erotic enthusiasm for experienced thought, to which Hannah Arendt refers when she claims that:

> More than anything else, Greek "theory" is the prolongation and Greek philosophy the articulation and conceptualization of this initial wonder.[19]

Philosophy was, in a word, an act, the unselfconscious act of loving wisdom actualized in *logos*, talk.[20] And it is again at this point of orality-as-experience that we must recognize rhetoric's inseparable link to philosophy. Where the philosophical transaction exhilarated, the rhetorical one charmed, but both partook of *peithein*, the arousal of delight-related emotions in the participants as an impetus to and consequence of direct oral interaction in the social realm.[21] Intellect thus reified itself in acts of discourse: thought was indistinguishable from its public display. Rhetorical theory, discourse *about* discourses, was simultaneously theoretical and political.

Had this conception of man-as-speaker persisted, rhetoric's place might well be as secure today as when it was taught and practiced by Protagoras, Gorgias, Solon, Aristotle, and Isocrates. But accidents of history preserved instead the Platonic attacks on Sophistry and upon Athenian public life in general and left for us only suggestive fragments of the dominant Sophistic motif. This fateful turn gave to Western thought a distinctively anti-rhetorical caste long after Greek Sophism had itself vanished. Confronted with the related problems of being, movement, and order, the Homeric-Sophistic tradition had focused on the nature of movement and tried to develop a philosophy of process; Plato chose to reject entirely the significance of movement and offer instead a solution which identified order with being. One consequence of his attack was to rupture the unity of thought and action which was so vital to a clear appreciation of rhetoric. It is therefore instructive to examine at some length Plato's posture in his debate with the Sophists.

At the outset Plato denied what was for Sophism the very foundation of man's humanness, his impulse to associate with his fellows within the social institution of the *polis*.[22] He claimed that social intercourse necessarily destroys the philosophic act. Hence, solitude became a precondition for thought as he would have it understood.[23] Contemplation could be consummated only in isolation. Note how this first Platonic claim flew in the face of the Greek experience, which held community to be the vehicle by which one achieved a superior life.[24]

Plato's commitment to philosophical solitude went beyond mere antisocial caprice. The pre-Socratic line of thought had, with a few exceptions, held thought to be an outgrowth of naive experience; Plato claimed that the entire sense world distracts and confuses the philosopher, that it is only the "eye of the soul" which can intuit pure being.[25] Rejection of the realm of appearances is thus a fundamental step in his account of a transcendent, invarient realm of knowledge.

This bifurcation of reality had a disastrous impact upon the conception of human communication, for it caused Plato to disclaim the validity of *logos* as an instrument of thought. He held that language merely approximated reality and so was bound to mislead us.[26] Effective discourse about philosophical matters was impossible.[27] The philosopher who employed discursive means to encounter Truth would become disoriented in his own mind.[28] Plato thus wrenched dialectic from its position as one of several language arts, stripped it of its relation to human experience, and made of it a kind of rapturous search after a static, transcendent reality.[29] It followed that the converse of this radical subjectivism would deny to rhetoric and the other "arts of appearance" any legitimate connection to genuine thought.

It followed also that, having divorced ideas from common sense and theoretical distance, Plato should allow the emotional component to become a dominant feature of the philosophical act. This meant that at the bottom, the conditions of wisdom became not so much intellectual as moral, that critical detachment gave way to a kind of obsessive coercion.[30] In the cave allegory (and the theme is echoed in the figure of the charioteer and the winged horse in the *Phaedrus*), the philosophical impulse is depicted as a compulsion which forces one to struggle at every step toward ultimate ideals.[31] Such a ready acceptance of *nous* as a compulsive pursuit of knowledge transformed philosophy into an enterprise at once lonely and dogmatic.

It was St. Augustine who completed the separation of thought from sense appearance begun by Plato.[32] Charles Norris Cochrane's masterly study, *Christianity and Classical Culture* has thoroughly documented the widening split between thought and action in the Roman period, and we need here only mention those Augustinian contributions to the division which bear directly on the nature of rhetoric. According to Cochrane, Augustine's response to and extension of Platonism grew from his understanding that it was:

> . . . simply classical poetry in cap and gown. For [classical] philosophy, like poetry, began by envisaging the 'subject' as in some sense 'opposed' to the 'object' world. It then proceeded to tell itself a story, the purpose of which was to establish an intelligible relationship between the two.[33]

While accepting the Platonic distinction between experience and knowing,[34] Augustine made "faith" the stimulus to experience as well as the starting point of *sapientia*.[35] Augustine himself recognized the danger such a concept might have if faith became confused with the impulse to rationalize. He called such a perversion of intellectual activity *fantasica fornicatio*, the prostitution of the mind to its own fancies. And he understood how the effort of the scientific intelligence to assert control over reality could result in such an error.[36] But his reservations were lost upon those less capable souls who followed after him. By the end of the eighteenth century, when "God" had been removed from the medieval equation, all that remained of Augustine's notion of revelation through faith was the "will to believe" that typified ideological adherence to *a priori* epistemological premises.[37]

Having re-affirmed in this fashion the existence of a Platonic realm of being, St. Augustine also pushed to its logical conclusion Plato's detachment of external and internal reality. This he did by positing the notion of self-consciousness through which God manifested himself to the mind, by claiming that it was awareness of one's selfhood that in turn represented the divine quality in man.

We must bear in mind that Augustine was a rhetorician by training, and that he was writing within the tradition of Roman rather than Greek rhetoric. Roman thought broke sharply with Greek in reverencing clever imitation in matters intellectual and cultural. This desire to copy lofty exemplars manifested itself in rhetorical theory where invention was understood as the selection of ideas from among concepts already known to all. In sum, Roman rhetorical theory concentrated on the adept use of commonplaces (loci) in situations of controversy.[38] And as a consequence, the Romans gave far more attention to *memoria* than had the Greeks.[39]

Given this common notion of thought, it made sense for Augustine to highlight memory in his treatment of consciousness. Indeed, his discussion of *memoria*, although new in the realm of philosophy, was for the most part a borrowing of the classical Roman notion of *memoria* from rhetoric. In brief, Augustine described memory as a kind of space, an information retrieval system replete with the loci one employed in debate, but expanded to include those additional loci of self and God needed to flesh out a total epistemology.[40] In its inception, Augustine's "self-awareness" was thus little more than an elaborated locus system for sifting through one's memory in a systematic manner. It derived its import from the fact that even as it appropriated the core of Roman rhetorical theory to the province of philosophical thought, it also made meaningful the fulfillment of Plato's search for an explicitly internal, innate, non-active notion of thought. From the viewpoint of rhetoric, however, this transformation of the canon of memory into the philosophic notion of self awareness was but another erosion of the by now tenuous link between thought and public discourse. How crucial a shift this was only became evident when Ramus made explicit the consequences for rhetoric already implicit in Augustine.

I have thus far explored some of the effects upon rhetoric of its divorce from its intellectual roots, the pirating of certain of its features (as *memoria*), the renunciation of others (common sense) by Platonism and its successors. The past four centuries have seen the reassertion of the significance of action, this time at the expense of philosophy, but again at further cost to the rhetoric. As the notion of action has been refined and elevated in our estimation, it has lost its political-experience features and come to represent physical processes. In these terms appearance too has severed its links to public action in a manner which has left rhetoric quite literally nowhere.[41]

A principal assault on the Idealistic faith in innate ideas came from Locke, who countered with his own faith in the notion that sense perception was the virtual origin of all thought.[42] This single change completely transformed the character of rhetorical theory. Henceforth, the New Science was to acquire knowledge by means of scientific rather than topical investigation. Rhetoric, if it was to have any justification whatsoever, was called upon to merely transmit the new learning after the fact of its discovery.[43]

Naive faith in sensation signaled renewed interest in physical reality, an interest which was to further diminish the significance of both philosophy and rhetoric. In the first place, language was again attacked as a legitimate vehicle of thought, this time not for its inability to capture the higher Platonic reality, but for its lack of correspondence to physical process. Professor Wallace, in his admirable study of a thoroughly non-ideological man, Francis Bacon, has pinpointed the factor which was to become a primary characteristic of ideologists in our own day—those disciplines which distrust verbal discourse eventually develop an urge to quantify:

> The old methods [of discovery] were methods of invention developed by dialectic, logic, grammar, and rhetoric. They were therefore tied inevitably and permanently to men's language. . . . If man were to uncover nature's secrets . . . . he must abandon old ways of search and inquiry and must devise new ways of querying nature directly. . . .
>
> How did the "new" induction differ from the old invention? The new method was a way of controlling observation and abstraction by setting up two contradictions. First, the understanding was to be tied directly to the senses and thus to increase the chances that a concept would emerge. . . . Second, the understanding was to be governed by an order and procedure designed to delay and control abstraction.[44]

In the second place, the distance between event and spectator, so crucial for ancient theoretical perspective, was eliminated. Spinoza, as well as anyone, represents this change. According to him, the external forces of Nature determined the body, which in turn determined the mind; thought as well as action were thus essentially passive.[45] As a result, virtue was taken to mean acting in accord with one's natural powers, and thought about action followed from the capacity to act. Intellect's highest objective was to become conscious of physical necessity.[46] Salvation (or as Spinoza would have it, reconciliation) with God was achieved through affirmation of recognized inevitability; metaphysics and theology must replace faith with a "super geometry."[47] This mechanistic denial of classical theoretical objectivity was extended in the scientistic positivism of Auguste Comte and Karl Marx, who held that human nature was largely determined by man's material existence, that one's inner life was a direct function of his environment.[48] In our own day it has culminated in the extreme positions of logical positivism and Skinnerian psychology, both of which deny entirely man's "experiential capacities" and limit their notion of man to that of an automaton consisting of a network of observable behaviors.[49]

To confine the range of permissible theoretical discourse to nonnormative statements had a dual effect on rhetorical theory (and in addition upon such other traditional theoretical studies of human affairs as ethics and political theory). In the first place, those efforts to account for the being as well as the appearance of human discourse—and this represented the bulk of what we have come to call rhetorical theory—was with bare toleration relegated to the disreputable estate of "armchair speculation." Secondly, like the rest of behavioral research, students of discourse who chose to accept the dominion of process over essence so contorted themselves in their attempts to become value free that they rapidly trivialized the objects of their study. A casual reading of any current behavioral science learned journal will reveal that a massive paralysis has now set in; to the extent that behavioral research meets its own metaphysical standards of "rigor," it usually dismisses its objects of study in favor of unending debate over the proper way to take measurements.

There are obviously many other factors to consider in the emergence of the realm of appearance as an independent category than the few contributions I have mentioned. I shall discuss just one more which bears on rhetorical theory's deterioration. That was Hegel's extension of Spinoza's "necessity" into the realm of human affairs. In a typically cryptic passage of the Preface to his *Philosophy of Right*, Hegel proposed to will philosophical inquiry out of existence:

> What is rational is actual and what is actual is rational. On this conviction the plain man like the philosopher takes his stand, and from it philosophy starts in its study of the universe of mind as well as the universe of nature. . . .
>
> To comprehend what is, this is the task of philosophy because what is, is reason. Whatever happens, every individual is a child of his time; so philosophy too is its own time apprehended in thoughts. It is just as absurd to fancy that a philosophy can transcend its contemporary world as it is to fancy that an individual can overleap his own age, jump over Rhodes. . . . Philosophy in any case always comes on the scene too late. . . . As the thought of the world, it appears only when actuality is already there cut and dried after its process of formation has been completed. . . . When philosophy paints its grey in grey, then has a shape of life grown old. By philosophy's grey in grey it cannot be rejuvenated but only understood. The owl of Minerva spreads its wings only with the falling of the dusk.[50]

Hegel thus tried to demolish the distinction between being and appearance by affirming the total predominance of appearance. For him, "thought" functioned only in retrospect, in the historical consciousness of the emergent, constantly shifting patterns of mankind's history.[51] Reason was a story, clear only at the end of a sequence of events whose possible variety was infinite. Man's task is to constantly update the story, reconciling the contradictions his own historical reality manifested, and internalizing them.[52]

The Hegelian emphasis on historical consciousness is most significant for our purposes in what it denies: common sense as understood by the Ancients (Hegel substitutes his murky notion of the Spirit, or Realization of the Idea[53]) and the weight of tradition. For in one sense Hegel's historicism is a rejection of history; his thinker maintains himself in an ahistoric condition, looking to the ideas of the past as quaint artifacts which serve only to give him perspective—he does not expect the past to speak to him as Cicero listened and responded to Plato.

As Hegelian attitudes have permeated the academy, rhetorical scholars have sought refuge in the study of the history of rhetorical theory, much as their humanistic colleagues have turned increasingly to endeavors such as intellectual and cultural history, the history of philosophy, and the history of science. But Hegel's substitution of Spirit for common sense makes any study of the past's artifacts at once unfocused and futile. Unfocused because there is no hierarchy among artifacts. One can as well find the Persian Spirit manifested in its pots as its speeches—so rhetorical study is one among an infinite number of co-equal investigations.

But the effort is futile because tomorrow's contradictions will inevitably rob today's scholarly insight of its validity and make of it farce. If the past speaks, it is listened to only insofar as fits the immediate needs of today's story; and if one objects that this form of scholarship is a perversion of the search for truth which is reason's most vital domain, the Hegelian will nod vigorous assent and probably contend that that is exactly the trouble with Reason.[54] So in rhetorical scholarship, as in the other historical disciplines, one feels a constant nagging sense that somehow the endeavor is absurd, that we are erecting a monstrous rationalization, that we are publicists for assorted messianic causes rather than objective analysts.[55] The charge of triviality and irrelevance, though not sharpened as an argument, may have more than superficial merit. Rhetorical study in any case finds itself playing no significant role in a world where appearance and sheer action are idolized and being is ignored; it tends to get lost in the crowd of antiquarians.

What conclusions can be drawn from this brief Hegelian analysis of rhetoric's erosion? I wish to make only one: as Western thought became ever more schizoid in its efforts to fragment self and social consciousness, it was no accident that rhetoric, lying at a strategically important juncture linking the two, should suffer exceptional damage in its attempts to maintain its integrity. Like a duchy located in an area of convergence between two enemies engaged in a maniacal civil war, it has been sacked by both sides for their own purposes until its resources are almost depleted. So long as the warfare continues, there is little hope for restoration.

The ever shifting fashions in intellectual method here considered have one common feature: scientific discoveries in all ages seem to have been preceded by comparable philosophic statements.[56]. Hence the scholastic tradition, in the process of detaching thought from the mundane realm of appearance, chose to regard rhetoric as inconsequential because it concerned the fleeting sector of public action. Rhetorical theorists of an earlier age were thus forced into an apologetic posture because their subject could not find total inspiration in the realm of inner dialogue.

Platonism is today in general disrepute in the academic world, but we should not expect the impending victory of the behavioral philistines to improve the possibilities for the study of rhetoric. "Social science" rests on a set of mechanistic assumptions which deny the legitimate reality of being in favor of idolatry of sheer appearance. To the extent that we allow ourselves to confuse the frenetic investigation of "behavior" with the human "experience" lying at the foundation of rhetorical transactions, we can expect our research to confirm an emasculated notion of rhetoric as a none too effective means of social manipulation. Such *post hoc* gestures of impotence as propaganda analysis, market analysis, and attitude change research currently enjoy the perverse notoriety of governmental subsidy; they are likely to be rightfully disdained by thoughtful men in the near future.

Given these two unsatisfying contemporary alternatives, one must conclude that, given rhetoric's territorial location at the concord of shared social experience and self awareness, the only hope that its exploration will become once more a fruitful endeavor is that men grant again the symbiotic relation of being and appearance.[57] Should that conception take hold, rhetoric's key position may make it imperative that it re-emerge as a viable discipline.

FOOTNOTES

1. See D. Germino, *Beyond Ideology* (New York: Harper & Row, 1967), pp. 1–6; L. W. Rosenfield, "Rhetoric, General Semantics, and Ideology," in K. Johnson (ed.), *Research Designs in General Semantics* (Washington, D. C., in press).
2. H. Arendt, *Between Past and Future* (New York: Viking Press, 1961), pp. 17–40.
3. The author has elsewhere dealt with the problem posed to writers of position papers to "outline a conception of rhetoric suitable to twentieth century concepts, learning, and needs." See *The Proceedings of the University of Minnesota Symposium in Speech-Communication* (Minneapolis, 1969), pp. 26–41.
4. Robert Gordis, in his profound essay, "Politics and Ethics" (a publication of the Center for the Study of Democratic Institutions, 1961) confirms the thrust of this argument with reference to the erosion of Old Testament ethics.
5. The consequences have extended into behavioral thought as well. See J. Deese, "Behavior and Fact," *American Psychologist*, XXIV, #5 (May, 1969), 515–22; W. D. Hitt, "Two Models of Man," *American Psychologist*, XXIV, #7 (July, 1969), 651–58; T. W. Wann (ed.), *Behaviorism and Phenomenology* (Chicago: University of Chicago Press, 1964).
6. Cicero, *De Inventione*, I. iv. 5 echoes this humanistic view. See also E. Hamilton, *The Greek Way* (New York: W. W. Norton and Company, 1930), p. 82; J. H. Randall, Jr., *Aristotle* (New York: Columbia University Press, 1960), pp. 121–23; Arendt, p. 63; Aristotle, *Politics*, 1253a 10–30.
7. Hamilton, p. 53; Randall, p. 101; T. J. Slakey, "Aristotle on Sense Perception and Thinking" (unpublished Ph.D. dissertation, Cornell University, 1952).
8. R. Price, "Some Antistrophes to the *Rhetoric*," *Philosophy and Rhetoric*, I, #3 (Summer, 1968); E. Janssens, "The Concept of Dialectic in the Ancient World," *Ibid.*, 177–79.

9. E. L. Hunt, "Plato and Aristotle on Rhetoric and Rhetoricians," in R. F. Howes, *Historical Studies of Rhetoric and Rhetoricians* (Ithaca, N.Y.: Cornell University Press, 1961), p. 69; J. Croissant-Goedert, "La Classification des sciences et la place de la rhétorique dans l'oeuvre d'aristote," *Proceedings of the 11th International Congress of Philosophy* (North-Holland Publishing Company, Amsterdam, 1953), XIV, 272–74. That at least the Sophists were in basic agreement on the unity of being and appearance can be seen from a careful reading of their judgments. See J. Burnet, *Early Greek Philosophy* (Cleveland: World Publishing Company, 1957), pp. 130–276; G. Vlastos, "Introduction" to *Plato's Protagoras* (New York: Liberal Arts Press, 1956), xiii-xiv.

10. Xenophon, *Memorabilia,* trans. E. C. Marchant, *Loeb Classical Library* (New York: Putnam, 1923), IV, v. 12.

11. Cicero, *De Oratore,* III, xv. 56; xvi. 61; xix. 72; R. McKeon, "The Methods of Rhetoric and Philosophy: Invention and Judgment," *The Classical Tradition: Literary and Historical Studies in Honor of Harry Caplan* (Ithaca, N.Y., Cornell University Press, 1963), pp. 25–26; Quintilian, *Institutes of Oratory,* "Preface."

12. Hamilton, pp. 27–28; B. Snell, *The Discovery of the Mind,* trans. T. G. Rosenmeyer (New York: Harper & Row, 1960), p. 24; E. Barker, *The Political Thought of Plato and Aristotle* (New York: Russell & Russell, 1959). The notable exception to this general condition was the intolerance displayed at the time of Socrates' trial. Yet even this case had political motivations; heresy was not at issue.

13. W. Barrett, "Phenomenology and Existentialism," in W. Barrett and H. D. Aiken, *Philosophy in the Twentieth Century* (New York: Random House, 1962), III, 130–131; Arendt, p. 39; Snell, p. 4.

14. Price, pp. 155–158; Aristotle, *Nicomacean Ethics,* 1139b 18–35.

15. A. Stigen, *The Structure of Aristotle's Thought* (Oslo: Universitetsforlaget, 1966), pp. 348–349; Barker, 2.

16. Randall, pp. 190–192.

17. See Aristotle, *Rhetoric,* 1355b 26–27.

18. Aristotle, *Metaphysics,* trans. W. D. Ross, *Basic Works of Aristotle,* ed. R. McKeon (New York: Random House, 1941), 982b 11–18.

19. Arendt, p. 115; see also, Snell, p. 33.

20. See D. Hyland, "Why Plato Wrote Dialogues," *Philosophy and Rhetoric,* I, #1 (January, 1968), pp. 42–43; J. Pieper, *Enthusiasm and Divine Madness,* trans. R. & C. Winston (New York: Harcourt, Brace & World, 1964), pp. 47–50; H. L. Sinaiko, *Love, Knowledge, and Discourse in Plato* (Chicago: University of Chicago Press, 1965), pp. 2–16.

21. See Gorgias, *Helen,* 10; Plato, *Protagoras,* 315b.

22. Aristotle, *Politics,* 1253a 20–30.

23. *Republic,* 491–496, 532–534; *Theaetetus,* 173–174. This interpretation is confirmed in the cave allegory (514–521), where the incipient philosopher is forced to make an "about face" (periagoge) from the world he has inhabited and to struggle up the lonely path of mathematical discipline toward intuitive knowledge. See Arendt, pp. 36–37; Hunt, p. 51.

24. See Snell, p. 170; Hunt, pp. 24–25. Aristotle seems at times to hint at a similar distinction between contemplative thought and public activity, but we must recall that for Aristotle, such philosophic isolation presupposes a polis and that thought is itself a form of action. Plato's notion of contemplation is more radical in that it denies any connection between thought and action. See *Gorgias,* 433e and *Apology,* 31d.

25. C. N. Cochrane, *Christianity and Classical Culture* (Oxford: The Clarendon Press, 1940), p. 419; Snell, pp. 137–52; Hunt, p. 33; *Theaetetus*, 51–53 and 151–53; *Republic*, 518; *Phaedo*, 99–100.

26. Snell, pp. 221–22; Plato, *Seventh Letter*, 342–44; *Sophist*, 233–35; *Phaedo*, 74–84. It is this notion that the senses are inherently deceptive to which Plato is referring when he likens the philosophical experience to dying; *Phaedo*, 64–69.

27. Plato, *Seventh Letter*, 341c: There is no writing of Plato's, nor will there ever be. . . ." See also *Cratylus*, 432.

28. Plato, *Republic*, 517; *Theaetetus*, 174–76.

29. Cochrane, pp. 422–26; Plato, *Phaedrus*, 249–52; A. Kojeve, "Tyranny and Wisdom," in Straus, pp. 160–61; Sinaiko, pp. 273–82.

30. David Bidney, in his *Psychology and Ethics of Spinoza* (New Haven: Yale University Press, 1940), 282, puts it very well when he remarks that for Plato, "to know the truth and to consent to its performance" were one and the same thing. See also Arendt, pp. 107–10; Cochrane, p. 451; E. Black, "Plato's View of Rhetoric, *The Quarterly Journal of Speech*, XLIV, #4 (December, 1958), p. 364.

31. Plato, *Republic*, 516; *Phaedrus*, 246–55.

32. For Augustine's debt to Plato, see Cochrane, Chapter XI.

33. Cochrane, p. 430.

34. St. Augustine, *Confessions*, VIII. viii; X. xxxv.

35. Cochrane, pp. 435 ff.

36. Cochrane, p. 418.

37. See Carl Becker, *The Heavenly City of the Eighteenth Century Philosophers* (New Haven: Yale University Press, 1964), for a thorough explication of this evolution.

38. Quintilian, *Institutes of Oratory*, II. iv. 22–27; X. i. 5-ii. 28.

39. Cicero, *De Oratore*, II. lxxxvii. 350-lxxxix. 361; Quintilian, XI. ii. 1–51.

40. Compare *Rhetorica ad Herennium*, III. xvi.28-xxiv. 40 with St. Augustine, *Confessions*, X, vi-xxvi for a parallel treatment of the spatial and temporal qualities of memory. See also Cochrane, pp. 402–03; pp. 432–33.

41. The growing split between rhetoric and appearance roughly paralleled the rise of modern science. In the necessarily brief sketch to follow I shall limit my discussion to only a few seminal spokesmen whose contributions to the separation of thought and action reflect the general tendencies of their times. For more complete treatments of the problem see W. S. Howell, *Logic and Rhetoric in England, 1500–1700* (Princeton: Russell & Russell, 1956); W. J. Ong, *Ramus: Method, and the Decay of Dialogue* (Cambridge, Mass.: Harvard University Press, 1958).

42. Germino, p. 48; W. S. Howell, "Sources of the Elocutionary Movement in England," in Howes, p. 142; H. D. Aiken, "The Revolt Against Ideology," *Commentary* (April, 1964), pp. 35–38.

43. W. S. Howell, "Renaissance Rhetoric and Modern Rhetoric: A Study in Change," in J. Schwartz and J. A. Rycenga (eds.), *The Province of Rhetoric* (New York: Ronald Press Company, 1965), pp. 293–303.

44. K. R. Wallace, *Francis Bacon on the Nature of Man* (Urbana, Ill.: University of Illinois Press, 1967), pp. 157–58.

45. Spinoza, *Ethics*, III; Bidney, pp. 59–61; R. A. Duff, *Spinoza's Political and Ethical Philosophy* (Glasgow: James Maclehose and Sons, 1903), pp. 24–27; R. McKeon, *The Philosophy of Spinoza* (New York: Longmans, Green and Company, 1928), pp. 202–15.

46. Spinoza, *Theologico Political Treatise*, I, chapter 1; Duff, pp. 30–42; Bidney, pp. 286–87; McKeon, *Spinoza*, pp. 304–09.

47. Spinoza, letter #62; *Political Treatise*, "Introduction;" McKeon, *Spinoza*, pp. 134–35; H. D. Aiken, *The Age of Ideology* (New York: New American Library, 1956), pp. 22–29.

48. J. Barzun, *Darwin, Marx and Wagner* (Garden City, New York: Doubleday, 1958), pp. 133–36; Aiken, *The Age of Ideology*, pp. 115–37; Germino, pp. 51–60; Barker, pp. 63–67.

49. See A. J. Ayer, *Language Truth and Logic* (London: Gollancz, Ltd., 1946); B. F. Skinner, "The Machine That Is Man," *Psychology Today* (April, 1969), pp. 20 ff. Responses to this positivistic extremism can be found in R. D. Laing, *The Politics of Experience* (New York: Partheon Books, 1967), pp. 17–38, and N. Chomsky, *Language and Mind* (New York: Harcourt, Brace, 1968), pp. 63–68 among other places.

50. G. Hegel, "Preface," *Philosophy of Right*, trans. T. M. Knox (London: The Clarendon Press, 1967), pp. 10–13.

51. See G. Hegel, "Introduction," *Lectures on the Philosophy of History*, trans. J. Sibree (London: Bell & Daldy, 1872), especially pp. 38–40 and pp. 56–60.

52. Cf. Hegel, *Philosophy of Right*, p. 11; Aiken, *The Age of Ideology*, pp. 71–97.

53. Hegel, *Lectures*, p. 12.

54. Cf. Kojeve, pp. 164–165.

55. Cf. Germino, pp. 38–40. To be sure, this reformist instinct is part of our Enlightenment heritage. As such it is but one more evidence of the consequence of contemporary preoccupation with changing observed symptoms and behavior instead of achieving a detached understanding of the being embodied in human experience. See Becker, pp. 36–51.

56. See H. Arendt, *On Violence* (New York: Harcourt, Brace & World, 1970), p. 39.

57. To be sure, an autopsy is too somber an occasion for the coroner to wax oracular. But we may take some comfort from a few recent instances of scholarship which seem alive to the insights possible if the delicate balance of thought and action is restored. See especially C. C. Arnold, "Oral Rhetoric, Rhetoric, and Literature," *Philosophy and Rhetoric*, I (Fall, 1968), pp. 191–210; R. D. Laing, *The Politics of Experience* (New York: Pantheon Books, 1967); H. W. Johnstone, *Philosophy and Argument* (University Park, Pa.: Pennsylvania State University Press, 1959).

5 / SOME TRENDS IN RHETORICAL THEORY

HENRY W. JOHNSTONE, JR.
Pennsylvania State University

It is only fair to say that while I am the editor of a quarterly journal,[1] I am not an expert. To some readers, this disclaimer will sound like a contradiction. Perhaps, they will say, the College Editor of a publishing house need not be an academic man; what is basically required of him is insight concerning market conditions; and with the help of reviewers who are academics, he can usually give a good account of himself. But surely the editor of a scholarly journal ought to be an expert in the field to which the journal is dedicated. Can anyone other than a professional chemist decide what articles on chemistry are original and timely? No more, it will be said, can someone not an expert on rhetorical theory decide which contributions he receives make an important step forward.

It is necessary to begin my defense by confessing a heavy reliance on the judgment of other readers. They have saved me from mistakes that could have ruined the journal. Their advice has been priceless. What is also remarkable, however, is the number of times I have found my own impressions of an incoming contribution confirmed by the judgment of the expert to whom I have turned it over. There may be several reasons why this should be so. In the first place, there are matters of general style and taste on which an academic person comes to have views regardless of the discipline. If a paper is badly written, or illogical, one can see this without knowing anything about the field to which it is intended to contribute. If it is nothing but a tissue of footnotes or if it consists of ruminations rather than arguments, its unacceptability is obvious. If an editor were required only to be sensitive to such shortcomings, a competent scholar, regardless of his discipline, could edit anything he chose, at least within certain limits.

But this is not, I think, the only explanation of the frequent coincidence of readers' judgments with my own impressions. By profession, I am a student of philosophy. Such a person has been trained to discern creativity in thought. He has developed an eye for statements that express a novel idea or thesis. When he sees such statements, he has been conditioned to work out their logical relationship to statements of other ideas and theses, past and present. Thus he may be led to judge whether a statement expresses realism, or idealism, or existentialism, and to what extent, if any, it deviates from certain established expressions of these views. He also tries to puzzle out the arguments that have led to the making of the statements; for each of them will seem to him to stand in need of rational justification. Thus he is inclined, as the result of his training, always to seek the contexts of statements; and this inclination gives him a sort of *ex officio* position as a witness of novelty as it occurs in a variety of intellectual enterprises.

The philosophically trained observer can be sensitive to broad trends as well as to specific statements. He can see movements and revolutions in the making. Of course, this insight is not purely oracular. It does not develop in a vacuum. One condition favorable to its development is exposure to a mass of evidence. Precisely such evidence is provided, however, by the flow of articles that cross an editor's desk. In this flow the editor comes to discern patterns. Checking one contribution against another, he comes to construct a picture of what is current, what is relevant, and what is new and promising in, for example, rhetorical theory. The picture can emerge from a cluster of unacceptable papers as well as from acceptable ones. What many people are struggling to write about, but none successfully, will surely one day have its proper spokesman.

In this paper I will try to describe the view from my editorial chair. I want to discuss the signs I have seen of developments that may take place in rhetorical theory over a certain period in the future. I have no reason to suppose that my remarks will be valid for any specific period of time; there is no way in which I can even guess how long the trends I now perceive will continue to be trends. For all I know, they may all come to fruition in three or four years, then to be replaced by newer trends that we cannot now even fathom. One cannot, I believe, project the future of a theory in the way one can project the future of a university or an industry. When a university plans its dormitories, it calculates in terms of assumptions that are likely to remain valid over the period of its projection: each student will need a bed, there will be so many beds per room, and so many students to be admitted. In other words, the planners assume that the needs to be satisfied and the equipment to satisfy it will in principle be the same ten years from now as they are now. This is precisely what the would-be projector of developments in theory cannot assume. He cannot know what needs future theory must satisfy because he cannot be sure in what ways present theory is deficient. Even if he had strong personal feelings concerning its deficiencies, he could not guess how people will later come to *regard* it as deficient, and hence what sort of new theories they will construct to overcome these deficiencies. We can exaggerate the difficulties of projection to an absurdity if we ask ourselves with what success Theophrastus or some other younger colleague of Aristotle could have predicted the future of rhetoric for the coming twenty-four hundred years. Obviously, modern rhetoric answers needs that could not have been foreseen in ancient Greece. Not only could they have not been foreseen—they would not even have made sense. But on a smaller scale, just this sort of thing happens over a period of, say, ten years. Trying to see ahead to rhetorical theory a decade from now is like trying to see infrared rays. The conditions for visibility do not yet exist. By this I mean that the problems that rhetorical theory ten years from now will have to cope with probably have not arisen yet. And they are problems that cannot even make sense to us until their time has come.

Thus I speak about trends now in evidence, not trends of the future. For all I know, all the movements that seem so urgent now will, within the next five years, have collapsed of their own weight or died on the vine. When that has happened, I do not presume to guess what the sequels to the theories that now seem so urgently needed can be. All that I am sure of is that as long as there are men there will be rhetoric. But from this axiom one can draw no conclusions concerning the form of rhetorical theory.

Having declared my refusal to speculate, I turn to the material I find on my editorial desk.[2] The need that seems most urgent is reinforced by the news. This is the need for an understanding of the rhetoric of the New Left. We need to understand the rhetorical function of shouts, obscenities, sit-ins, and interruptions of lectures. It is not sufficient to dismiss such tactics as uses of violence; for the users of these tactics are not usually violent people, and refuse to be violent in most of the familiar ways; for example, they do not crack skulls. A new criterion of the distinction between rhetoric and violence is needed. There is the violence of nightsticks and the quite different violence of words.[3] A sober discussion of the rhetorical effects of shouts and obscenities is needed. It would also be of great importance to decide what, in view of the rhetoric of the New Left, is becoming of the concept of reason. Shouts and obscenities seem to be a rejection of reason. So do the non-negotiable demands, and refusals to consider proferred compromises. One mark of the New Left is its refusal to argue with the establishment. Is that refusal based on the presumption that to argue is already to be on the side of the establishment—that the establishment is simply a subculture defined by its insistence on argument? If so, what kind of a rhetoric is it that proceeds precisely by refusing to argue? But perhaps the refusal on the part of the New Left to argue with the establishment is *not* based on the presumption I mentioned. Perhaps the New Left does not reject all argument. If this is the case, it becomes imperative to characterize the arguments that remain available to the protestor, and possibly new arguments that have been invented to supplement these. The role of such arguments in the deliberations of the New Left itself needs to be explored. It would seem that whatever arguments the radicals use in deciding their own courses of action, they are not the arguments that make it possible for a democratic society to survive disagreements on the part of its members; for groups representing the New Left rarely survive any but the most superficial intramural disagreements.

The rhetoric of the New Left has deep philosophical roots, and these need to be laid bare. I keep hoping for a manuscript that would do justice to the title "Wittgenstein and the Rhetoric of the New Left." Wittgenstein's rhetoric is not addressed to reason, and uses few arguments, if any. It is a rhetoric intended to stimulate intuition, to evoke what we know about our language and its grammar. Instead of arguing, Wittgenstein *shows*. Can we say that the rhetoric of the New Left is similarly intended to stimulate intuition? Certainly it has been associated with the hippy's instinct to seek the immediate and the simple. For Wittgenstein, philosophy should be immediate and simple; the pages of *Philosophical Investigations* offer the philosophical equivalent of a love-in or pot party. Not that I think Wittgenstein had any direct influence at all on the rhetoric of the New Left. It is just that he articulated, at a relatively early date, attitudes toward reason that are now of wide currency.

A theme whose connection with the one I have just discussed is obvious is the relationship between rhetoric and ethics. Every three months or so I get a paper with a magnificent title like "The Moral Measure in Rhetoric." It fills me with expectancy. When I have read the paper, however, I am usually ready to weep. Such unfulfilled promise! Typically the author begins by assuming that rhetoric can be used for good or bad ends. He tries to decide what makes an end good or bad. Usually the effort leads the writer to rediscover an old moral platitude, like the Utilitarian formula of the greatest happiness for the greatest number. Since the writer doesn't know that he has merely paraphrased John Stuart Mill, he is also ignorant of one hundred years or more of criticism of Mill's formula, as carried out by some of the most astute contributors to moral theory. So the "moral measure" remains to be satisfactorily formulated. But what becomes of rhetoric in this process is worse. For the writer of the sort of paper I am describing is thinking of it as completely subservient to an ethical standard wholly external to it; rhetoric is to be no more than the means used to achieve an end nonrhetorically certified as good. But once this position is taken, and the autonomy of rhetoric surrendered, it becomes impossible to say why rhetoric rather than some other means—perhaps a more effective means—should be used. If the hedonistic calculus tells us that x should be brought about, and x can be brought about by sticks or drugs as well as by rhetoric, then why not use the sticks or drugs? In the end, there is no longer any way to identify rhetoric except as a relatively weak kind of *force*.

But this is not the only sort of essay that is written under the title "The Moral Measure in Rhetoric," and sent to me. Some contributors take the position that rhetoric must be subservient not to ethics but only to itself. They distinguish an effective from an ineffective rhetoric. To my genuine regret, however, they are unable to say what makes rhetoric effective except that people are persuaded by it. The old question about the effectiveness of Hitler's rhetoric arises at this point. The writers know that in order to make their case they must be able to take the position that Hitler's rhetoric was in some ultimate sense ineffective, but the search for this sense seems inevitably to lead to a standard of rhetoric *outside* rhetoric.

The people who are trying to write papers on "The Moral Measure in Rhetoric" are trying to say something that needs to be said today.[4] In a technocratic world, a world controlled by computers, where plans often reduce to calculations, they are trying to restore to rhetoric something of its ancient autonomy. Rhetoric's worst enemy has been the rationalism first formulated by Descartes in the seventeenth century; the belief, in Pascal's language, that *l'esprit géometrique* can supersede *l'art de persuader*. But today this rationalism is itself being identified as the enemy, and such an identification is implicit in the attempt to shift the locus of the moral measure from reason, where it has been for three centuries, to rhetoric. The attempt is as much an attack on "the establishment" as is the posture of the New Left. On the part of both positions there is a rejection of traditional arguments and a summons to a nonrational immediacy.

A theme obviously related to this is that of communication. A decade of work resulting in the development of contemporary communication theory—a theory with computational, mathematical, sociological, psychological, and linguistic ramifications—cannot help leaving its mark on rhetorical theory.[5] Depending on one's attitude toward the scientific establishment and one's conception of communication, one will hold either that rhetoric is or that it is not a form of communication. Social psychologists tend to regard rhetoric as an aspect, dimension, or kind of communication subject to scientific measurement and control. For them, communication covers a broad spectrum of activities, exemplified by persuasion as well as by the transmission of information. There are those, however, who distrust the embrace of communication so broadly construed. They see the autonomy of rhetoric as threatened by a cancerous growth. Such theoreticians tend to limit the applicability of the concept of communication to situations in which information in some objective form is disseminated. Their view of communication thus judges it by mathematical standards; for example, as exhibiting a certain minimum signal-to-noise ratio. Their problem is to show that there is some relationship between communication, construed in these terms, and rhetoric. You don't have to use rhetoric to get a machine to accept information; why should you have to use it to get a human to accept information? And if rhetoric is no more than a device for getting people to accept information—a stick inserted in the jaw so that the truth can be poured down the throat—it seems in danger of losing the very autonomy that the act of distinguishing it from communication was supposed to instate. Rhetoric must itself somehow be informative. How it can be informative without becoming a mere variety or instrument of communication is a question that must be thought through. The process of thinking it through is something I see on the agenda for the next few years in rhetorical theory.

Those who assume, or argue for, the autonomy of rhetoric, are close relatives of another group of thinkers who I believe are beginning to break through to the places of influence in rhetorical theory. Those are the ones who see rhetoric as a necessary activity, and want to exhibit its necessity. The title "The Ontological Basis of Rhetoric" is not strange to their pens. Ontology, especially as the term is used today, is the study of the conditions of human existence. If rhetoric has an ontological basis, it is one of those conditions. It is not clear that any traditional thinker regarded it in this way. Rhetoric has usually been regarded not as a necessary condition of human existence but as a device needed only because men are not as perfect as they might be. In a society of perfect men, rhetoric would not be needed. This view is opposed in our time, however, by those who believe it impossible to conceive man apart from the "rhetorical situation" (to borrow Lloyd Bitzer's phrase). The human condition, according to such views, is essentially rhetorical. Man is a rhetorical animal, and to strip him of his rhetorical faculties is to strip him of his humanity; it is to make him into a computer. Philosophers like Maurice Merleau-Ponty and Paul Ricoeur have expressed this position with great plausibility. Rhetorical theoreticians are beginning to become aware of and to study their works. They are also beginning to develop their own versions of "The Ontological Basis of Rhetoric." This trend seems to be in the offing for at least the next few years.

From ontology it is but a stone's throw to phenomenology. A phenomenology of the rhetorical transaction would begin by assuming that rhetoric has an ontological basis, that it is a necessary condition of human existence. It would proceed to describe as faithfully as possible the role played by rhetoric in human life. It would make use of procedures first introduced by Edmund Husserl, the most important of which is "bracketing." To bracket a phenomenon is to consider it wholly apart from the claim that it exists or causes other phenomenon to exist. Thus suppose we wish to make a phenomenological study of our perception of an object like a table. The important thing is to suspend judgment as to whether the table exists or not—to describe our perception of it as it would be whether the table were a real object or an illusion. In this way we could describe the structure of our perceptual field wholly apart from existence claims. A similar bracketing would be required for the phenomenological study of rhetoric. What we would be looking for would be a description of the structure of the rhetorical field wholly apart from any question of the objective validity of the issues or even of the objective existence of the speaker. It might turn out, for example, that a dimension of this field consisted in a sort of rhetorical *distance*—a distance from the speaker to hearer or a distance from the issues to the hearer. To describe this distance in the most accurate way possible would be the task of the phenomenological rhetorician. It is, I should add, a most demanding task, because if rhetoric is a necessary feature of the human condition, its use is clearly not limited to formal speeches. It must rather be an ingredient of every human encounter. In eliciting its phenomenology, we are supplying an essential piece of the panorama which Husserl called the "Life-World," the world of everyday life and ordinary experience in which all of us are immersed most of the time.

To see rhetoric as capable of occurring in ordinary experience, wherever else it may occur, is to be prepared to hear that there is a rhetoric of the mass media. I think I detect signs of an interest in this rhetoric. The problem is not so much to develop the rhetoric of broadcasting and advertising along traditional lines but to submit radical reinterpretations of them, such as that supplied by Marshall McLuhan, to critical scrutiny. We need to test McLuhan's apocalyptic picture of an electronic age and traditional models of rhetoric against each other, in the expectation that there will have to be revision in both places. We ought to ask whether McLuhan's assertions are borne out by what we know for sure about rhetoric; but we also ought to ask whether these assertions do not require us to modify rhetorical theory in some ways.

The "Life-World" is also the territory of the ordinary language philosophy that has been dominant in professional circles in England and America in recent times. This philosophy, like phenomenology, seeks to extract the essence of a philosophically interesting situation. Its peculiar form of bracketing is to concentrate on the *language* we use in talking about the situation. But the ordinary language philosopher has until recently paid scant attention to the language we use to describe rhetorical transactions and activities. This deficiency, however, is beginning to be overcome. The pioneering work of Alexander Sesonske, to mention one of our contributors,[6] is stimulating an interest in what it is that we mean when we talk, for example, about freedom of speech.

A philosopher thinking of McLuhan may be reminded of Korzybski, whose excesses are certainly no greater than McLuhan's. General semantics is still a lively movement in America; it exists wherever speech departments for one reason or another cut off from professional philosophy have felt the need to take a philosophical stance. General semantics has much to say about the rhetorical transaction. It can correct traditional rhetorical theories, and be corrected by them, in much the way that McLuhan's views can interact with traditional rhetorical theories. Perhaps in making this point I am expressing an editorial hope rather than an expectation; I would like to have contributions from general semantics but have received few so far. I think there is a need for them.

Rhetoric has two faces, persuasion and argument. My comments so far have emphasized its persuasive face. Not that argument can ever be absent from the phenomenon of persuasion, even in a McLuhanesque world. But there is an interest nowadays, in argument as such; and this interest takes many forms. The *Topica*, Aristotle's handbook of the sources of arguments, is being studied with especial vigor. One proposal that seems pretty clearly prefigured is that the idea of the topics be extended from the legislative chamber and the courtroom to all the areas in which augmentation occurs. If there are arguments peculiarly suitable to certain political situations, are there not likewise arguments peculiarly suitable to certain scientific situations? Even to certain philosophical situations? In other words, can we not generalize the topics to cover all human discourse? If we can do this, we shall see arguments as leading lives of their own, no longer subservient to the generally unattainable ideal of formal validity. Stephen Toulmin took a step in this direction in *The Uses of Argument*, but there remains the suspicion that he was simply dealing with enthymemes which would meet the formal criteria once the suppressed premises were supplied. By "an argument with a life of its own" I do not mean merely an enthymeme.

Interesting sociological questions concerning topics have been raised. If arguments are clustered in the way Aristotle supposed, what account can we give for this clustering in terms of more ultimate modes of explanation? My journal has already published an article on this theme,[7] and will probably bring out others. Another intriguing topic concerns the relation between topics as the places of arguments and places of other sorts. In Aristotle's world everything had its proper place. What happens to the places of arguments when nothing else any longer has its place, as nothing does in the infinite universe of modern science? Can the shift in the status of rhetoric between Aristotle's time and the seventeenth century be accounted for, at least in part, by this loosening and relativization of the idea of place? A correspondent is, I hope, now hard at work revising a previous paper on this theme.

Meanwhile more traditional concerns with the topics are being carried forward, especially by those with legal training and especially in Europe.[8] The work that has been done here is mainly an attempt to ascertain whether legal arguments are distinctive, subject to their own canons and not to those which apply to arguments of other kinds. Evidences of this interest occasionally reach me in the mail; I think we shall be hearing much more about this movement in the next four years.

A moment ago I mentioned enthymemes and their connection with formal logic. It is not only in its use of enthymemes that rhetoric offers material for an investigation of the role of formal logic in persuasion; and Toulmin has not said the final word on the subject. The time is ripe, I think, for standing the world on its head, to use Hegel's felicitous phrase. Instead of timidly measuring rhetoric by its conformity with formal criteria, why don't we turn the whole problem upside-down and derive formal logic from the rhetorical concerns and transactions of human beings? What in the end can we make of the concept of formal validity except as the refinement of a very familiar rhetorical argument —the "You might as well say" argument? To call the syllogism "All men are mortal, and Socrates is a man; therefore Socrates is mortal," valid is to declare that you might as well say "All whales are mammals, and Moby Dick is a whale; therefore Moby Dick is a mammal." Some of the papers I have received contain intimations of the bold and imaginative reversal that ought to be accomplished here.[9]

The rhetorical theoretician is condemned not only to being constantly reminded of formal logic but also to having to hear *ad nausem* about dialectic. No one really knows what dialectic is, but it is an excellent word to use to bait the rhetorician. It suggests a domain of purer, more rigorous, more powerful arguments lying beyond the messy arena in which rhetoric holds sway. But the nature of dialectic is obviously in need of clarification. Dialectic cannot simply be whatever private preserve a philosopher may set up for arguments that he wishes to exempt from attack. At the same time, it would be a mistake if the removal of its privileged status resulted in the collapsing of dialectic back into rhetoric. In using the term, Plato, Aristotle, Hegel, and Marx were trying to tell us something. What they were trying to tell us, and what more there is to say on the relation between rhetoric and dialectic,[10] is a theme that I expect to see developed during the next few years.

I turn to the only area in which I would claim to be prepared in any way—that of philosophical argumentation. This topic is attracting the attention of an increasing number of contributors. One crucial question is whether the study of philosophical argumentation is part of rhetorical theory at all. Perhaps it is relevant to rhetoric only as contrasted with it. Eleven years ago I expressed this view in my book *Philosophy and Argument.* My position then was that the soundness of a sound philosophical argument must be judged wholly apart from its persuasiveness. I saw persuasiveness as deliberately accomplished through the use of unilateral techniques, employed by the speaker but concealed from the audience. I felt that sound philosophical argumentation ought by contrast to restrict itself to the use of bilateral techniques, by which I meant techniques available to the audience precisely to the extent that the speaker made use of them. Many people, including contributors to our journal, have taken issue with this attempt to draw a hard and fast line between philosophy and rhetoric. They have felt both that my presuppositions concerning the nature of rhetoric were too restrictive and that my views of what happens when philosophers argue was wrong. To begin with the first point, rhetoric need not be limited to a technique of persuasion, and even if it were so limited, there is no reason why it could not achieve persuasion by the use of bilateral techniques. Rhetoric has certainly not always been thought to concentrate on persuasion. One of the contemporary views concerning its nature that I myself have come to feel to be attractive is that rhetoric is concerned with *adaptation*—of issue to audience, and vice versa. But when the philosopher argues, he clearly adapts his thesis or his refutation to his audience; this in fact is precisely what would be involved in the argument I have long regarded as paradigmatic in philosophy, the *argumentum ad hominem.* What is it to argue *ad hominem* if not to adapt one's message to the particular man one addresses, taking account of his own deepest motives and attitudes? And what if a peculiar form of adaptation that we might want to call "persuasion" should occur here? There seems no reason why the philosopher would necessarily regard the occurrences of this persuasion as a taint, or why the persuasion so accomplished should not be equally open as a possibility to both members of the conversation.

My view of the nature of philosophical argumentation itself has also shifted in the last decade. I used to think of philosophical criticism primarily as the attempt to expose an internal inconsistency in the position criticized, forcing the holder of the position to revise or abandon it. Since this interpretation assumes that consistency is the highest aim of anyone taking a philosophical position, it is at root a rationalistic interpretation of the philosophical enterprise. Indeed, I used to think of philosophy as primarily an effort to apply reason to the issues that occur at a certain level of generality. I regarded the fact that philosophers ultimately argue rather than just assert and dogmatize as evidence of a concern on their part to expose all their findings to the test of reason. Philosophic truth, it seemed to me, occurs as the conclusion of an argument, not as the utterance of an oracle.

I still believe in the essential role played by argument in philosophy, and I still want to have no traffic with oracles. But my interpretation of what philosophers are doing when they argue is changing. I am no longer sure that they are appealing to a sense of consistency on the part of the listener. In fact, I have always been bothered by this notion of consistency. I am a pluralist in philosophy; I believe in the possibility of a plurality of different philosophical views of the world, each defining it in radically different terms. How, then, can I avoid being a pluralist with regard to the very meaning of consistency? In other words, how can I suppose that there must be just *one* version of consistency, appealed to in the arguments of all philosophers? And yet if there is a plurality of versions, the very possibility of arguing seems to vanish. The sense of consistency to which *I* appeal in criticizing another may well not be *his* sense of consistency at all; so there may be no reason in the world why he should listen to my argument.

My rationalism has accordingly been unstable and precarious. On several occasions I have attempted to buttress it, but the attempts were mere stopgaps. I think it is now a thing of the past. I no longer see philosophical argumentation as an attempt to appeal to a standard of consistency in order to get an interlocutor to revise or abandon his position. I think of it now as an appeal to the other person to be more responsible for his own position, whatever that may be. It is an attempt to evoke on his part a fuller consciousness of presuppositions that may have been merely implicit in his philosophical position. In the somewhat more technical language I have recently been using, I would say that philosophical argumentation is an appeal to the self. One could also use Heideggerian language and characterize it as a call to authenticity.

An argument that *calls* could hardly avoid manifesting a rhetorical dimension, however we may wish to construe rhetoric. Thus the abandonment of rationalism has made it possible for me to adopt a view of philosophical argumentation according to which rhetoric has a natural and proper place in the discussions and debates of philosophers. But it is not only in such academic debates that I see it as having a place. My main concern is no longer with philosophical argumentation at all; it is with the self (to which it seems to me such argumentation appeals) and with the person. I will not now recapitulate the technical considerations that have led me to distinguish self and person. But my present view of the person is that he is encountered as absolutely irreplaceable and fully actualized. This impression that a person makes on us when we encounter him is nothing that could be objectively verified; it is a claim, not a fact. It is, furthermore, a most extraordinary claim. What else in our experience, after all, is absolutely irreplaceable? What besides Aristotle's God is fully actualized? We are led, then, to ask ourselves how a person whom we encounter can make such an extraordinary claim, and why we find the claim irresistible. The answer to which I am now inclined is that rhetoric is involved here wholly apart from its involvement in philosophical argumentation as such. It is the way the person's claim to irreplaceability and actuality is made. It is his presentation of himself. Here, I think, there are echoes of ancient theories of *ethos*.

All this needs to be worked out. There is here a project of sufficient scope to occupy me for at least ten years. It is dimly prefigured in my forthcoming book *The Problem of the Self*,[11] but here I do no more than to *describe* the claims of the person, without attempting to elicit their rhetorical dimension. Nearly all the work has yet to be done. Hence even though I cannot be at all sure what my colleagues will be doing ten years hence, I have a fairly good idea what *I* will be doing, if I am still around and able to do anything.

FOOTNOTES

1. *Philosophy and Rhetoric* (University Park, Pennsylvania: The Pennsylvania State University Press).
2. Some of the items I am about to enumerate appear in the report of the McKeon Subcommittee (Chap. XII). That report also lists many other topics for rhetorical research—topics which did not occur to me as I was writing this paper but which seem to me clearly valid.
3. Barnet Baskerville, in his Response, takes the position that the violence of words is still violence, with all the disastrous consequences of any violence. I agree that there can be a violence of words which is indistinguishable from a violence of bricks and clubs. But there is a humanitarianism present in the use of shouts to stop a lecture—a humanitarianism absent when bombs are used for the same purpose. Besides, even the most violent shouts can *arouse*; and here there is a need for rhetorical research.
4. Karl Wallace, I believe, has succeeded in saying it—in the very paper which appears in the present volume. I am tempted to add a P.S. on the *frustrations* of being an editor!
5. Samuel L. Becker's paper in the present volume, like Karl Wallace's, would be ideal for publication in *Philosophy and Rhetoric*.
6. See "Saying, Being, and Freedom of Speech," *Philosophy and Rhetoric* I, No. 1, 1968, pp. 25–37.

PART TWO

WINGSPREAD:
RESPONSES

6 / THE SCOPE
OF RHETORIC TODAY:
A POLEMICAL EXCURSION

WAYNE C. BOOTH
University of Chicago

A piece of rhetoric about rhetoric to a group of rhetoricians who already know more about the subject than I do? Impossible, clearly. Every stroke will give me away. I have seen their papers (having failed to meet the deadline), and I know just how formidable a group they are. Not only will they be immune to every possible blandishment—one would never dare flatter them, for example, in one's introduction—but they will already have thought of everything I might say. I could of course begin on the offensive, scrutinizing each piece, especially the introductions, for weakness of *ethos*, or locating the fallacies in every argument, exposing the. . . . But it is easy to see where *that* would lead. It would be like opening a conference of psychoanalysts with a paper psychoanalyzing each of the other analysts. Every statement would soon dissolve into the *true* reasons (hidden, "rhetorical") why it was made: "Oh, I know why you said *that*. Your eccentric definition of the nature and function of rhetoric leads inevitably to . . . ." "Ah, yes, but *I* know why *you* say *that*. *Your* picture of us as audience requires . . . ."[1]

There is probably no secure way to cut through such games of one-up-man-ship, and it may be a mistake to bring the danger out into the open; the other papers do not even hint at it. But I feel forced to it, forced by that age-old rhetorical principle: "It's harder for an opponent to call you a fool if you've said it first." Returning to serious systematic study of rhetoric after five years of absorption in the practice of rhetoric as a college administrator, I feel rather like a skittish ingenue forced to perform before grand masters. How can I get them to accept this interim report, written just as I am getting well into M. Perelman and before I have had time to make any real inroads into that stack of books on my desk at the British Museum: the McKeon, to read and re-read, the John-stone (will everyone else have read everything in *Philosophy and Rhetoric*?), and indeed the whole lot? Since I am in fact trying to rid myself of the presuppositions of an "English teacher," perhaps I can get away with the stance of a wide-eyed novice, coming into the troubled province of theory for the first time and asking, without shame, whatever questions pop into my rhetoric-filled, but theory-emptied, head.

In assuming my naiveté, I must, however, draw the line some-where, and I choose not to be so naive as some of the British colleagues I have been meeting in the last few months. "You're planning to spend more time now on *rhetoric* than on *fiction*, you say? Pity! I just don't see how you can turn from the great literature of the world to study trivia—those long lists of devices! I must say to our credit that nobody in England troubles much about that sort of thing any more." This speech, or something like it, I have heard at least five times since arriving in September. One Professor of Anglo-Saxon was terribly annoyed, at a cocktail party, when I insisted that there is a quite respectable tra-dition behind my effort to broaden the meaning of the term "rhetoric." "Oh, well, if you think you can use a word any way you choose!" And he drew away in disgust.

He and his kind—"literature" teachers in most if not all western nations—have left a vacuum which is inevitably filled by peddlers of various rhetorical nostrums. I find in the morning *Times* (London) a fea-ture article on one Warren Lamb, who makes his living as a personnel consultant. I wish I could duplicate here the six pictures showing Mr. Lamb as he adopts the characteristic gestures of six types of "business executive": The Investigator, The Explorer, The Confronter, The Decider, The Anticipator, and The Operator. But perhaps you can imagine what they must look like, using a little help from the classical comments on Gesture and the hints in the text describing his work:

> Talking to Warren Lamb is an unnerving experience. As you tell him what you want to do he is looking at your feet, when you ask him a question he is looking at your hands. For Mr. Lamb speech has lost much of its significance . . . he says he can learn more about a man's character by watching his physical behavior during an interview.
>
> Mr. Lamb, in fact, makes his living doing just that. He is a business management consultant who specialises in advising on the hiring of new executives and the best use of men already working.
>
> He first became interested in 'attitudes' (the combination of gesture and posture) during the war. He was a seaman who saw action . . . and had time to study men under stress. It soon became apparent that the way

a man talked was not a good indication of how he would behave. 'After a time I relied less and less on what men said and started to look for more reliable indicators of personality. Then I began to realize that each man had a number of characteristic gestures and postures . . . These were constant, no matter what the circumstances were and I realized they could be codified.'

Since he started his own firm in 1950 . . . Lamb has identified twelve 'action requirements' which he says all executives need . . . He has been consulted by firms like Colgate-Palmolive . . . He also gives seminars on his methods and travels to America to lecture . . .

You can just bet he does travel to America to lecture, and that as visiting rhetorician he gets paid very well for his lecture on reducing the arts of rhetoric to attitude-ology.

Some of our definitions of rhetoric would exclude Mr. Lamb's study and practice, but as a naive visitor to the realms of persuasion, I can hardly leave him out. He is studying one way in which men change each other's minds. It occurs to me, as a naive visitor, that there may be some use in a rapid survey of what other practices and theories would be included, in our time, if we took seriously a pragmatic definition as broad and loose as that: rhetoric will for now be *all* the arts of changing men's minds. I hope it will trouble no one that this huge net catches many fish that he would throw away. There is plenty of time for sorting, later on, when some of us may want to accept Mr. Wallace's exclusion of "experts speaking to experts" and others may reject, with M. Perelman, all "non-discursive" forms of persuasion. But for now, I face the whole buzzing, blooming, impossibly complex world of "efforts to change men's minds." About the only mode of changing men that is left out is the use of force or violence to change actions without changing thoughts. *Threats* of force will be included—they are so clearly an important means of producing changes in thought and motive. If for no other reason, a rough and ready catalogue of this kind is useful as a preliminary to my second naive survey, which will be of the currently practiced modes of *studying* "rhetoric" in this grotesquely bloated conception.

I. SOME OF THE WAYS MEN IN OUR TIME TRY TO CHANGE OTHER MEN'S MINDS

If the naive visitor to this rhetorical planet happened to read some Marshall McLuhan and take seriously what he says about the new iconic non-verbal age, he would no doubt be greatly surprised to discover how much of the traditional kind of rhetoric still goes on behind McLuhan's back: openly polemical oratory and pamphleteering about public policy, debate about who was to blame in the Kennedy assassinations or in the death of Miss Kopechne, attacks on and defenses of men like Garrison or institutions like the university. I wonder whether there can ever have been a time in America when people took the power of public speaking and pamphleteering more seriously than they do now. When Kennedy spoke on Civil Rights, the nation attended, and everyone seems to agree that some men were changed. When Johnson and Nixon have spoken on Vietnam, the world seems to take what goes on with a seriousness that hardly accords with claims about the unimportance of verbal messages in an "electronic" age. It's true that these speeches are usually *seen* on TV as well as heard, which makes them different from Roosevelt's speeches—but not from Pericles'. The political significance of the addition of TV as a device for getting visual effects to masses of people may be very great indeed, but the rhetorical demands on Nixon, his rhetorical resources (except for relatively trivial matters like make-up and lighting), and the analytical problems given his hearers are essentially what they would have been in all ages. It is simply untrue to say that a *new* rhetoric is needed to deal critically with the flood of speeches and pamphlets and editorials that threatens to swamp us daily: to make up one's mind about whether to accept Nixon's statements I can think of no questions one would ask that one would not ask of any speech in any age (except perhaps for questions of the kind raised by Mr. Becker about the context of the viewer—it *may* be that they could be more easily taken for granted in earlier times). I am not, of course, saying that the answers to the questions will reveal a rhetorical practice identical with that in all times and places. Nixon's speeches on Vietnam, for example, are sometimes long on efforts at ethical proof and emotional appeal, short on arguments (I've been reading, in my catch-as-catch-can visit to the provinces of rhetoric in this age—the young Churchill's speeches in the House of Commons early in this century, and it is enough to make a man weep to see the contrast—even taking into account the different audiences and the fact that Churchill, as his son says, "reserved his invective largely for the public platform," and "gave the House of Commons the best fruit of his thought and the most reasoned arguments in his power. Often in later years he would say: 'The House of Commons is a jealous mistress: you must give her the cream of your thought'." A nation of democratic "viewers" ought to be a jealous mistress, too!).

The point is that in the modern world speeches come at us from every side—open efforts to persuade, calling for a conscious decision about whether to agree. Similarly the polemical pamphlet or broadside flourishes—usually with no appeal whatever in the "medium," with, in fact, nothing but "message" scrawled, and often misspelled, on mimeograph paper. Someone calculated that in one of the sit-ins at the University of Chicago, something like 2,000 pages of argument had been distributed by both "sides," all on the assumption, as old as writing, that a written argument may change someone's mind or strengthen his allegiance or do *something* to him that the writer wants done.

Aside from the sheer quantity of such rhetoric, perhaps the most striking thing about it is how much of it is addressed to what might be called the community of the blessed and how little of it is addressed to the outsider in an effort to convert him. It is often said of Hutchins' splendid speeches about education that they never converted anybody; all they did was enspirit the already enspirited troops while further enraging the already enraged enemy—that horde of established plotters which he characterized, in so many delightful ways, as irremediably benighted. Whether this is true of Hutchins' speeches—and as a man who had his life changed (however slightly) by reading him at the age of nineteen I know it to be at best a half-truth—it seems to be true of a great deal of rhetoric today. It is written or spoken as if the community of believers were already determined, the only thing left to decide being whether to act on the belief or not. It is as if all hope were lost of winning outsiders to become insiders, or—to put it another way—as if no *reasons* were needed to prove the essential rightness of one's cause, only reasons for stepping up one's energy level. The New Left addresses itself, on the whole, to the community of saints, and every rhetorical stroke seems designed to sharpen polarization: as one Lita Lepie, a Vassar senior, sees the rhetorical problem, "It's very hard for any person who's seriously interested in improving the general quality of life in America to pose any kind of tangible threat to the populace. If you pose a political threat, like the Panthers, you're shot. If you pose a cultural threat, you're either censored or thrown in jail for drugs." To "pose a threat" is a curious rhetorical purpose for anyone wanting genuinely to improve the quality of life, and it is matched in its blissful rejection of outsiders by those who oppose the left: witness the language of Mr. Hayakawa as he attacks "student gangsters" and "bastards."[2]

There's nothing especially new in this aspect of our openly polemical rhetoric. In a sense it is an aspect found in most classical rhetoric, which also assumed a "band of insiders," sharing a set of fairly obvious places of argument: Who is guilty of having violated the laws *we all agree on?* who is right in arguing for political policy that will preserve values *we all agree on?* who at the present moment deserves highest praise for exemplifying the ideals that *we all share?* The Aristotelian tradition is suited best to analyzing the cogency of such rhetoric, from the point of view of someone who is at least in some sense on the inside. It is not quite so helpful—but then what theory is?—on the question of

what to do if you want to construct a unifying rhetoric that will penetrate what seem to be totally hostile circles. An Athenian addressing a
Spartan—assuming that weapons can be laid aside long enough for some
talk—has a categorically different problem than the one he faces when
talking to the Athenians. Though it can be said that he still has only the
problem of finding what places are in fact held in common (though as
yet undiscerned by either disputant), and then arguing from them, the
fact is that such places are often extremely difficult to find—far more
difficult than classical rhetorics would imply.

What our naive survey finds, then, at this point, is that there is a
good deal of rhetoric going on for which the classical analysis seems
more appropriate than it actually is. The temptation (as I have found in
practical affairs) is to a self-satisfied exposé of the opponent's fallacies
and absurdities, without making the slightest effort to "move into his
circle of assumptions" and argue from there. In Chicago's sit-in last
spring, for example, we discovered at one point that each side—and by
that time to talk of only two sides was tragically appropriate—was du-
plicating the rhetoric put out by the other side, *without adding comment*,
and distributing it as widely as possible. To each side it seemed that the
opposing rhetoric was self-evidently damning! This did not mean that
none of the rhetors was achieving his purposes. One student told me
later on that the sit-in had at least succeeded in one of its major purposes, that of polarizing the campus; presumably he would have said
that the rhetoric "succeeded" in the same sense. Only to those of us who
were trying to hold the university together was there this kind of rhetorical failure.

One could argue that the failure was one of intelligence or education in the producers of the rhetoric: surely professors of English (and
we English teachers were prominent among the university spokesmen)
should have been able to see beyond the surface arguments and find
topics that would have a common appeal. Much of my own time during
those harrowing days was spent, in fact, trying to discover with students
what were in fact our common assumptions; often what I discovered
were simply the widening chasms of difference.

This characteristic of our rhetorical situation presents itself most
dramatically in those many moments, duly noted as "rhetorical" by the
naive observer, when one side decides not to let the other side state its
case. The speaker has an assumption that the situation calls for an effort
of one kind or another to talk things through; the auditors, some of them,
assume that the time for talk is past, since the speaker and his kind are
so clearly evil that to listen to them would in itself be an evil. At such
moments, any chance for a rhetoric of the classical kind disappears. Two
inaccessible communities are formed, communities which are then free

to harden their lines by addressing their "closed rhetoric" only to themselves.

This is precisely what the cliché, "loss of community," means, rhetorically; or in Dewey's terms we can say that we have destroyed "the public" and built a variety of hostile publics, more or less sealed from each other. A black student comes to me privately and says, "Mr. Booth, you must not pay attention to what we say to white people when we are in groups. What we say is said for each other, not for you, and you should be smart enough to realize that."

What I would like someone to provide for me—and I am speaking now in my role as a person who has to live in this society, not as the naive observer—is an "art of invention" that would help me deal with such moments, or with the fact that two of my former students, students with whom I worked closely for a full year, are now members of the Weatherman crowd. I have sat meditating a long letter to the one I think is most likely to be accessible. But what do I appeal to? I have thought of using *his survival,* but I know that one of the key assumptions of his rhetoric of attack is that personal survival does not matter in a world as evil as ours. I have thought of trying to use whatever common ground we share—and there is some—in our views of what's wrong with America and what would be a desirable future. But I've not been able to write the letter yet, and I probably won't be able to: what is called for is not a piece of "rhetoric" at all, in the traditional sense. We have reached the stage, he and I "together," at which our *essential* commitments, our most cherished myths and symbols, seem to be at war. What is called for here is something different from a letter, on the one hand, or Hayakawa-like epithets or an escalation of violence on the other.

I suspect that it may be some notion of rhetoric that will take into account those essential shifts of mythic worlds that we ordinarily call "conversion." I shall want to return briefly to the notion of such a "rhetoric of religion," or "rhetoric of metaphysical transformations," or whatever it would be, later on. For now I must return to my naive observer as he shifts from the openly polemical forms of rhetoric to a second kind, less open, more likely to make unacknowledged appeals to the values of a closed community, or even to produce "conversions" without the converter quite knowing what has happened to him: not speeches and pamphlets, not open conclusions openly arrived at, but secret conclusions secretly imposed. Of the many forms of disguised rhetoric, our observer is most impressed by three: advertising, the drama presented on TV and in movies, and fiction. It is true that one finds open polemic in all three of these "forms." Much advertising, perhaps most, makes its argument explicit; many novels and movies are openly didactic and thus fairly amenable to traditional modes of analysis. I open the *Sunday*

Times (London) and see a picture of a troubled-looking lady standing in front of an old-fashioned sash window. "Double glazing? You couldn't fit it here," she is saying, and the advertisement goes on with a direct and simple appeal: "Oh yes, we could! Everest double-glazing units fit sash windows, bays, and almost every other kind of window. . . . The slimness, trimness and simplicity of . . ." And so on—all entirely open and direct except for the choice of a matronly, visibly responsible woman rather than a sexy model. The major is, it is true, suppressed: double glazing is what everyone will want if it *can* be made to fit. But all of the appeals—to possibility, to economy, to aesthetic values, to safety (they "deter burglars") and to popularity ("More homes are fitting Everest . . . than any other make") are straightforward and thus subject to the sort of analysis we all know how to make. But in the same issue I come to a full-color page showing a "Boutique" with four attractive young girls, obviously on an exciting shopping spree. At the bottom of the full page, in print less than a third the size of the sign, "Boutique," "Lloyds Bank looks after people like you." And then, in *very* small print, which I did not notice until I had decided to study the ad: "Anne Malton and her friend Jane Mortimer are at London University on grants. This means that they have to watch their budgets and take care of expenses. Luckily Lloyds Bank understands about student life—so much so that they handle students' accounts free of charge. To help organise slender resources to best advantage."

On the face of it, this is a fairly mild example of what we have all learned to recognize as an oblique appeal, much of the content of the appeal left entirely unstated. But if we think of what might be called the mythic content of the ad, what Lloyds relies on to make the explicit appeal for Lloyds, we see that very large issues are at stake when one tries to decide whether to approve or disapprove of it. Imagine what an intelligent member of SDS would say of it!

The whole art of disguised appeal to snobbery, vanity, sexual desire and fear, fear of disease and death, and indeed to all of the human vices and weaknesses, has been developed professionally in our time, and I cannot believe that we have developed an adequate rhetoric to deal with it in our education. The communications movement, so-called, tried a few years ago to introduce study of "the media," and criticism of advertising, into all "Freshman English" courses, but without an adequate theoretical base and with little intellectual content—or so it seemed to me. It is not surprising that these courses soon proved dissatisfying; there are, I believe, few of them left. But they were onto a good thing, as we say, and I think it is too bad that McLuhan and others have so badly fouled the waters of the media that no one knows anymore which way the current of the electronic age is running.

Perhaps it is enough for now to note that the rhetoric of the image, reinforcing or producing basic attitudes towards life that are frequently not consciously faced by the rhetor, constitutes an enormous part of our daily diet of rhetoric. Awareness of its power is one of the things that protesters mean when they say that there's no use trying to remove this or that abuse, because the whole "system" is corrupting. This part of the system *is* corrupting, even though it is also true, as Daniel Boorstin has pointed out, that the advertising for certain products succeeds in building a kind of community among those who finally buy the product— a community that partially makes up for the lack of more genuine forms of community in the lives of the buyers ("I always honk my horn when I pass another Mercedes-Benz driver").

Perhaps an even more interesting phenomenon to our imaginary observer (and certainly one that interests me strongly quite aside from any poses here) is the way in which many art works, particularly fiction and drama, have become explicitly or at least noticeably responsive to a rhetorical situation. It is true that critical theory in the arts has been predominantly anti-rhetorical, at least until recently; there have been many "objective" aesthetic theories in this century, arguing that the artist should pursue his ikons purely. But the arts have refused to conform: novelists and playwrights have written in full awareness that the high-brow audience is fragmented (or thinks it is) and that the lowbrow audience has a very low common denominator. On the one hand, the artist who rejects what has been thought of as "commercialism" laments the fact that he can find no ready-made cultivated audience. Virginia Woolf once expressed envy of writers in earlier ages who could depend, as she thought, upon readers who shared public norms, while she had to impose her private vision on the reader through the work or feel that she was writing only for herself. Many have echoed her lament. Some have faced the problem openly and tried to embody in their fictions the kind of rhetoric which could create its own audiences. Saul Bellow seems to me highly effective in this subtle and difficult transformation. Others have withdrawn into privacy, convinced that any thought of the reader poisons true creativity; but their very withdrawal is often visibly audience-centered. And on the other hand, fiction and drama, especially TV and cinema, have tended, with rare exceptions, to be produced in what seems to be an elaborate effort to "psych out" the audience in advance, deciding what it wants and then giving it to them.

When the arts become rhetorical in this sense—when artists try to please audiences with whom they in no sense identify themselves—degradation is inevitable. But the whole process has been abetted, it seems to me, by ostensibly anti-rhetorical critical theories. If all good art has no rhetorical dimension, as so many have argued, then the "rhetoric" is left to those who will use it for the devil's purposes (we have here something analogous to Augustine's decision that men of God should learn rhetoric, since the devil's minions will surely master it). How much better it would be if we could develop a way of understanding how great literature and drama does in fact work rhetorically to build and strengthen communities. Reading *War and Peace* or seeing *King Lear* does change the mind, just as reading *Justine* or taking a daily dose of TV fare changes minds. A movie like *The Graduate* both depends on commonplaces shared much more widely than our slogans of fragmentation and alienation would allow for, and strengthens the sharing of those commonplaces; like *The Midnight Cowboy* or *Easy Rider*, it can be said to make a public as well as finding one already made. All of them work very hard to *appear* nonrhetorical; there are no speeches by anyone defending the graduate's or the cowboy's values against the "adult" world that both movies reject so vigorously. But the selection from all possible worlds is such that only the most hard-bitten or critical-minded viewer under forty is likely to resist sympathy for the outcasts and total contempt for the hypocritical aging knaves and fools that surround them. If sheer quantity and strength of pressure on our lives is the measure, the rhetoric of such works, though less obvious, is more in need of study than the open aggressive rhetoric of groups like *The Living Theatre*.

Another observation that should be made by anyone surveying the rhetorical scene without prejudice, is that most young people now seem to derive their basic beliefs, at least those that are capable of articulation, more from fiction and drama than from forms that at one time were more influential: sermons, scriptures, epideictic orations—to say nothing of systematic discussions of theology or philosophy. Among our undergraduates, there are probably ten who have seen *The Graduate* for every one who has read *Magister Ludi*, ten who have read *Magister Ludi* for every one who has read *War and Peace*, and ten who have read *War and Peace* for every one who has read (aside from class assignments, which don't count for much here) Plato or Aristotle or even Jaspers or Heidegger. All of them have read or seen some works which imply or state that all institutions are hypocritical; few have ever read a serious discussion of the role of institutions or the uses of authority. Most of my students have read *Catch-22* along with other good novels, like *One Flew Over the Cuckoo's Nest*, that imply or state that virtue lies mainly in "the opposition." Their lives are molded by such works, and if a discipline sets out to deal with what changes men's minds, it must face these squarely.

But this leads back once again to that vast neglected area of rhetoric, the rhetoric of "conversion," of transformation—the rhetoric with the effect, whether designed or not, of overturning personal ties and changing total allegiances: what my colleague Charles Wegener has been calling *psychogogics.* We all know that Aristotle does not pretend to deal with such matters in the *Rhetoric*, and that they are more characteristically the preoccupation of the Platonic tradition. Yet if our naive visitor looks around at the changes attempted and achieved in our society today, he can only conclude that vast tracts of our rhetorical landscape are left out by those who use the word rhetoric. We are the age, for example, of psychoanalysis, perhaps next to Christianity the most ambitious and evangelical of rhetorics in the history of man: Come to us and we will change not just your beliefs but we will change *you*, change you into another and more desirable person. We are also the age—to continue with this rashly pontifical tone that the naive visitor adopts in his uncritical survey—of group therapy, of group dynamics, and of a host of staring, touching, praying, bathing, and copulating groups that spread across the land in a great ecstatic glow. We are also the decade of the revival of astrology as something taken seriously by people who claim to be educated; I know a graduate student who says, "Well, I know the evidence is not conclusive either way, but to me it *means something.*" If we are tempted to deny the importance of such matters, we need only talk to a few of the serious— not to say over-solemn—young people who actually join these groups. They talk of their conversions as religious converts have always talked: the essential message is, "I have changed my life." "Until I went into that building [for the sit-in] I wasn't even alive; I didn't know what life was *about*. Something permanent happened to me in there; I'll never be the same." "Well, I'd say the turning point for me came when I discovered Yoga; that's what taught me what I was and what I could become." "It may sound silly, but I've been totally different ever since The Living Theatre was here; I've been dancing, sometimes quite literally—last Sunday afternoon it was barefooted on the dormitory lawn—but sometimes just metaphorically—so much is possible, if you just let down the old barriers and *embrace* everybody."

You and I may enjoy—I certainly do—poking holes in the logic of statements by leaders of such groups (I'm especially amused by how narrow their conception of "everybody" turns out to be; they're as exclusive as the Exclusive Brethren). But our analytical poking has no effect, because these transformations lie deeper than our logic can penetrate; they are like the changes that are claimed by psychoanalysis or brainwashing techniques or Christian missionaries.

One has to say for Marshall McLuhan, silly and irresponsible as he can sometimes be, that he has at least tried to grapple with some of these more difficult rhetorical problems. Father Ong, less capriciously, and George Steiner, more gloomily, have also dealt at length with what happens to the Word when men "retreat from reason" to levels of "silent" psychic processes too deep for words. Many of us may choose not to follow their "probes" (note the rhetorical thrust of McLuhan's key terms like "probe"), but we should never forget how much we rule out if we do so. There are many aspects in the present gropings of the young that resemble Biblical utterances more than classical orations; the San Francisco *Oracle* presumably changes minds, but if we want to understand how, we must look not to our Aristotle or Cicero but to Kenneth Burke's *Rhetoric of Religion* or to some as yet unwritten rhetoric that would explain how gospels work their miracles. With new religions and new saints being created all around us—Martin Luther King, Malcolm X, President Kennedy—the very least we might hope for would be a rhetoric of the new communions as useful for today as was William James's great "rhetoric," *The Varieties of Religious Experience*. Such a work would attempt a sympathethic treatment of what is happening in an age of "happenings" that "blow your mind," of transformations through drugs or other routes to mystical vision, of total political transformations that claim to slough off, like old and ugly skin, the old life and bring in a new millenium of peace and light. You and I may not palpitate to these things, but a surprising number of men in our time are proving "convertible." In being so, they are of course vulnerable to charlatanism but, by that same token, they are hungry for any art of rhetoric that will help them choose between the liberating and the destructive.

I do not know what such a rhetoric would be, though I have found valuable hints towards it in McKeon's four kinds of architectonic productive arts and in Kenneth Burke. Elements for it will no doubt be found from many different fields and approaches. When law is no longer taken as something to respect but rather something to be violated to make a superior rhetorical point, forensic rhetoric must somehow expand to take on the very task of reasoning about the need for law itself and its true bases in human reason (here M. Perelman is of major importance). When the crimes and heroic achievements of the past are no longer treated as historical truths to be recaptured or lived with, but as fodder for memory chutes, the simple rational processes of debate about who was to blame are radically insufficient. When deliberation about the future is subject to deep doubts about whether there will in fact be a future, men look for a "deliberative" rhetoric of "mythical comfort and communion," a "symbolic" of unification more than for a rhetoric of simple persuasion about this or that policy. Finally, when a country is, like ours, riddled with suspicion of vast conspiracies, when we find ourselves talking about whole generations being untrustworthy, when entire races are taught to hate all other races, we need a rhetoric that will search far deeper than the simple pursuit of an epideictic rhetoric dealing with the praise of honorable men.

The naive observer's tour could be continued indefinitely, as he returned from these high spiritual regions to note the ubiquitous rhetoric of "factual" reporting, from the news media through political biography and literary autobiography (he would like to give us a page or two alone on *Time Magazine's* curious notions of what a fact is); the rhetoric of literary criticism as practiced by those who, like Leslie Fiedler, write to a program; the rhetoric of the press conference; of congressional hearings; of dress, hair, buttons, and placards. But though he has many more kinds of rhetoric on his list, we must leave him now. He has filled his purpose, which was to startle us, once and for all and forever, out of any notion that "rhetoric" is the special province of any one of our disciplines. If the the whole catalogue has seemed laborious and obvious to you, perhaps you should chalk it up to my own need to get out of my system the notion that rhetoric is something properly confined to the English department.

II. SOME OF THE WAYS MEN IN OUR TIME STUDY HOW MEN CHANGE EACH OTHERS' MINDS

Because the study of "how men change each other's minds" has no clear boundaries, because it can in fact be fruitfully applied to every mode of communication and every subject matter, it has always attracted popularizers like Mr. Lamb. America is full of these popularizers today, few if any of them calling themselves rhetoricians or students of rhetoric: Mr. Flesch with his reduction of all the arts to the arts of simplifying; Mr. Carnegie, with his reduction of all the arts to the art of flattering with an air of sincerity; Mr. McLuhan with his reduction of all of the arts to the art of a-logomancy—prophesying the future by spotting the latest antiverbal trend (I hope you have all seen the ads for his *Newslitter*); the advertising agencies and business consultants, with their various reductions to this or that fragment of ethical proof or emotional appeal or mode-for-disguising sophistical enthymemes, or gimmick of arrangement, or program for inducing creativity; the journalism schools, some of which, I understand, have been developing quite scary rationalizations for playing fast and loose with the facts. We also seem to produce a constant flow of somewhat more serious academic studies purporting to bring intellectual order into our rhetoric-bombarded lives. The first one I ever embraced was semantics, in the curiously truncated form spread by Stuart Chase's *The Tyranny of Words*; he really convinced me, for a while, that intellectual clarity in one's reading could be found by substituting a meaningless noise—I remember it as something like buzz or bosh—for every abstract term. It is not hard to see why *that* road to rhetorical salvation was soon abandoned, but it is really astonishing to note how many rhetorical fashions have touched lightly at the fringes of this skittering century and then been passed by: systems of semantics, communications, linguistics and rhetoric by the dozen.

How are we to avoid this fate for the new fashion in serious rhetorical study? I think only if we repudiate once and for all the notion of a takeover and embrace rather the notion of a pluralistic set of arts, learning from all relevant disciplines and indeed willing to be absorbed by other disciplines at appropriate moments. The study of rhetoric would be, in this view, universal (as rhetoric is itself a universal art) but it would not be universally encompassed by any one student and it would not aspire to a single universal methodology for ascertaining either how men's minds are in fact changed or whether they should have been changed. Though it would by its nature aspire to the improvement of human communication in all its forms, it would know in advance the truth that Perelman and Johnstone and McKeon have been reminding us of, namely that there are many kinds of effective reasoning. It would thus be a kind of pluralistic philosophy not just of "argument" but of *the whole of man's efforts to discover and share warrantable assent.*

Such a philosophy of suasion would seem vulnerable to the charge that has always been levelled at rhetoric: "you have no subject matter." Having many subject matters, and different "methods" to suit the special needs of each, rhetoric in this view would become indistinguishable from philosophy, or at least that form of philosophy which avoids dogmatic or fixed or final formulations and throws all questions of validation back into the rhetorical situations which gave rise to them. Just as the notions of what makes a good public speech are discovered in the give and take of speech-making communities, and the notions of what makes sound proof in physics are discovered in the give and take of physicists, so the notions of what makes good political argument in our time would be referred to the political arena; as Mr. McKeon says in his paper, there is no point in deploring political demonstrations, for example, for being illogical when they do not set out to make a logical case. For all we know, before looking as closely and sympathetically as possible at the content and form, a given demonstration may be the vanguard of the chosen people marching to the promised land.

In one interpretation, such a pluralistic view would leave nothing whatever for the student of rhetoric to do: each field would take care of itself, and as it became more and more expert at its own standards of validation, it would find less and less of a place for the rhetorician-philosopher to meddle. (This is of course an old problem for philosophers, solved by some modern philosophers—wrongly I think—by retreating into a corner of linguistic analysis.) But in another view, the student of rhetoric finds a place as a kind of general coordinator of what he and others can find about how suasion works. Since we are used to thinking of rhetoric as this or that traditional slice of what I am now calling rhetoric, it may be annoying to be asked to think of our discipline under a more general rubric. It may even be that we shall want a new term for the philosophy of suasion, reserving rhetoric for either a sub-branch of the study or (as I would prefer) for the practice of the art. In either case, we shall find, on any honest view, that the workers in the vineyard I have been clumsily defining are far more numerous and various than we ordinarily admit. I have space to discuss only a small number of the disciplines now actively studying how men discover and share (what they take to be) warrantable assent. I shall say nothing of speech departments (leaving that to the participants from that field) or of English departments (leaving that as perhaps the area most in need of whatever re-organization we can provide of educational aims), and I shall say very little more about philosophy (hoping that everyone will read everything that Mr. Johnstone, Mr. McKeon, and M. Perelman have written).

Let me just run very briefly over some of the disciplines that are today giving serious treatment to one or another of the aspects of rhetoric. Though it is unlikely that any one of us will ever master what is now known about rhetoric in this broad sense, at least we should be able to reduce somewhat the present ridiculous duplication of effort and unfortunate dissipation of results.

1. PSYCHOLOGY

A. PSYCHOANALYSIS

Psychoanalysts have not been eager to look at their theory and practice as one system among many for changing men's minds. But there is a sizeable literature by now, some of it summarized in Jerome Frank's stimulating little book, *Persuasion and Healing*, that touches problems dealt with in traditional rhetorics. It takes no great skill in translation of terms to recognize that when the analyst talks of transference he is dealing with the processes that underlie what we mean by ethical proof. The emotions he deals with are the same emotions that a traditional rhetorician would deal with, and regardless of his particular school of therapy—and of course there is a very babel of schools—the effort to move behind superficial emotional responses or symptoms to a superior reality would be matched by any rhetorician who sought some way either to understand the emotion-ridden political movements of today or to produce some kind of healing. I think it is no accident that analysts have always been fascinated by political leaders. Perhaps the study that most completely dramatizes the common rhetorical ground that underlies some political movements and some views of therapy is the recent biography of Gandhi by Erikson, *Gandhi's Truth*. Unfortunately there are few analysts who can rival Erikson's breadth of interest and insight into the rhetorical meaning of political acts, but I cannot believe that any student of rhetoric would fail to learn from his study of what might be called the rhetoric of sainthood.

The psychology of sainthood (in this sense) is one of the most pressing subjects we face today, when so many young men and women are attempting total immersion—and sometimes even immolation—in this or that utopian cause. It may very well be that no nation can survive without saints, and that one of the things we are suffering from is a kind of withdrawal symptom of a people all of whose saints have been debunked: if we have no leaders who can be idolized, then we will idolize first the Schweitzers and Gandhis and Thoreaus of the present or near past, and then the various new prophets who announce themselves almost daily—the Christs and Satans and Gods and Buddhas of the California scene. If we cannot save ourselves in rational modes, we will embrace "irrational" modes, even if they destroy us, in order to convince ourselves that our lives have point. Psychoanalysts have dealt with the irrational more effectively—with all their factions and internal warfare—than have students of rhetoric, and any new rhetoric must be ready to learn from them.

B. Experimental psychologists

There is so much going on here relevant to how we persuade that I must simply choose one branch, "operant conditioning," and hurry on. I have myself been so mistrustful of Skinner's theories, and so fearful of the effect on us all of his notion of how human beings work, that it is only with the greatest effort that I can give a sympathetic hearing. But I am impressed by what some "Skinnerians" have been able to do with, for example, autistic children, leading them to take the first steps from their crazed isolation into a world of language and human life. I still palpitate —in theory—much more readily to Rogers or Chomsky when they attack Skinner than I do to Skinner and his simpleminded models. But the fact remains that human behavior is (as our friend The Philosopher too believed) in a very fundamental respect dependent on "habits," and habits can be induced, initially, by rewards and punishments. And the operant conditioners are able, in certain cases, to produce radical changes in behavior and belief that no traditional rhetorician could either produce or easily explain. Even if one chose to repudiate such techniques as beneath human dignity, the student of rhetoric must understand them if he is to earn the right to repudiate. If, as I am arguing, the purpose of studying rhetoric always has a two-fold practical dimension—to improve one's **own** rhetoric and to protect from mistakes about other men's—then even the most abhorrent devices fall within our ken.

These are only two from many examples of how the psychological study of "motives" should interest us and might inform what we do. I can think of nothing more irresponsible for a modern student of rhetoric, aware that the first great *Rhetoric* was loaded with psychology, than to ignore the psychology of his own time.

2. SOCIOLOGY

No doubt a lot that has been going on under rubrics, like group dynamics or T-therapy, is intellectually shoddy, and some of it looks to me immoral as well. But we shouldn't let this scare us away from those sociologists who have done systematic study of how convictions work for men in groups, of how community is built and destroyed, of how language works to build and destroy institutions and of how communal norms are built, reinforced, and exploited by works of art. I have been struck, for example, in looking at some of what is done with "content analysis," by how much it overlaps my interest in the study of topics—and also by how ignorant the sociologists are of the rhetorical tradition in such study. Similarly, when David Riesman analyzes the norms in children's books, he teaches *us* something, yet his own good work would probably have been better if he had worked closely with a rhetorician. Finally, how many of us really know our Weber? And how many followers of Weber know that we have common interests with them?

3. ANTHROPOLOGY

In what I said earlier about mythic worlds and the conversions that move men from one to another I implied that the study of rhetoric should include the study of mythic systems, of how they interrelate, compete, and capture believers from each other. One branch of anthropology (about which I know very little) seems to be doing a good deal with this kind of topic, and I should think that a systematic exploration of what has already been done, by someone trained in classical rhetoric, would prove fruitful. From my reading in Levi-Strauss it seems clear that much of what he has to say about the structures of mythic systems is relevant to anyone trying to understand current rhetorical problems (why, for example, is a piece of rhetoric which is deeply moving to a professor an object of mockery to many students, and vice versa?)

4. LINGUISTICS

Less likely to be neglected, at least by English departments, this field or collection of fields has often bid fair to take over the whole of rhetorical study. But despite the extravagant claims for what linguistics can do—claims which are found much less frequently these days—there is obviously a good deal that any student of rhetoric (in any sense of the word) can learn from the scientific study of language.

Many linguists are now willing to distinguish between the study of how language "in fact" works, and the study, by "rhetoricians" and "literary critics," of questions of value in the use of language. Now that they are abandoning their imperialism, I'd like to see us stir up the waters a bit by attempting some reverse imperialism: surely a rhetorician cannot turn over this whole field of the "factual" study of language to another discipline without at least asking whether "in fact" the value question can ever be ruled out. Every statement is in some sense rhetorical, in my definition: it can be said either to succeed or fail in the task of changing the mental state of *somebody* (even if only the speaker as his own audience— see Perelman). Therefore the question of value is present even in the "cleanest" scientific study of language. And if this is so, "rhetoric" cannot surrender any territory here. Though each of us must, as an individual with finite time and energy, surrender vast territories to other students, the subject of mutual mind-changing is by its nature imperialistic, and "rhetoricians" cannot rule out from their interest the current lively growth of linguistics and the heated controversies between universal grammarians like Chomsky and the many who have questioned his deductive models. It is obvious, for example, that McKeon's hope (which I share) for a "universal architectonic productive art" in a technological age has a good deal more chance for realization if Chomsky turns out to be accepted—if, that is, all men speak, in one very real sense, a common language. And if, on the contrary, there are no linguistic "places" that are really common to all men, then I don't see how we are to find a meeting ground in a new rhetorical world community. (I know that there are larger philosophical issues pushing to be heard here, such as whether or in what sense there are "universals" of the kind debated in the old nominalist-realist controversies; but I must ignore them, except to lament that when linguists debate the Whorfian hypothesis about how each language imposes a radically different world upon its learners, they have not generally profited from philosophical inquiry into the same question put in different form. But this may be simply another way of saying that in our time it may be more profitable to debate the old question in the new terms of linguistics and rhetoric; men seem much more comfortable when someone like Chomsky, flashing his scientific credentials, claims to prove that we are innately programmed to a universal than when a traditional philosopher argues that universals really exist.)

5. PHILOSOPHY

Wittgenstein said, or seemed to say in one of his guises, that we cannot really reason together about the things that matter most; before the really important value questions, the philosopher can only remain silent. As M. Perelman and the other philosophers at this conference have been reminding us, rhetoric seen as the philosophy of argument has always insisted that there are many ways to be reasonable, that in fact good (though perhaps not "positive") reasons can be shared by men even in debating the most difficult questions of all, the grounds of reason itself. Of all the fields one might unite under rhetoric as I have defined it, this one is the most thoroughly tilled.

Indeed, if rhetoric is, as a study, the philosophy of suasion, our whole conference will be about "philosophy," and I will therefore say little about it here, except for one brief point about the need for effective philosophical critique of the commonplaces uses in intellectual argument, or argument by people who think of themselves as intellectuals. Popular "thinking" is now ridden with platitudes about the "meaningless universe," about the beastliness and hypocrisy of life, "the horror, the horror," about, finally, "the death of God." Whereas men at one time wrote books to prove such matters, one now finds them relied on as assumptions needing no support. Since some of the most popular philosophers, most notably some of the existentialists, have seemed to argue for intellectual despair (even while recommending that one shake one's fist in the face of nothingness), the everyday rhetoric of non-philosophers finds itself resting either on places that have ostensibly been bombed out of existence by modern thought (the patriotisms and pieties of speeches by Nixon or Agnew, for example) or on the new despairing places: reason is helpless before the truths of existence, therefore choose your own poison, throw your bomb, join your party, take your drug, depending on whether it feels good to you.

Many philosophers, even from within the analytical school, have been working at new ways of talking about the old questions (e.g., Toulmin, *The Uses of Argument*; Karl Britton, *Philosophy and the Meaning of Life*). But it seems to me that there is a special need for philosophers interested in rhetoric to find the right rhetoric to get their arguments heard. It is of course true that the philosophical expert faces the same problem faced by all experts who try to write for a general literate public; it is never easy, and the dangers of distortion are real. But if anyone ought to be good at finding ways of translating ideas from one language to another, the student of rhetoric is the man.

One could move on, with the same easy superficiality, through many more fields—through the rebirth of explicit rhetorical concerns in literary criticism; through the blooming science of information theory, as adumbrated in Mr. Becker's paper; through history, in which we would find some intellectual historians tracing the history of commonplaces relied on in different periods (Mr. William Smith's recent book, *The Rhetoric of American Politics*, is the one I know best); and on through political science (where my ignorance is almost total, but where I am told that rhetorical studies under one name or another flourish); on through the new ethnology, professional and popular, with its discoveries about communication among animals and its (premature?) analogies with human communication about territory, conflict, and community; on through business schools with their courses in advertising and group dynamics and effective management; back through the more traditional, but still valuable, work of speech departments; "forward" again to propaganda specialists and brainwashing analysts, students of psychological warfare, thinktanks with their programs for stimulating invention; then on a side journey to the academic work on "creativity," ranging from the careful studies of Frank Barron and his colleagues through the loose but provocative speculations of men like Koestler and Ghiselin and on to the host of popularizers and frauds who make their fortunes teaching men how to be creative; on to the new centers for the study of culture, at places like Utrecht (under Betsky), and the University of Nottingham under Hoggart; and finally (but by no means exhaustively) to the schools of journalism, of communications, of education . . . (The trouble with any "universal" subject is that it is overwhelming. If anyone is still under the delusion that rhetoric is a subject to be mastered by any one man—even under Mr. Wallace's or M. Perelman's definition, let alone mine—he might take a quick look at the titles in the current bibliographies under terms like "Communications," or for that matter even the cross references under "rhetoric," though the makers of the Cumulative Book Index, say, or the subject index of the British Museum have not thought as much about the real meaning of the term as you and I. Where would you expect to find the topic "Belief and Doubt," for example? Why, under "Consciousness," of course!)

What does this hopelessly long list of "rhetorical" studies mean to us? One could take it as simple proof that the effort to see rhetoric in this kind of universal view is ridiculous in the first place; I can easily understand anyone who decides to choose a very narrow definition and carve away at what it covers, hoping for time and the bibliographers of bibliography to build some unified picture of how men in our time work on each other's minds and theorize about their workings. In practice all of us must follow this path to some degree. But even though I feel overwhelmed by the prospect of trying to sift out the genuine knowledge from the immense amount of chaff in all of these areas, I see no way in which we can collectively dodge the task. Unless we are contented to struggle to learn what is already known or to duplicate in one language what other men have already said, we will want a survey—not naive and fragmentary like this one of mine, but as complete and systematic as can be made—a survey of what our fellows now know or are trying to discover about how men work to discover and share warrantable assent in our time (and, of course, this necessarily entails how they work to *stimulate* the discovery and sharing of warrantable assent—bad rhetoric and bad morality can never be dodged in rhetorical studies).

I should like to conclude with five practical suggestions that seem to me to follow from our knowledge (for which this paper is but a long footnote) of how many students share our general interest in rhetoric, and our knowledge (which this conference has already demonstrated) of how many men are now thinking philosophically about a possible new rhetoric.

1. There is simply no point in debating about how wide a field the term rhetoric covers or should cover, as if there were hope of fixing the word in a right usage. I assume that my definition is broader than anyone's here except perhaps for Mr. McKeon's. But this should not trouble anyone: simply note where your definition ties into mine, record why you cannot include this or that kind of effort to change minds, and try to get me to listen to your results when you come to them. It is too late in the history of ideas for us to allow ourselves to fall into arguments about words or battles about semantic systems.

2. Though there is no doubt a great need for more work with theory at varying levels of abstraction, it seems clear to me that in a practical subject like ours we greatly need, without further delay, as many concrete analyses of rhetorical situations and of pieces of rhetoric as possible. It sometimes looks as if America is full of men trying to be first in the arena with *the* new rhetoric and relatively lacking in men who are willing to teach each other how to analyse particular bits of rhetoric. Under any definition, under any theory, America is badly in need of improved rhetorical practice—many of us would say that we are in a kind of rhetorical crisis with a really threatening diminishment in men's capacities to discover warrantable assent. A student last year said that he was disappointed in the Chicago faculty not so much for opposing the protesting students as for not even beginning to understand what they were trying to say. "They spent their time picking holes in the logic of our hastily written pamphlets instead of going behind the words to what we were really saying." At the time I thought he was asking entirely too much of any group under seige. But now I think that what he said made sense: it is

precisely "behind the words" of controversy that we must look, and that can be done best in concrete analyses of what men say and of the gestures and symbols they choose in making their demonstrations, verbal and visual and physical.

3. We need a clearinghouse for a constant scholarly and practical sifting of what is learned from our theorizing and our analyses. I'm aware that we already have some—departments of speech that have become interdisciplinary, committees like Mr. McKeon's Committee on Ideas and Methods, Mr. Johnstone's journal. But I suspect that nobody has yet gone far enough in gathering together at one spot men from the diverse disciplines to learn from each other.

4. I think we need more scholars of rhetoric who are willing to dirty their hands in actual controversy. We "rhetorologists" are peculiarly vulnerable to any charge that our practice is not improved by our knowledge: if a student of rhetoric cannot persuade, it may not in fact prove that his theories are false, but it will seem to most men that it does. A revival of rhetorical studies that produced a bunch of logic choppers and schematizers would be bad for the field, as we say. But I am thinking of something more important than this: if America's crisis is in fact largely (though of course not exclusively) a crisis of rhetoric, our chances of doing anything about it will depend on our finding ways of addressing persuasively men in all fields, and also men who resist the very concept of a "field." Much of the best study of rhetoric in the past has come from men like Cicero who had learned in practical affairs what works and what does not. While I would not ask that Mr. McKeon or M. Perelman take time from their theoretical investigations in order to address popular rhetoric about rhetoric to laymen in this rhetorical age, it seems clear that anyone who has any hope of adapting our various messages to more popular audiences should work at the task without shame or fear.

5. In all of the educational planning and innovation going on today nothing seems as promising as the effort to organize a new version of liberal education as education in the rhetorical arts. If the graduates of our "liberal arts" colleges were in fact masters of the arts of discovery, criticism, presentation, and systematization outlined by McKeon we might find that a rhetorical age need not be simply deplored or exploited; it could become a time of intellectual and spiritual flowering.

FOOTNOTES

1. In the conference as it developed, there were in fact two or three moments when I found myself thinking back on this paragraph as perhaps too prophetic for comfort. Fortunately we moved beyond them to what seemed a quite remarkable level of understanding.
2. *Newsweek*, December 29, 1969, pp. 30, 36.

7 / THE NEW RHETORIC

CHAIM PERELMAN
University of Brussels

The conceptions and the importance of rhetoric have varied in the course of time. It has been regarded during certain periods, as the crowning feature of a liberal education; yet Jacob Burckhardt described the interest the ancients showed for rhetoric as a "monstrous aberration"; besides, the teaching of rhetoric has been struck from the programs of both high schools and universities in Europe for over fifty years.

This change is coupled with a change in the conception of the object of rhetoric. If, for most cultured people in Europe, it evokes the idea of "figures of style" with their learned and exotic names, if it is pejoratively associated with such phrases as "glib tongue," "speechifier," with the idea of men on the look out for "artificial ornaments," averse to the simplicity which is good form in today's world, this attitude is by no means new. There are examples of it in the works of moralists and of all those who are interested in "serious matters," such as the Stoics, and particularly Epictetus who declares: "But this faculty of speaking and of ornamenting words, if there is indeed any such peculiar faculty, what else does it do, when there happens to be discourse about a thing, than to ornament the words and arrange them as hairdressers do the hair?"[1]

If rhetoric is an ornamental art, it no more deserves to be a central element in the education of every cultured man than the art of the hairdresser. That is the reason why the very word rhetoric is not mentioned either in the *Encyclopedia of Philosophy* or in the French philosophical dictionary by Lalande. This is the outcome of a conception which, in opposition to Aristotle, makes rhetoric a counterpart of poetics and regards it as the art of making beautiful speeches or the art of literary prose. Indeed, for Aristotle, rhetoric does not aim at the production of a literary work. It is not a poetical discipline but a practical technique with a view to producing an effect on an audience; if the resulting discourse has artistic value, that is but a consequence, not the aim of the orator's endeavors.

Unfortunately, Aristotle himself encouraged this confusion between the producing of a work and the exercise of an action by his own grossly mistaken conception of epideictic discourse. Whereas he saw without ambiguity that the deliberative and the forensic genres aimed at influencing the decision of the men deliberating in political assemblies and of those who have to pass a legal sentence, he thought that in the epideictic genre the listeners only played the part of spectators and that their decision was concerned merely with the speaker's skill (*Rhetoric* 1358b 1–7).

We know that, in actual fact, during the olympic games, oratorical contests took place on the same lines as athletic competitions and that the best orator received a crown. But it is preposterous to set forth as the character of a genre what is but its literary imitation. Indeed, there is no objection to staging a lawsuit or a political debate, but we would not therefore say that the aim of these oratorical genres is to enhance the author's talent. If such were the case, the speech delivered before the grave of a lost friend, which is the very epitome of epideictic discourse, the latter being, according to Aristotle, about praise or blame (*Rhetoric*, 1358b 12), would have no further object but to prove the speaker's talent! In the same way, the Christian preacher who speaks in praise of humility and repentance would only wish to see his virtuosity admired. There is no more absurd idea, and moralists, from Epictetus to La Bruyère, have never ceased to deride it.

Since the aim of every discourse is in reality to influence an audience, its action can only concern the future: the point is to bring people to act, to decide, to create or to reinforce in them a disposition to act. In that respect, although their end is not to urge people to immediate action, epideictic speeches are nevertheless essential because they increase in us a commitment to the values which make it possible to justify action. Patriotic ceremonies aim at reinforcing in us the love of our fatherland and the virtues of the good citizen. Private ceremonies exalt the virtues of the good father, of the exemplary son, of the devoted mother and of the faithful friend, thus fashioning the model of the man one should be in the various circumstances of life. Political discourse reveals the evils from which the city suffers and calls forth remedies, or presents the image of an ideal city which men should strive to bring into being.

If, as Aristotle points out, we only deliberate over means, a basic and sustained education should have provided us with all the ends which make of man a cultural being, not an animal driven by his instinctive and spontaneous desires. Now, without the epideictic genre, which is the educational genre "par excellence," we would have no rhetorical technique enabling us to create and to reinforce a communion concerning values.

It should be noted that the distinction between oratorical genres, although useful from a pedagogical point of view, should not be taken literally. A discourse can aim at reaching various results either simultaneously or successively. Thus we know that the communion, on the occasion of his funeral, around the victim of a political murder, may give the orator who will sing the praises of the deceased the opportunity to strengthen the people in their struggle against the Establishment and even to create a popular commotion, a riot, or start a revolution. These various stages can be clearly brought to light by an analysis of the famous oration of Mark Antony in Shakespeare's "Julius Caesar."

An old tradition, which is frequently referred to in Plato's writings, contrasts rhetoric and dialectic, the technique of long speeches on opposite sides and that of questions and answers. At the beginning of his *Rhetoric*, Aristotle alludes to these two techniques and makes rhetoric the counterpart of dialectic (*Rhetoric* 1354a 1). Both techniques have in common the fact that they can be used for any object, since both aim at persuasion by means of dialectical reasoning. However, rhetoric is presented as essentially dependent on the audience, particularly a nonspecialized audience. Hence, "commonplaces," that is, the commonsense notions and ideas, hold a central place in it (*Rhetoric* 1355a 24–28). Dialectic, on the other hand, puts opposite theses to the test, starting from generally accepted opinions. This can happen in any field since the examination of the first principles of any discipline cannot occur in any other manner (*Topics* 101a 38–101b 4). That is why we are told by Professor McKeon that dialectic is addressed to a universal audience whereas rhetoric is intended for particular audiences. In reality, however, Aristotle mentions audiences only in his *Rhetoric*. In the *Topics*, the very idea of an audience is strangely absent, perhaps because he considers that in a dialogue the speakers alternately play the part of orator and listener, as in the case of inward deliberation. That is how, conformably to tradition, rhetoric has been identified with public discourse even by the very authors who want modern rhetoric to study the effects of mass media on the public at large. Professor Becker's attitude is typical in this respect: His interesting study encompasses the whole range of modern media, yet he begins, traditionally by identifying "rhetoricians" and "public address scholars."

For Professor Karl Wallace, rhetoric concerns popular, nonspecialized discourse: "The principles and rules of its art refer to, and have relevance for, the subject matter or 'content' of everyday discourse when men act as social creatures in their families, neighbourhoods, communities, and political associations, and are not speaking as experts to experts."

It is easy to understand that this view of rhetoric which makes it a technique for ignoramuses, or at least for nonspecialists easily aroused and led astray, should have brought it into poor repute. The rhetor would then be the unqualified man, able by his skillful discourse to throw dust into the unknowing's eyes, like the demagogue of the *Gorgias* who, because he has managed to obtain the crew's goodwill by flattery, gets the management of the ship although he knows nothing about the art of pilotage.

However, if we reflect for one moment on the starting point of Aristotle's *Topics*, which consists in generally accepted opinions (*Topics* 100a 30–32), it is obvious that these opinions are accepted by the mind of those to whom the orator addresses his discourse. Hence the topics as well as rhetoric are concerned with dialectical reasoning fashioned with an audience in view. Likewise, when Professor Wallace sees the foundation of rhetoric in the study of good reasons, the main point is to note that good reasons are always relative to an audience which appreciates them as such.[2]

Aristotle opposed dialectical to analytical or formal proofs establishing truth, falseness, necessity, and impossibility, and determined by rules and criteria which are independent of all reference to an audience. Now, if the dependence on an audience, whatever its composition, is made the distinctive feature of dialectical proofs, the interest of evolving a discipline serving as a counterpart not for dialectic, but for the "Analytics" or formal logic, is at once obvious.

This discipline would unite the topics and rhetoric in one single branch of the study of reasoning with an audience in view. Are we to call it dialectic or rhetoric? I believe there should be no hesitation in calling it rhetoric, for our cultural milieu has for over a century identified dialectic with the conceptions of Hegel and Marx, and rhetoric is the only discipline traditionally concerned with an audience. We shall then call this new discipline the new rhetoric. I will now enlarge on some of its characteristic features which will, I hope, make it clear that it should be a main element in any humanist education.[3]

.   .   .   .

The new rhetoric thus owes its specific character to the relation between speaker and listener, between the man who tries to persuade and those whom he seeks to persuade. Its object of study should therefore be wholly general, not restricted to the techniques designed for a particular audience (for example the nonspecialized public), or to a particular medium of communication (oral or written, direct or indirect) or to any single form of persuasive communication (discourse or treatise, formal or informal discussion, inward deliberation) or to the contents of this communication (political discourse, counsel's speech, philosophical treatise, academic address, report at a scientific congress, etc.).

The very nature of the rhetorical act involves certain common characteristics. Rhetoric has not been given its due philosophical status because it has suffered from a major confusion. Rhetoric in all its generality has been identified with the particular cases such as the political discourse addressed to the people's assembly, the counsel's speech or the preacher's sermon, which are samples of the political, forensic, or sacred oratory. Rhetoric should not be reduced to what is generally called the theory of public address or of eloquence, even though these are important applications of the theory.

The rhetorical dimension is unavoidable in every philosophical argument, in every scientific discussion which is not restricted to mere calculation but seeks to justify its elaboration or its application, and in every consideration on the principles of any discipline whatever, even in the programming of a computer. As long as men are not reduced to intellectual robots, as long as their reasoning is not restricted to mere calculation or to the automatic working out of a program, whenever they act on other men by means of a discourse or are acted upon, they are engaged in an activity which is of interest to the rhetorician.

Man thus appears to be an essentially rhetorical animal. Hence, every education aiming at what is specific to man must rest on the two poles of reasoning, the formal, logico-mathematical pole and the rhetorical pole, each being easier to understand when compared or even opposed to the other.

Formal, impersonal thinking unfolds within a system that can be wholly detached from its context. This makes it possible to build calculating machines and various types of computers. But rhetorical thinking presupposes a contact of minds and always occurs in a psychical and social context. In the case of inward deliberation, the speaker and the listener being different parts played by the same person, the social aspect relating to the contact of minds is suppressed. We are, anyhow, left with the linguistic categories, the values and norms, the traditions and beliefs which reflect on the whole the social community in which the person has been educated and exert a continual influence on every one of its members. Freud even points out in his first introductory lecture on psychoanalysis that, when deliberating, a man is apt to hide from himself those motives for his acts which do not tally with the image he wants of himself.

The influence of society may be general, expressing the common-sense of its milieu. But for questions relating to a particular discipline, this influence is the outcome of the methodology of the discipline on which the personal reflection bears. This methodology will be all-pervasive, it may even be exclusive, when the problems under consideration are of a highly specialized nature.

When the audience the speaker addresses is composed of a large number of persons, various institutions exist which either make the contact of minds easy, or sometimes impossible, or which may grant or refuse audience to a speaker, the latter's prestige being thereby either enhanced or questioned. Such are schools, churches, courts of justice, the press, learned societies, mass-media, advertising, and censorship.

The social aspect of rhetoric makes it easier to understand the attitude of all kinds of protesters and contestants who cannot find in the established order adequate means to obtain a hearing and who seek to attract attention on their grievances by provocative gestures.

Considered from our point of view, political institutions and legal procedures could form the subject of fascinating studies. A list could be made of all the political and religious, public and private ceremonies which periodically offer the opportunity to foster social communion in the exaltation of common values. The rhetorician could thus make use of a great deal of social psychology and of the sociology of persuasive techniques.

The commonplaces of each audience, their variation in time and space, would be an object of study for the sociology of knowledge. The examination of values and their hierarchies, according to the ages, temperaments, social status, and political ideologies could also provide copious information about present and past audiences. Next to empirical inquiries in the most varied spheres, which would be useful to add to the actual practice of rhetoric, a study of the samples of discourse found in history would yield a lot of information about the audiences of the past.

The great speaker knows his audience. He knows the values to which they adhere and to what extent, and the arguments they accept and those they question. We may therefore presume that he is rarely mistaken about these points, especially when we know that his discourse has been effective.

In political discourse, recourse is had to commonplaces, to the common beliefs and interests of the audience. Hence the psychology of the listeners, their beliefs, prejudices and passions play an all-important part. Technical discourse, on the other hand, whether it be judicial or scientific, is composed with regard to the methodology of the related discipline. A knowledge of precedents will inform us as to the reasons which have prevailed in the past and which involve a particular interpretation of the law. The rule of justice which asserts that it is just and reasonable to treat essentially similar situations in the same manner will incline us to hope that, all other things being equal, the same reasons will prevail in the future, that an argument which has proved strongest will remain so in a similar situation.

We also learn from the various methodologies which arguments are regarded as relevant or irrelevant in each particular discipline. Analogy enables us to transpose the use of arguments from one discipline to another.

Every philosophy presents a vision of man and of the Universe. It thereby gives preponderant value to a certain type of argument while disqualifying certain others. Thus the argument from essence is known as typical of Aristotelianism, while the argument by analogy is characteristic of Neo-Platonism and the pragmatic argument, also called argument by consequences, is presented as the only valid one in Utilitarianism. Criticism of a doctrine is therefore correlative with the reevaluation of the type of arguments despised in this philosophy. I have shown elsewhere how criticism of the pragmatic argument, while setting other types of argument against it, constitutes a criticism of Utilitarianism.[4]

By generalizing, we could thus study the various philosophical systems from the point of view of the type of arguments favored or disqualified. The appeal to reason so typical of philosophical discourse could be analyzed as an appeal to a peculiar type of audience which I have called the universal audience.[5] The manner in which each philosopher visualizes this ideal audience, to which he assigns a place and a part in his system, could be usefully elucidated thanks to the rhetorical point of view.

The view I uphold, according to which rhetoric constitutes the common structure for all discursive action from one mind on another, would show its special use and even its indispensable character in the methodology of the social sciences, of law and philosophy. We could proceed to develop a common theory and to put it to the test in the field of linguistics and literature and through investigations in psychology, sociology, morals, and politics.[6]

It would also show how this structure must be specifically determined in each particular case, for the principles of rhetoric get more accurately defined through the subject-matter and context. It would reveal the conditions of efficacy for a political discourse or a sermon, for a counsel's speech or a scientific report. In each case the knowledge of the audience and the establishment of a contact with it occur on different bases. Here the oratorical action is essential, there it is negligible; sometimes it is important to know the listener's psychology, in other cases, it plays no part, for only a thorough knowledge of the subject and of its methodology make it possible to convince a specialized audience. At times, the techniques aiming at creating *presence* are all-important; at other times, they will be looked upon with distrust by a specialized audience.

Many such researches would necessitate a close cooperation between rhetoricians and specialists in a particular field, such as literature, psychology, sociology, history, law, morals, political science, history of science and of culture, pedagogy, and philosophy.

Thus, since the Colloquium on Proof which was held in Brussels in 1953, immediately after the IXth International Congress of Philosophy,[7] researches have been undertaken by the Centre Belge de Recherches de Logique in the field both of law and history. These researches have given rise to studies of a remarkable value which have established the importance of the Brussels group in legal reasoning.[8] Two volumes have been published containing studies devoted to the methodology of history and to the historian's reasoning.[9] Research in that field is proceeding regularly. Literary or pedagogical studies should also be envisaged in common.

Argumentation in all its forms has held a brilliant place with the ancients thanks to the technicians of rhetoric. We hope that the analytical and experimental study of this essential branch of reasoning will be pursued even more efficiently along the lines laid down by the new rhetoric. The latter will now encompass all the aspects of dialectical reasoning which are complementary to those analyzed by contemporary formal logic.

Translated by E. Griffin-Collart

FOOTNOTES

1. Epictetus, "Discourses," Book II, Sec. 23, *Great Books of the Western World.*
2. "The Substance of Rhetoric: Good Reasons," *Quarterly Journal of Speech,* XLIX (October 1963), 239–49.
3. Since my first contacts with the members of the Speech Communication Association in 1962, I have found that among the views most akin to mine are those expressed by Prof. W. E. Brockriede in his two articles: "Toward a Contemporary Aristotelian Theory of Rhetoric" and "Dimensions of the Concept of Rhetoric." See *Quarterly Journal of Speech,* LII (1966), 33–40 and LIV (1968), 1–12.
4. Ch. Perelman, "Pragmatic Arguments," in *The Idea of Justice and The Problem of Argument* (New York: Humanities Press, 1963), pp. 196–207.
5. Ch. Perelman and L. Olbrechts-Tyteca, *The New Rhetoric* (Notre Dame: Notre Dame University Press, 1969), pp. 6–9.
6. Cf. Ch. Perelman, "Recherches interdisciplinaires sur l'argumentation." Lecture delivered at the Sixth International Congress of Sociology, 1966, and published in *Logique et Analyse* (1968), pp. 502–11.
7. Cf. the readings of this colloquium in the *Revue Internationale de Philosophie* (1954), No. 27–28.
8. Cf. "Le fait et le droit," Bruxelles, Bruylant, 1961; "Les antinomies en droit," Bruxelles, Bruylant, 1965; "Les lacunes en droit," Bruxelles, Bruylant, 1968.
9. *Raisonnement et démarches de l'historien,* Bruxelles, Editions de l'Institut de Sociologie, 1964; *Les categories en histoire,* Bruxelles, Editions de l'Institut de Sociologie, 1969.

8 / TRENDS IN THE STUDY OF RHETORIC: TOWARD A BLENDING OF CRITICISM AND SCIENCE

WAYNE BROCKRIEDE
University of Colorado

The five papers by Professors Becker, Johnstone, McKeon, Rosenfield, and Wallace manifest a variety of concerns about many topics, each pointing out directions in which rhetorical scholarship is now moving or may or should move in the future. The purpose of this paper is to underscore some of those directions. First, I shall discuss briefly six trends in the study of rhetorical communication. Then I shall develop somewhat more extensively a relationship between criticism and science, an idea that grows out of some of these trends.

TRENDS IN THE STUDY OF RHETORIC

1

The trend perhaps most commented on in the five papers is a growing emphasis on the contemporary. The day is passing when a student focusing on a theoretical level is limited to the ideas of someone who wrote before the twentieth century, or when a student analyzing and evaluating someone's rhetorical practice has to wait until his figure dies. The study of contemporary theory and practice is becoming fully legitimate. Many people doubtless agree with Samuel L. Becker's concluding suggestion that:

> we devote at least as much serious, sophisticated, scholarly work to contemporary communication phenomena as we have to that which occurred in the past. Too many scholars of rhetoric and public address have been concerned only with the discourse of the past—discourse on which one can, presumably, gain a more "objective" perspective. Whatever perspective and objectivity is gained is more than overbalanced, however, by the loss of sources of data through time.

So long as past theory and past practice are not altogether ignored, it is good to move in contemporary directions and place much more stress on what is conceived and practiced now.

2

Another trend is to make conceptual models approximate contemporary practice more closely. To narrow the gap between what is studied and the conceptual models with which we study it is always important. The reduction of the distance becomes especially important, however, when what is being studied undergoes enormous change.

Under a variety of labels, "body rhetoric,"[1] "the rhetoric of the streets,"[2] the rhetoric of "confrontation,"[3] of "agitation,"[4] of "coercion,"[5] and others, students have noted radical changes. If contemporary rhetorical practice is experiencing a revolution, conceptual models for that practice must also be revolutionized. As Karl R. Wallace puts it, "Contemporary man doubtless needs a modern rhetoric." Such an idea is implied strikingly by the title of a lecture presented by Franklyn Haiman: "The Rhetoric of 1968: A Farewell to Rational Discourse."[6] The task, as L. W. Rosenfield contends, is "broader than simple renovation."

At any rate, the traditional concept of a speaker constructing a persuasive discourse to influence other people has been called into question. Three targets for the criticism are especially worth noting. Some of the criticism has been aimed at the perspective that places the speaker at the center of the transaction, a pervasive one historically. From the practice of the sophists and the writing of Isocrates and Cicero to the thrust of many twentieth-century textbooks in public speaking, the rhetorical transaction has been seen as one in which a speaker seeks to have his way with an audience—both to achieve an immediate end and to achieve power or glory as a respected member of society. Although some writers, certainly, have stressed the importance of the audience, most have conceived the audience primarily as a target for the speaker's art. Even Aristotle and George Campbell, perhaps the two luminaries least vulnerable to this indictment, can be read and have been read in this way. Professor Becker offers an intriguing alternative to the focus on a speaker as a persuasive agent when he suggests that public address analysis be guided by an equilibrium model. Other possibilities include seeing the transaction from the point of view of the auditor or as an interaction between people.

Another object of criticism has been the idea that persuasion is the principal, sometimes exclusive, function of a speaker's art. No one can deny that in some rhetorical transactions a speaker influences an audience, but to assume that persuasion is the *only* function of rhetoric is to limit unnecessarily and unwisely the study of how people and ideas interact. Some of the other functions of rhetoric, to mention a few, are to aim at identification, at alienation, at adaptation, at self-discovery, at interaction, and at the development or maintenance of a group.[7]

Still other criticism is directed at the view of rhetoric as a set of signals or symbols organized and expressed in conventional ways. Some behaviorists are as vulnerable to this criticism as are some traditionalists. The assumption that the ultimate object of study is the form of the message, whether seen as a "speech" by traditionalists or as "code" or "information" by behaviorists, runs the risk of ignoring what is vital—that *people* are encoding and decoding and organizing the message. The ultimate measure of a message's effectiveness lies in how people respond to it. The function of people must have higher priority in our study than does the form of the message. Henry W. Johnstone, Jr. makes this kind of suggestion in relation to formal logic, and his premise can be extended to other instances of the form vs. function issue. He says, "Instead of timidly measuring rhetoric by its conformity with formal criteria, why don't we turn the whole problem upside down and derive formal logic from the rhetorical concerns and transactions of human beings?"

A more accurate conception of rhetoric might result if the primacy of the speaker were replaced by an emphasis on people interacting in a situation, if an exclusive emphasis on persuasion were replaced by a recognition that people relate in various ways, and if a preoccupation with the form of a discourse were replaced with a focus on how people act together functionally.

3

A radical reconceptualizing of rhetoric is called for by those who object to the idea that the most appropriate unit of rhetoric is the "speech," a one-shot attempt at persuasion, the idea that a rhetorical transaction is bounded by a speaker's introduction and his conclusion. Even when a speech is placed within a social and political context and what occurs before and after a speech is taken into account, the focus of study traditionally has been the speech.

Several writers, using different primary terms, have proposed antidotes to such a limited perspective. Leland M. Griffin has urged rhetorical critics to study "movements" rather than single speeches.[8] David K. Berlo has insisted that communication is a "process," having no beginning and no end;[9] for purposes of analysis one starts and stops somewhere, but the beginning and the ending of a speech may often prove to be meaningless terminals. Wallace Fotheringham has spoken of a persuasive "campaign,"[10] a recognition that rhetorical effects are likely to require more than a single speech. All three of these writers imply that they are calling for more than an additive study of a number of speeches, that the categories of analysis appropriate for the study of a single speech may be useless in the study of a movement, process, or campaign.

Their analysis is extended significantly by Professor Becker's contribution to this project. He argues convincingly that the speech is not an appropriate unit of analysis. More important is his provocative idea that each person receives a unique campaign message. If one considers a message from the point of view of what a person perceives from available messages disorganized over time and across space, he engages in a different kind of study than if he sees the message as an entity perceived alike by all who are exposed to it, whether that message be a single-shot speech or an extensive campaign.

I hope Becker's idea is read very carefully and not assimilated as a minor modification of a traditional concept of rhetorical communication. It is revolutionary. Anyone who accepts it can no longer design research in traditional ways. Both critic and experimenter have tended to assume a simplistic model of that which they study. Becker's contribution to a more sophisticated model adds an enormous amount of methodological complexity.

4

Another tendency is to move from a linear, mechanical model to one of a complex set of interacting dimensions that form an organic configuration. Such linear relationships as cause-effect, stimulus-response, and evidence-claim no longer seem appropriate for much contemporary communication.

A contemporary model of rhetorical communication should embody at least two significant features. It must recognize that people often perceive message-events configurally. Convincing support for this idea appears in Professor Becker's paper. He argues that:

> various message sets are, in effect, overlayed to form the large and complex communication environment or "mosaic" in which each of us exists. This mosaic consists of an immense number of fragments or bits of information on an immense number of topics. . . . Each individual must grasp from this mosaic those bits which serve his needs, must group them into message sets which are relevant for him at any given time, and within each message set must organize the bits and close the gaps between them in order to arrive at a coherent picture of the world to which he can respond.

Unfortunately, most of our current thinking and research stem from a linear conception of *the* speaker presenting *the* message to *the* audience.

A second important feature of a contemporary model is to view rhetorical communication as a matrix of interrelated dimensions, each of which is capable of exerting influence on the others and on the total configuration. In an earlier essay I sketched three families of dimensions—the interpersonal, the attitudinal, and the situational.[11] Although these may not be the ones that best represent the process of rhetoric, I am still committed to the idea that the rhetorical transaction is best viewed as a set of interacting dimensions. The idea of studying only a few of the relevant dimensions, whether in a critical or an experimental study, is not a productive one, I think, because it denies the essential unity and configuration of a rhetorical transaction. The experimenter, for example, who merely studies whether source credibility does or does not exert an influence on a communication attempt, making an effort to hold all other variables constant, is not asking an important question. The more interesting question is under what combination of variables (and the number of combinations is many) it exerts what kinds of influence.

5

Over fifty years ago Charles H. Woolbert voiced an eloquent plea to make greater use of quantitative and experimental research techniques.[12] Until the past fifteen years or so, however, experimental studies were relatively rare. Experimentalists, at first, were opposed; then they were accepted on a kind of token basis ("Professor Jones is our quantitative man"); and finally they emerged as part of a dualistic establishment ("they do their thing, and we do our [different] thing").

The conflict between traditionalists and behaviorists is understandable. Most people who learned research techniques before 1955 or so were not exposed either to the philosophical rationale or to the specific procedures of experimental research. What was not understood was feared. In addition, some experimental studies justified such fears by leaving people and numbers unrelated, or by relating them unconvincingly. On the other hand, the sterility of much traditional research fed the behaviorist's distaste for historical-critical techniques.

By 1970 the increasing emphasis on experimental research is beyond question. Whether some traditionalists like it or not, experimental research is here to stay. The issue should no longer be how to arrest such a development but how the "we" and the "they" can blend competencies in a common search for a better understanding of rhetorical communication.

6

Both traditionalists and behaviorists appear to be placing a greater emphasis on the concrete transaction and less on theoretical models. Rhetorical critics are moving away from a preoccupation with applying Aristotelian or Burkeian categories with a severe compulsion to touch all bases. Such a method seems singularly to have left unilluminated the transaction under scrutiny. The new injunction is to let the transaction itself suggest its own analytic categories. Behaviorists are evidencing a greater interest in the individual transaction from which general hypotheses are to be tested. This evidence comes in two forms—a growing interest in field studies that utilize the real actions of real people in real situations, as well as a growing concern in laboratory experiments for external validity, that is, to take pains that the communication event contrived artificially in the laboratory will sufficiently approximate real communication to warrant the generalizations that will be made.

Although a concern for the concrete event is laudable, one wonders if the theoretical model is not at least as important as the data. Whether made by a critic or an experimenter, the study of a concrete event that does not relate to a general model of rhetorical communication, or is not relatable to one, would seem to have only limited value.

7

Several of the trends discussed above may imply the kind of distinctions and dichotomies that have long plagued the history of rhetoric, many of which have led enthusiasts to stress one point of view toward rhetoric and ignore its counterparts. For example, some have focused on being and excluded appearance (or vice versa), on persuasion instead of conviction (or vice versa), on content rather than form (or vice versa), on the individual and not on society (or vice versa), and others.

An idea that may result in a more promising choice than any one of the pairs in the preceding paragraph is suggested by a word Professor Rosenfield used in the conclusion of his paper. That word is "symbiotic." The idea is developed in a doctoral dissertation soon to be completed at the University of Colorado by Evan Blythin. The particular form of symbiosis Blythin discusses is the relationship between concrete data and general principles. He argues that the development of an open system making information possible requires a symbiosis of general theory and universal principles (what should be) with the concern for the concrete situation (what is), and that an exclusive interest in either one or the other leads necessarily to a closed system from which information cannot flow.[13]

Symbiosis may be a useful construct in relating the contemporary with the historical, the persuasive speaker with people interacting in a situation for many reasons, the microscopic look at a speech with a macroscopic look at a campaign, the linear with the configural model, the efforts of the traditionalist with those of the experimentalist. But it relates most squarely to the idea to which Blythin has attached it. The rhetorician so intent on the preservation of his traditional canons and categories that he looks at concrete situations only to torture them into serving as illustrations of the tradition has fulfilled the prophecy that his universal principles are enduring. This sort of approach leads to such movements as scholasticism and to such studies as cookie-cutter criticism. On the other hand, the empiricist so intent on describing concrete behavior that he asks only descriptive or normative questions about details and disdains questions of value or theory dooms himself to be trivial.[14] If one wants to understand the workings of one rhetorical transaction or the general principles of rhetoric, he must somehow blend the universal and theoretical with the concrete and hypothetical.

TOWARD A BLENDING OF
CRITICISM AND SCIENCE

1

Over ten years ago, C. P. Snow discussed what he called the two cultures of science and literature and argued that "the intellectual life of the whole of western society is increasingly split into two polar groups. . . .

Literary intellectuals at one pole—at the other scientists. . . . Between the two a gulf of mutual incomprehension—sometimes . . . hostility and dislike, but most of all lack of understanding."[15] Furthermore, Snow contended, matters had grown steadily worse in recent years: "Thirty years ago the cultures had long ceased to speak to each other; but at least they managed a kind of frozen smile across the gulf. Now the politeness is gone, and they just make faces."[16]

The applicability of such a two-cultures analysis to rhetorical communication is obvious. Members of the scientific culture—those persons interested in the empirical, the experimental, and the behavioral—tend to read and write their own literature, talk their own language, and pursue their own goals. Members of the other culture—those persons interested in the literary, the aesthetic, and the humanistic—likewise tend to pursue their own separate courses. The relationship between empiricists and traditionalists in rhetorical communication, like that of Snow's larger analysis of the two cultures, tends to range from overt hostility to peaceful but separate coexistence.

Another way of saying that last sentence derives from my colleague Donald K. Darnell's analysis of goal relationships among communicators, based on logical truth tables.[17] Darnell sees six classes of goal relationships, three of which are especially pertinent to the point I am making. An equivalent relation is one in which success for one person implies success for another person, and failure for the one implies failure for the other. An independent relation is one in which success or failure for one individual has no implications for the success or failure of another. A contradictory relation is one in which success for one person implies failure for another, and failure for one implies success for the other.

Among humanists and scientists interested in rhetorical communication, the perceived goal relationship is most often one of independence, sometimes one of contradiction, and hardly ever one of equivalence. Even the most tolerant of advocates for one or the other of the two points of view rarely sees his goals as equivalent with those of an advocate of the other point of view. One can imagine a "tolerant" traditionalist, for example, saying, "Some of my best friends are scientists."

And yet unless one adopts a thoroughly Manichean view of the world, assuming the wickedness of the other side, he has to wonder if he may have something to learn from another person who looks at similar phenomena from a somewhat different perspective. The underlying assumption of this section of the paper is that humanists and scientists can make and use knowledge about rhetorical communication more productively if they do so in full cooperation with one another.

A good plea for scientists to move in humanistic directions is made by Warren Weaver. He summarizes his case by saying:

If one looks deeply within [science], . . . instead of meeting more and more dependable precision, . . . instead of finally reaching permanence and perfection, what does one find? He finds unresolved and apparently unresolvable disagreement among scientists concerning the relationship of scientific thought to reality. . . . He finds that the explanations of science have utility, but that they do in sober fact not explain. He finds the old external appearance of inevitability completely vanished, for he discovers a charming capriciousness in all the individual events. . . . For those who have been deluded . . . into thinking of science as a relentless, all-conquering intellectual force, armed with finality and perfection, the limitations treated here would have to be considered as damaging imperfections. . . . I do not myself think of them as unpleasant imperfections, but rather as the blemishes which make our mistress all the more endearing.[18]

Weaver goes on to discuss the "dangerous gap between science and the rest of life,"[19] and he concludes by arguing that scientists must help to close the gap:

We must bring science back into life as a human enterprise, an enterprise that has at its core the uncertainty, the flexibility, the subjectivity, the sweet unreasonableness, the dependence upon creativity and faith which permit it, when properly understood, to take its place as a friendly and understanding companion to all the rest of life.[20]

Members of the other culture can also close the gap by participating in the scientific process of making knowledge. If they do, they may help to turn a relationship of independence or contradiction into one of equivalence. They can do so because scientists and humanists (specifically, critics) are more alike than they are different, both in the method they use and in the goals they pursue.

2

In regard to method, my claim is that although behavioral scientists and rhetorical critics use different techniques of gathering data, although they may be preoccupied with somewhat different focuses, they share the important common function of advancing the best *argument* they can for the conclusions their interpretations of the data require.[21]

If one views science as unassailable and infallible, the idea that scientists argue is a strange one. That concept of science implies that scientists merely explicate truth. But if one accepts Weaver's interpretation of science as uncertain and flexible, the concept of scientist-as-arguer is sensible. True, scientists move as close as they can to objectivity, and they take pains to give their claims every chance of being proved wrong. They employ a rigorous procedure for collecting data, and they expose that procedure to the readers of their argument. They make inferences from those data by means of warrants that colleagues are willing to accept, and they also make the steps in their reasoning process visible to readers.

The critic is also an arguer. That critic who merely presents a synopsis of a speech; he who asserts that a speaker used *logos*, *ethos*, and *pathos*; or he who appreciates a speech without giving reasons for his delight —these are not arguers. But the critic who starts with a set of theoretical assumptions or a set of criteria which are intended to yield explanatory or evaluative claims about a rhetorical transaction is an arguer. This view of the critic has been developed in two important recent writings on rhetorical criticism. Edwin Black says this:

> A critical statement is, in some sense, verifiable. A critical statement, even a critical judgment, is one for which reasons can be given, reasons that may gain the agreement of rational people to the statement. . . . Neither the physicist nor the critic should expect their inferences or their findings to be accepted on faith. Both carry the burden of proving their claims, and that proof must be of a sort that is accessible to others as proof.[22]

The other statement is from a provocative essay by Lawrence W. Rosenfield, who insists that criticism is "a special form of reason-giving discourse."[23]

Critics and scientists share, then, the function of being users of argument. Although scientists often maintain claims with more confidence than can critics, such a difference in qualifiers should not obscure the essential unity of the method of argument they employ.

Critics and scientists also pursue similar goals in relation to similar phenomena. If rhetoric represents the symbolic interaction of ideas and people in a situation, then it occupies essentially the same territory as the interest of theorists of human communication.[24] But do they have the same goals? Some people distinguish the two by saying that the critic wants to understand, interpret, and perhaps evaluate the individual transaction, whereas the scientist wants to develop general communication theory. This distinction can be accepted only if it is interpreted as meaning that the probable primary focus of the one may differ from the probable primary focus of the other. It should not be taken to mean that the critic has no use for theory or that the scientist has no use for the individual transaction.

The critic cannot even engage in systematic description unless a theory aids him in the selection and ordering of data. He certainly cannot argue convincingly his interpretation or evaluation of a rhetorical transaction unless he looks through the lens of a theory and employs inferences derived from that theory. Useful criticism is necessarily comparative, and theory provides a model against which to set the object of one's criticism. This claim is in accord with Professor Rosenfield's suggestion that critics employ a model modality or an analog modality, the former comparing a discourse with an ideal, the latter with another discourse.[25]

For his part, the scientist cannot afford to forget that the hypotheses he tests, the generalizations he formulates, and the theory he builds are made of the stuff of living people, actual messages, and real situations. Unless the scientist abstracts from individual human experiences the experimental situations he constructs and uses as a model, his generalizations are not likely to apply to the real world and he is not likely to predict much beyond the laboratory.

In short, both critic and scientist pursue the goal of understanding rhetorical communication. As Carroll Arnold puts it, "For any critic, as for any behavioral scientist, the question remains: what interactive processes occurred with what consequences *within* the neatly defined context."[26] The critic may more often interpret the individual transaction, but he must use theory to do so. The scientist may build generalizations and theory, but he must know what happens in individual acts of human communication if he is to do so. Each rhetorical transaction is a test of theory, whether it occurs in the laboratory of the scientist or the real world of the critic.

3

Since the critic shares with the scientist the method of argument and the goal of understanding, how can he participate in the process of making knowledge? Richard Rudner delineates two contexts in which the making of knowledge occurs—the context of discovery and the context of validation.[27] The critic can make a contribution in each.

A critic can make discoveries in much the same way a scientist does. When experimental results do not follow expectations, one of the possible explanations is that the theory is inadequate and must be altered or replaced. The experimenter may be able to conceive a new or revised theory that can account for the surprising result and also square with previous experience and knowledge. Likewise, a critic may find that some of his interpretations of a rhetorical transaction are not consistent with his theoretical assumptions. He may be able to conceive a hypothesis consonant with his interpretation and with what else he knows.

When a critic makes discoveries, he is engaging in what John Waite Bowers calls "the pre-scientific function." Bowers contends that rhetorical critics in the past have concerned themselves primarily:

with the explication and evaluation of a single piece of work in a single context. . . . Rhetorical criticism [can] . . . contribute to an economical set of scientifically verifiable statements accounting for the origins and effects of *all* rhetorical discourses in *all* contexts. This point of view requires that rhetorical criticism be viewed as an early part of a process eventuating in scientific theory. . . . The rhetorical critic's principal task is to produce testable hypotheses.[28]

The critic, like the experimenter, cannot always make pre-scientific discoveries, but he can sometimes produce testable pre-scientific hypotheses.

This claim may be illustrated by two examples. In the process of criticizing the structure of Truman's speech in 1947 enunciating the Truman Doctrine, Robert L. Scott and I observed that the speech did not follow the traditional model of a logical brief.[29] In that model each major contention supports directly the proposition; each contention, in turn, is supported by arguments and sub-arguments; and these, finally, are supported by evidence. Furthermore, a speaker is expected to say everything he is going to say about one topic before proceeding to the next. Judged by that model, the structure of Truman's speech is chaotic and confusing, and Truman violates over and over again the principle of putting all of an argument in one place.

We wondered whether a model derived from the concept of musical counterpoint might more appropriately explain, in part, how Truman's auditors could have responded positively to a speech structured as it is. Contrapuntal form may be defined as the combination of "two or more melodic lines in a musically satisfying way."[30] Each of the melodic lines may recur several times in a musical composition in company with different combinations of other themes that also come and go. We identified ten themes in Truman's speech and viewed them as threads that developed horizontally in several places, combining with a variety of other themes that also developed similarly. After tracing the argument-threads we engaged in some speculative hypothesizing, wondering about the extent to which speeches structured along the contrapuntal model could have significant and salutary effects on understanding, attitude change, and behavioral influence, and wondering about the conditions of interpersonal, ideational, and situational variables under which such effects might be predictive.

We thought several factors might point to the effectiveness of a contrapuntal structure. Many short exposures to parts of an argument may under some conditions be more effective than one long exposition of a complete argument. In addition, a juxtaposition of an argument into a variety of contexts that included references to highly compatible attitudes may enhance its effectiveness. Furthermore, the slow and gradual unfolding of an argument may give it a suspense and a momentum that might result in a cumulative effect. Finally, by exposing the auditor to bits and pieces of an argument, a speaker may encourage him to feel a sense of interest, participation, and involvement he would not feel if he were handed the fully developed argument in one continuous passage. This set of hypotheses, we think, could be subjected to experimental investigation.

A second example is an M. A. thesis conducted at the University of Colorado in 1969 by Gregory W. Oswald. The study began as a classroom exercise in the critical analysis of argument. Oswald set out, by means of the Toulmin model, to analyze arguments in selected television commentaries by Eric Sevareid. In the process of doing so, Oswald discovered that although Sevareid's commentaries appeared to function as arguments, the Toulmin model did not work very well in analyzing them. The Toulmin assumption that an argument involves a linear relationship between some data and a specific claim supported by those data was not able to explain what auditors were supposed to do in response to a discourse by Sevareid.[31]

Having satisfied himself of the inadequacy of the Toulmin model to explain Sevareid's use of argument, Oswald looked for a better explanation and developed what he called a theory of configural argument. He postulated that instead of presenting an array of evidence leading to an unambiguous claim, Sevareid presented narration and description as data and left the claim unstated. Had the unstated claim been unambiguous, the classical doctrine of the enthymeme might have accounted for Sevareid's argumentation within the linear concept. But not only did Sevareid not state a claim, he left no very definite clues concerning what claims should be supplied by auditors. Oswald hypothesized that (1) some auditors would crave closure, (2) they would most likely supply a claim consistent with their own attitudes, (3) they would assume the claim they had supplied was the one Sevareid had intended, (4) they would conclude that Sevareid was a credible source, and (5) they might decide to hear more of his commentaries.

But whereas a single commentary might be highly ambiguous to an occasional auditor, Oswald argued that a group of commentaries on the same theme over time would develop a campaign claim much less ambiguous to an auditor who had heard many Sevareid commentaries. The campaign argument would be configural: the data and ambiguous claims of a sequence of messages would ultimately form a mosaic that would reduce uncertainty and ambiguity.[32]

Oswald's study constitutes a discovery made through criticism, and his theory of configural argument constitutes an attempt to do what Toulmin diagrams had been unable to do: to explain how Sevareid's arguments functioned. Although this much is valuable, if it had ended here, if the critic had stayed in his own culture, the criticism could not lead to general knowledge. Oswald's criticism was a rare event in two senses: Oswald was a unique critic, and Sevareid was a unique object of criticism.

But a critic-blended-into-scientist might ask two series of questions. First, would other critics interpret Sevareid as Oswald had? Would auditors respond as Oswald had hypothesized they would? Could Oswald's interpretations be objectified into an interpretation of some reliability? By utilizing scientific assumptions and techniques for gathering data and making inferences, could Oswald build a more convincing argument that a theory of configural argument represents a good interpretation of Sevareid's commentaries? Oswald tried to answer some of these questions through a pilot study.

A second set of questions concerns the generalizability of the theory. If the Oswald interpretation proved reliable as measured empirically, to what extent is it generalizable to other speakers, on other topics, with other functions, to other auditors, through other channels, and in other situations? These questions invite large-scale experimental investigation, prepared for by the theoretical discovery of a critic.

4

Critical techniques can also be blended with empirical techniques in the context of validation. Whereas discovery creates a hypothetical conceptual model, validation tests how far and under what conditions the model is generalizable. Although validation has been pursued almost exclusively by laboratory experiments, a critic can complement experimental validation in a subsidiary but significant way.

Experimenters have recognized the problem of the artificiality of laboratory conditions. Since academic empiricists have students more easily accessible as subjects than anyone else, the temptation to use them is almost irresistible. Some writers voice the concern that experiments are generating a rhetoric of the college sophomore that may not justify generalizations about the behavior of auditors outside the classroom.[33] Furthermore, the necessities of laboratory controls dictate that an experimental situation *must* come from abstracting elements and dimensions most appropriate to the hypothesis to be tested. At any rate, for whatever reasons, even the most expertly constructed experimental situation has at least the faint aura of artificiality.

A critic's contribution could be to test the explanatory and predictive power of a theory in the real world of historical and contemporary rhetorical transactions. This enterprise, which John Waite Bowers calls "predicting backwards,"[34] must involve such fundamental techniques of experimental research as operational definitions, sampling procedures, reliable measuring instruments, and the like. He must also select historical and contemporary situations so they approximate the theoretical model he is investigating. He must conceive a rigorous design that puts himself in genuine jeopardy; he must give himself every reasonable chance of proving himself wrong.

One example of a critical study that supports the adequacy of a theory is by Michelle Bray Davis and Rollin W. Quimby.[35] Davis and Quimby studied a speech by Senator Proctor of Vermont in 1898. They argue that Proctor's speech was influential in developing support for U. S. intervention in Cuba, but they contend that traditional standards of persuasiveness fail to account for that influence. They then try to show that Proctor's speech had the effect of restoring cognitive consistency—both for Americans who favored intervention and for those who opposed it. Davis and Quimby conclude that those auditors in 1898 behaved very much as today's cognitive consistency theorists might have predicted.

A second example of critic-as-validator is Don Beck's study of the presidential campaign of 1860.[36] Beck tried to determine whether the social judgment-ego involvement approach to attitude theory of Muzafer Sherif and associates could explain what happened to Stephen A. Douglas during that campaign.[37] Sherif predicts that ego-involved auditors will tend to distort messages in two ways. If a message is close to the attitude of an auditor, he will tend to *assimilate* it in the direction of his own position. If a message is too distant, on the other hand, the ego-involved auditor will tend to *contrast* it and see it as even more distant than it is.

By examining newspaper accounts and other evidence of reactions in the north and in the south to the speaking of Douglas, Beck supported his hypothesis that an explanation for some of Douglas' difficulty in the campaign was that ego-involved auditors contrasted him. Many northerners saw Douglas not as taking a moderate position somewhere between those assumed by Lincoln and Breckenridge; rather, they contrasted him as a southern sympathizer little better than Breckenridge. Many southerners saw Douglas as an abolitionist little better than Lincoln. In short, Beck found that ego-involved auditors in 1860 behaved as the Sherif formulations a century or so later might have predicted they would. The empirically derived discovery of the 20th century had received one bit of historically derived validation from the 19th century.

The function of validating conceptual discoveries cannot, of course, be taken over entirely by critics. A critical validation merely provides one example from a real transaction to support or deny a theoretical position. Validation by an experiment provides another kind of example from an artificially produced transaction to support or deny a theoretical position. Just as a debater makes a convincing case by using varied evidence, so the research scholar can argue a theoretical position more convincingly by blending the powerful evidence of experimental research with the vivid evidence of criticism.

The research studies cited above do not demonstrate that a blending of critical and scientific techniques is an easy or surefire way to produce knowledge about rhetorical communication. Far from it. But they do, perhaps, illustrate the possibility. My hope is twofold: that critics will pursue that possibility and that scientists will welcome the pursuit. When the inhabitants of the two cultures begin to cross the boundaries and to communicate with one another, they may recognize that their goal relationship is equivalent. Then they can seek knowledge together to the profit of themselves and their discipline.

FOOTNOTES

1. Leland M. Griffin, "The Rhetorical Structure of the 'New Left' Movement: Part I," *QJS*, L (April 1964), 127.
2. Franklyn S. Haiman, "The Rhetoric of the Streets: Some Legal and Ethical Considerations," *QJS*, LIII (April 1967), 99–114.
3. Robert L. Scott and Donald K. Smith, "The Rhetoric of Confrontation," *QJS*, LV (February 1969), 1–8.
4. See Charles W. Lomas, *The Agitator in American Society* (Englewood Cliffs, N.J.: Prentice-Hall, 1968) and Mary G. McEdwards, "Agitative Rhetoric: Its Nature and Effect," *Western Speech*, XXXII (Winter 1968), 36–43.
5. James R. Andrews, "Confrontation at Columbia: A Case Study in Coercive Rhetoric," *QJS*, LV (February 1969), 9–16.
6. In *The Ethics of Controversy: Politics and Protest*, ed. Donn W. Parson and Wil A. Linkugel (Lawrence, Kansas: Department of Speech and Drama, University of Kansas, 1968).
7. See Johnstone and Becker essays.
8. "The Rhetoric of Historical Movements," *QJS*, XXXVIII (April 1952), 184–88.
9. *The Process of Communication* (New York: Holt, Rinehart and Winston, 1960), *passim*.
10. *Perspectives on Persuasion* (Boston: Allyn and Bacon, 1966), *passim*.
11. "Dimensions of the Concept of Rhetoric," *QJS*, LIV (February 1968), 1–12. A parallel idea is Hermann G. Stelzner's proposal to develop an "organic" model to replace our present "mechanical" model. See his "Analysis by Metaphor," *QJS*, LI (February 1965), 52–61.
12. "Suggestions as to Methods in Research," *Quarterly Journal of Public Speaking*, III (January 1917), 12–26.
13. "Rhetoric and Communication: Toward a Symbiotic Theory of Knowing." I am indebted to Blythin for the idea on which this section is based. Richard McKeon seems to argue for a kind of symbiosis when he says (pp. 53–54) that theory and practice must be reunited "by the constitution of a technology which is theory applied, the *logos* of *techne*. We seek to produce it in concrete experience and existence by rejoining reason and sense, cognitive and emotive, universal law and concrete occurrence."

14. Although a person who performs a scientific function may at specific points in the procedure try to avoid value judgments, "preferences about what is better or worse," as Wallace (p. 17) suggests, the total process of making knowledge cannot and should not avoid such choices.
15. *The Two Cultures and the Scientific Revolution* (New York: Cambridge University Press, 1959), p. 4.
16. *Ibid.*, p. 17.
17. Unpublished paper, University of Colorado, 1968. Many of the ideas in this paper, especially those in the second major section, are products of conversations with Professor Darnell.
18. "The Imperfections of Science," in *Science: Method and Meaning*, ed. Samuel Rapport and Helen Wright (New York: Washington Square Press, 1964), p. 29.
19. *Ibid.*, pp. 29–30.
20. *Ibid.*, p. 30.
21. Professor Johnstone's analysis of philosophical argument (pp. 87–88) appears altogether compatible with the sense in which I claim that critics and scientists argue.
22. *Rhetorical Criticism: A Study in Method* (New York: Macmillan, 1965), pp. 7–8.
23. "The Anatomy of Critical Discourse," *Speech Monographs*, XXXV (March 1968), 50.
24. Professor Wallace (p. 4) says that "the interests of rhetoric and communication overlap." I cannot conceive any topic of rhetoric that could not be the concern of a student of communication, or vice versa. People who prefer the label "rhetoric," however, have tended to focus interests differently from those who prefer the label "communication." Part of my argument is that the interests of these two groups of people might, with great profit, overlap much more than they do.
25. "The Anatomy of Critical Discourse," 65–68.
26. In *Conceptual Frontiers of Speech-Communication*, ed. Robert J. Kibler and Larry L. Barker (New York: Speech Association of America, 1969), p. 187.
27. *Philosophy of Social Science* (Englewood Cliffs, N.J.: Prentice-Hall, 1966), pp. 5–7.
28. "The Pre-Scientific Function of Rhetorical Criticism," in *Essays on Rhetorical Criticism*, ed. Thomas R. Nilsen (New York: Random House, 1968), p. 127.
29. In *Moments in the Rhetoric of the Cold War* (in press).
30. Kent Kennan, *Counterpoint: Based on Eighteenth-Century Practice* (Englewood Cliffs, N.J.: Prentice-Hall, 1959), p. 2.
31. "Sevareid and a Theory of Configural Argument."
32. Oswald's theory of configural argument seems highly compatible with ideas expressed in Professor Becker's paper.
33. See, for example, Roger E. Nebergall, "A Critique of Experimental Design in Communication Research," *Central States Speech Journal*, XVI (February 1965), 15 and James C. McCroskey, "A Summary of Experimental Research on the Effect of Evidence in Persuasive Communication," *QJS*, LV (April 1969), 176.
34. Bowers, p. 136.
35. "Senator Proctor's Cuban Speech: Speculations on a Cause of the Spanish-American War," *QJS*, LV (April 1969), 131–41.
36. "The Rhetoric of Conflict and Compromise: A Study in Civil War Causation" (Ph.D. dissertation, University of Oklahoma, 1966).
37. For a development of this approach to attitude, see Carolyn W. Sherif, Muzafer Sherif, and Roger E. Nebergall, *Attitude and Attitude Change: The Social Judgment-Ego Involvement Approach* (Philadelphia: Saunders, 1965).

9 / THE NEED FOR CLARIFICATION IN SOCIAL MODELS OF RHETORIC

HUGH DALZIEL DUNCAN
Southern Illinois University

AUTHORITARIAN MODELS OF RHETORIC IN SOCIETY

Contemporary theorists of rhetoric in society must take into account both European and American ideas of communication. After the grim sociodramas mounted by Mussolini, Stalin, and Hitler, who can deny the power of ritual victimage? But if ritual invocation of the sacred, however perverse, is the only way of reaching order in social relationships, democracy is doomed, and the vision of equality among men will become a dream. Yet, if we love democracy, and believe that equality need not end in servitude, but in freedom, how do we propose to create and sustain order among sovereign selves? For, as the Latin proverb reminds us, being first among equals is the most difficult of all forms of leadership. And when we accept equality as a form of authority which can be studied within the American tradition of the act, how do we go about creating a model of action which *normalizes* disagreement, rivalry, competition, and conflict?

We can begin by analyzing how conflict is resolved in the dominant models of symbolic action now prevalent in American social thought. The mechanistic model deals with conflict as "imbalance," or "disequilibrium." This implies that whatever disturbs equilibrium is a kind of "breakdown," and that change is a threat to permanence. But human interaction exists in pain and pleasure in the action and passion of social relatedness. Mechanical images of interaction are images of function as motion in space, not as passion, will, and thought among men.

The ritual model of struggle between the "sacred" and the "profane" is at least a model of action as symbolic action, and is much closer to our concerns with rhetoric. But it is a very authoritarian model. The "secular" is the realm of change, the "sacred" the home of permanence. Secular truths are particular, while sacred truths are eternal. Difference and conflict are resolved by transcendence, an upward way to a "higher" principle of order. Those who do not believe in these "higher" principles live not merely in disagreement, but in sin, guilt, treason, or blasphemy. Killing them becomes an act of purification, and even kindness, for sinners are not happy, and upon death face eternal suffering. The torture of inquisition and the heavy burdens of penance to purge them of sin are only "temporary." The execution of traitors becomes a rite of purification; cells of torture and death are transformed into altars of the state. The political prisoner becomes a sacrificial victim whose suffering and death absolves the community of sin and guilt.

This model of victimage is familiar enough in our time. We turn in horror from Stalin's purges and Hitler's death camps, but we face still the terrible revelation that victimage works. Man is a *social* beast of prey. He does not kill for food, but to achieve "order" in society. Thus before we create models of social order which tell us what happens *after* or *before* conflict, as we do in Utopian and Edenic myths, we must develop models which tell us something about what goes on *during* conflict. The question, then, is simple enough: how does victimage *resolve* conflict?

The ritual act of Frazer, Durkheim, and Malinowski, and the dramatistic act of Kenneth Burke have many common elements. Burke places great stress upon the sacrificial principle of order which, he says, is intrinsic to all ideas of Order. For him the "iron law of history" is discovered in "Order and Sacrifice." Order leads to guilt, guilt needs redemption, redemption needs a redeemer and, therefore, a victim. Order based on guilt leads to victimage which ends in the cult of the kill which expresses the "curative" function of victimage. We blame our troubles on others in the belief that if the other were eliminated all the problems we encounter in our own order would be eliminated.

But while Burke accepts the integrative power of religious victimage as both religious and social, the source of this power for him is in language. He is concerned with the nature of religion as a rhetoric. In his logosocial analysis theological dogma is a body of spoken or written words. As he says: "Whatever else it may be, and wholly regardless of whether it be true or false, theology is preeminently *verbal*. It is words about God."

Thus while Burke finds ritual to be an "ultimate" expression of social relationships, it is the expression itself, the *ways* in which ritual is staged,
that engrosses him. And while few rhetoricians have paid greater homage
to the power of authoritarian victimage, Burke's analysis is intended as a
cure for the horrors of victimage through the creation of a method of
analysis which will open authoritarian mystification to reason.

FORM AND CONTENT IN
SOCIAL ACTION

The sociodramatic model (or at least my version of it) uses institutional form as the basic social form of experience. In theoretical proposition 5 of my *Symbols in Society*, I list eleven such forms. These are (1)
the family, (2) government, (3) economic institutions, (4) defense, (5)
education, (6) manners and etiquette, (7) entertainment, (8) health and
welfare, (9) religion, (10) art, (11) science and technology. These institutional forms can be observed easily, and their study does not require
highly abstract schemes of interpretation.

I can see a house, just as I can observe family life within the home,
the roles played by members of the family, the ways in which these roles
are expressed, the kind of social hierarchy in which these roles are ordered and the principle of order invoked as necessary to social order dependent upon family life. Stage, action (as institutional action), role,
means of expression (especially the arts of social expression such as architecture, the forms of eating, dressing, etc.), and order (in all its variants of order, disorder, and counter-order)—the *structure* of social action
as sociodramatic action—can be observed with a minimum of interpretation. As Charles Horton Cooley said in his 1927 essay, "Case Study of
Small Institutions as a Method of Research", the institutional approach
opens a view of social relations as an actual dramatic activity, and allows
us to participate in those mental processes which are a part of human interaction, and are accessible to sympathetic observation by the aid of language.

Observation, such as any observation of "facts," depends upon the
models we use. "Facts" are derived from the model, not from sensory experience, or direct observation of raw experience. When our abstractions
are complicated and very general, and much explanation of the model as a
model is necessary, we are never sure whether our explanations clarify
relationships in society or in the model itself. This is not to say that facts
can be observed without *some* interpretive scheme or model. "Facts" do
not leap out of their social context, nor do our instruments alone order
them for study. Social facts are facts of relationship which are observed

in the way they are because of the ways we think about them. We construct models to interpret social relationships, but until sociology shows signs of sophistication similar to modern physics, it will be best to keep our models and systems of interpretation close to the observable data of social experience.

The problem of model construction and use is not brought nearer to solution when we justify models as fictions, analogues, or metaphors. This view of the model assumes that there is some kind of reality which the model itself does not "contain," but does "express." A thermometer, it is argued in this view, is but a tool whose gradients are only arbitrary notations of measurements of temperature. Obviously, there is no zero, anymore than there are negatives, in nature. The same argument is used for the use of fictions. In themselves they mean nothing; it is only the inquiry they make possible, the testing of hypotheses, which is of value.

But even if our models are tools, surely the *form* of the tool determines what we can do with it. And if a model (such as the sociodramatic model of social interaction) is only a metaphor, or an analogue, of *what* is it so? If there is some kind of social reality "beyond" the forms of language, what is this reality and how do we *observe* it? To discover social reality in *content* alone as when we "explain" social relations by sex, economics, religion, or politics simply explains the known—the forms of communication—with an unknown.

The sociodramatic model is not intended to be a metaphor, an analogue, or a fiction, but a *representation* of social relationships which arise in, and continue to exist through, communicative forms studied best in models derived from dramatic form. The way we communicate *is* the way we relate. Drama *is* the form of communication in which the psyche, as a social psyche, *works*. Even dreams are dramatic in form. And while it cannot be said that Freud paid much attention to the form of dreams, it is worth noting that he turned to drama to construct his Oedipus Complex, and that he argued that we know what dreams mean because we know the meaning of symbolic forms such as tales, legends, narratives and jokes. The same may be said for Frazier and other anthropologists who use ritual models. The rite is a drama, a communication, and like all drama means what its form means.

MEANS OF EXPRESSION
AND AUDIENCES

In sociodrama means of expression are not thought of as a kind of wire which "contains" a message, but as symbolic forms which determine as well as transmit experience. The medium alone is not the message. To say that how we communicate determines what we communicate implies that our instruments of communication determine what we communicate, or that only when we know how a message is communicated do we know what it means. Even a simple message sent over television cannot be understood unless we understand the situation in which it was sent, the kind of act in which the communication took place, the roles of the communicators, and the purpose in sending the message.

A description of communicative means must also involve a description of audiences reached by these means, and this description must be based on the *forms of relationship* between speaker and audience. The speaker's status longings and position, his class interests, his style of life, his sexual habits, his religious affiliations, are of interest in communication theory only insofar as they serve as clues on how the forms of communication affect conduct. How a man communicates, whether through talk, oratory, press, radio, or television tells us nothing about the meaning of communication until we know how these are related to the situation in which he speaks, the act in which the speech takes place, the kinds of speakers involved, and the social purpose of the speech.

When we ascribe social characteristics to an audience and then derive these characteristics from the audience's response to the speaker, or discover them in the message itself, we are not defining but illustrating. An audience is not a fixed body whose class interests, ethnic interests, drives, fate, or destiny, compel its members to courses of action. For even when we know the characteristics of our audience we must still gain their attention through skillful address. We are audiences to each other, as we are speakers. In this sense audience is a phase of response within the act, not a fixed or permanent role. Even the lowly student who submits to many hours of lectures, makes us his audience in campus politics or in the football stadium.

Different audiences must be addressed in different ways. If we could isolate audiences according to class, status, party, or ethnic derivation, and control the situation, the act, the roles, the means, and the purpose of our speech, bending audiences would become a simple matter of rhetorical technique. When communication becomes ritual (as anthropologists describe primitive communication) the voice with whom the gods communicate becomes the voice of the people. But the gods themselves admonish us to beware of evil communication from devils, just as "true" prophets warn us of "false" prophets. Even in sacred communication there are many discordant voices. We are saved only through God's grace, some say; through works, others tell us. Reconciliation of sacred and secular voices, and of competing sacred voices in prophecy, is sometimes as difficult in religion as it is in the realms of art, science, and politics where many voices are raised.

The small homogeneous audience, familiar to Aristotle and to modern anthropologists, no longer exists in the public life of modern times. We do not believe, as Greek orators did, that Athenian reason is universal reason. Nor can we assume that appeals directed only to elites will decide action. The voice of the people is no longer the voice of God, but it is still the voice of profit, of mass armies, and of the ballot box. And in democratic society, where differential status prevails, elites in one role are "the people" in another.

It would be absurd to argue that the interests of an audience do not affect the efficacy of communication. But it is equally absurd to disregard the forms in which speakers and audiences communicate. Even on the level of sensory experience symbols directed to hearing, seeing, smelling, testing, or touching must be affected by the different forms in which the senses function. We know far more about the effects of words and visual images than we do about the effects of symbols formed in tones, dance, space, taste, or smell. The simple question, asked of the most practical of artists, architects, how do your architectural forms affect relationships which occur within these forms?—is answered poorly, if at all.

TYPES OF AUDIENCES

A social typology of audiences, considered in forms of relatedness between speaker and audience, can be described in five types. First, there is an "I" speaking to a general public, a "they." This occurs in all kinds of mass communications where we speak in our public roles as professors, deans, presidents, and so forth. Second, there is address to community guardians who are delegated by the community as guardians of order. Third, there is address to others significant to us as friends and intimates. Fourth, there are audiences we address in soliloquy and all forms of talking to oneself (this includes fantasy, night and day dreams, memory, etc.). Fifth, there is the "final" audience we invoke to sustain order in social relationships.

We speak to one of these audiences in the company of others. In public address the general public hears what is said to the community guardians who, in turn, hear what is said to the general publics. The close friends of a politician hear his promises to the people, and his plea for help from the community guardians. Invocations to God, Americanism, Democracy, Peace, or the "sacred bonds of the family" are heard, and on television seen, by all. Since these audiences are often in sharp disagreement, or even in conflict, pleasing all is very difficult. In rare, very rare, occasions these audiences may agree, but even in cooperation there is a great amount of antagonism. Football players who cooperate on the field soon part in the locker room.

Nor can we assume that people even *want* to agree among themselves, or through their champions. It may be that conflict is more enjoyable than harmony. The moment of victory excites us because of the contest in which victory was achieved. We train our young in America to believe that nothing succeeds like success but, at the same time, we admit that nothing is more boring. It is the game, as well as victory, which sustains play. Enough has been said about man's need to satisfy aggression. But is it aggression or the enjoyment of contest which motivates us in struggle? If the cat is "satisfying aggression" when he catches the mouse why does he not kill it immediately? Why does the cat release the mouse only to hunt it down again?

And what of the audience in the dream? The father, Freud says, is the primary audience. But could not groups outside the family be audiences? If dreams are not simply "repressions" but attempts to solve problems, problems which must be solved if there is to be order in our relationships, to what audience in society do we turn to play out the shadowy dramas of the night? We do not have a sociology of the dream, yet as Freud argues in his discussion of symbolism in dreams, we can explain the dream by what we hope to do in the future, as well as by what we have done in the past.

INTEGRATION AND SOCIAL ORDER

Principles of social order, the systems of belief which bind us together in social relationships, function in three ways. First, we accept a certain order as "necessary" to group survival. Second, we doubt and question the efficacy of certain principles. Third, we reject an order. In this view systems of belief function as rules for action. These rules are learned in communication. We are taught to assume that others will respond in predictable ways to what we say to them. Symbols experienced mutually by speaker and hearer are predictable and public; those which do not have mutual meaning and which must be internalized (because of fear, guilt, ignorance, repression, etc.) are private. When public communication increases fear and anxiety we turn inward to mount in private the dramas we cannot mount in public, just as we joke in absurd and puzzling ways when we cannot communicate "seriously."

Individual and private symbols must have universal and public references, if they are to have social meaning. A unique self is beyond communication, for how can we know the meaning of a unique other? This is not to deny that there are private meanings to symbols, nor to overlook the fact that no symbol means quite the same to speaker and hearer alike. But the sociologist gains little by accepting the timeworn dichotomy "subjective-objective" as polarizations of symbolic interaction. Nor will he gain much in debate with those who uphold what they call "individual psychology." Such psychologies often turn out to be institutional, not individual. In Freud's "individual psychology" the "individual" is the mother, father, son, or daughter, who act as they do because of their family roles.

From the sociodramatic view communication cannot be studied as symbolic action between "subjects" and "objects," anymore than it can between "inner" and "outer" selves. Communication arises in attempts to overcome differences in roles. We must, therefore, investigate the ways in which conflict occurs, and the means by which it is resolved. Models of communication in society which are based on what occurs in communication *after* conflict is resolved must be used with great caution. If we assume that only moments of "equilibrium" are moments of order, and that such moments are normal, we reduce conflict (and all its variants from debate to war) to what we call "social disorganization."

Disorganization is not necessarily a *lack* of organization, but a *negative* organization of a positive form of order. There is no crime until laws are passed, no adultery until marriage laws exist, no crimes against nature until what is "natural" is defined, no broken rules until there are rules to break. And since those in power make the laws it is only natural for them to assume that conditions for living under the laws are the same for all. Any man, we hear, can get a job if he will look for one. But in a rural area how does one look for a job without transportation? Every husband should be satisfied with his wife, but when husbands become soldiers away from home, or prisoners for many years, how can they relate to their wives? All we can say about any law is that it "works" so long as social conditions remain the same, but social conditions seldom remain the same, and when they do it is only for periods of time. Thus all "eternal" principles of order are subject to mutability and change. Survival depends, not on denying need for change, but facing change in the name of principles of order. When this cannot be done revolt occurs, and a new order counter to the old is proposed.

We ask of any model of social action: does it deal with disorder and conflict as normal to agreement or are they reduced to "imbalance" or heresy? The religious model of social order as used by Frazer, Durkheim, and Weber has been of great service. Kenneth Burke's *The Rhetoric of Religion*, an analysis of the extraordinary power of religion as a "unifying principle," offers many clues to integrative factors in all types of communication in society.

But ritual models, as developed by Frazer, Durkheim, Malinowski,

Radcliffe-Brown (the list could be larger), fail to stress conflict as well as harmony in religion. Yet, as we know, the history of religious accord has been a history of great discord. Religious models of social action can be used as guides to the study of conflict as well as harmony or equilibrium. Burke's analysis of victimage indicates the value of this approach. For in religious life we run into the paradox of all authority. How can men disobey an all wise, loving, powerful god, who dwells in eternity beyond time?

Whatever the limits of religious models of communication we cannot accuse religious thought of disregarding evil. The sociologist concerned with conflict models can avoid the labyrinth of theological disquisition on good and evil; but this should not lead to the neglect of the rich and ancient dramas of religion which tell us so much about conflict, discord, and disagreement. The ways in which religions "explain" evil, the forms of victimage used in sacrifice to the gods, the types of purification, expiation, atonement, and redemption adopted in various religions, offer many clues for the construction of conflict models. We may disagree with the ways in which religion deals with conflict, but we cannot deny the power, or the cogency, of religious drama as a social drama of struggle between "good" and "evil" principles of order.

PROBLEMS IN THE CONSTRUCTION
OF A THEORY OF DEMOCRATIC
RHETORIC

Monistic models of communication have served their purpose. There is little need to argue further about the primacy of territory, social institutions, status groups, classes, political parties, or castes in our analysis of the social effects of rhetoric. Nor is it necessary to repeat that role enactment determines social order. And after the recent wave of emphasis on means as determinants of ends in communication there is no need for further exposure of the dangers of confusing means and ends in communication. And, finally, we ought to know by now that invoking gods, however solemn and terrible, produces disorder as well as order in social life. It is not the invocation of ends alone, but the expression of means-ends relationships as they exist in various symbolic structures, that ought to be studied.

Monistic theories of rhetoric still persist as we discover in the writings of those who discover "laws" of communication in the environment (as in equilibrium theory); in the act of communication itself (as in propaganda studies); in the roles in which we communicate (as in role theory); or finally in sacred invocation (as in ritual theory). Sophisticated students of communication do not need to be convinced that where and when we act, in what kind of action, in what roles, by what means, and to attain what kind of social order, determine the effect of rhetoric in society. But selection of any *one* of these factors, to the exclusion of all others, must be done with great care.

Nearly a hundreds years ago, Charles S. Peirce proposed a triadic theory of meaning. Some seventy years ago George Herbert Mead brought Peirce's triad within the act as a communicative form of interaction. In the twenties Malinowski developed the "context of situation" as the source of meaning. In the thirties Burke began his analysis of what he called later the "socioanagogic" elements in communication. In 1945 Burke's *Grammar of Motives*, followed in 1950 by his *Rhetoric of Motives*, offered a synthetic model of communication in which scene, act, actor, agency, and purpose were *all* taken into account.

Monistic and eclectic models of communication tell us little about the *integrative* function of rhetoric in society. Critics who deny the value of models of communication based on ritual and drama on the basis that such models confuse language with reality are repeating an ancient charge against symbolic analysis in general. What is the "reality" known to such critics? If it is non-linguistic, the study of rhetoric must be abandoned to those who know "reality" in human communication. If "reality" is still linguistic but not of the kind described in the dramatic model, what then is it? Simple logic dictates that knowledge of error must come from knowledge of truth. If we know what is wrong with a model we must know this from the "right" construction of other models.

In the face of accusations that social reality is not dramatic; that there is no "proof" for assuming that what goes on in symbolic texts (viewed as dramatic texts), is not what goes on in social relations; that symbols are "subjective," and so forth, we wait for enlightenment derived from better analogies. But we wait in vain. Thus far no one has offered a substitute model. Every now and then some prophet arises to bring light into the symbolic jungle. At the moment in social science circles it is Claude Levi-Strauss, while in philosophy Wittgenstein's musings on "language-games" hold attention. But, as even reviewers favorable to Levi-Strauss point out, he is an eclectic. For all his brilliance, subtlety, and wide range of learning, Levi-Strauss fails to produce a *model* of symbolic action. And while it would be pointless to deny the importance of Wittgenstein's search for a social model, it is not a new search to Americans raised in the tradition of Peirce, James, Dewey, Mead, Malinowski, and Burke.

Burke's model can be used to analyze how symbolic expressions work *both as symbolic expressions, and as charters for action in society.* Burke does *not* say that when we know what a text does for the speaker we know what it does for the audience, nor does he say that when we know the social characteristics of audiences we know the meaning of symbols used in communication between speaker and audience. Symbolic form has qualities of its own, but it would be idle to pretend that economic and political acts (among others) reach reality only through symbolic reality. We must learn to analyze *both* social *and* symbolic elements in social action. This involves acceptance of the reality of symbols as symbols, of needs which we can satisfy only through the responses of others, and, finally, of the *relationship* between the two. For it is the form of *relationship* between symbol and society that contains socioanagogic reality.

I have said that a model of rhetoric as used in democratic society must be a conflict model. Conflict of all kinds, ranging from government by opposition under parliamentary rules, to war, must be accepted as normal to rhetoric. We must accept the fact that as we perfect rhetoric we *increase* our chances for hate and doubt, as well as love and certainty. Democratic communication involves risk to superiors, inferiors, and equals alike. In this it differs little from ritual communication as used in authoritarian relationships. It is comforting to think that the victim of authoritarian ritual has been transformed in democratic dramatism into the "loyal opposition," but our inability to understand the rise of Hitler ought to warn us not to assume that democratic opposition will "somehow" or "inevitably" replace victimage. Social theories of rhetoric based on dramatic form (both as ritual and dramatistic) as the definitive communicative form still supply many clues to the meaning of all forms of symbolic action. In democratic as in authoritarian society dramatic forms prevail. The use of dramatic forms by Frazer, Freud, and by Kenneth Burke in our own time, is proof enough of the vitality of this model. Much can still be done with the dramatistic model, and other disciplines will join anthropology, psychoanalysis, and literature in their use of it.

10 / RESPONSES, QUERIES, AND A FEW CAVEATS

BARNET BASKERVILLE
University of Washington

As one of those invited to comment upon the creative efforts of a number of distinguished scholars, I would begin by expressing my gratitude to the Planning Committee for their wisdom and generosity in allowing the responders such welcome latitude. We are instructed to offer a critique of a particular position paper, of several, of all, or of none. Alternatively, we may address ourselves to the charge which generates these papers, discussing some concern which the papers omit or treat scantily.

Encouraged by such permissiveness, I shall try to record my reactions to selected passages in several of the essays, and then set down a few concerns growing out of my reading and listening during the last year or so. Such an approach may result in a mere elaboration of the question marks, exclamation points, and cries of "well said" which I have scribbled earlier in the margins of the position papers, to which are appended some querulous warnings of pitfalls to be avoided, but I shall try not to stray too far from the central focus of the conference.

The charge to the writers of position papers is an awesome one: "What is the outline of a satisfactory contemporary theory of rhetoric?" We have observed in the past a certain reluctance to make frontal attacks upon topics of this magnitude. Writers of journal articles frequently avoid the appearance of pretentiousness by using such titles as "Toward a theory of . . . " "Notes on a philosophy of . . ." "Prolegomena to . . ." Writers of our position papers also reveal a becoming modesty. Wallace declares, "I shall not try to outline a theory. . . . I simply want to suggest the start-

151

ing points for theorizing." Becker offers no "new conception of rhetoric," but says he has some questions to raise and some suggestions toward the development of new conceptions. Johnstone declines to predict the form of future rhetorical theory, but proposes to discuss "trends now in evidence," signs of developments that may take place. Rosenfield passes over the primary commission and deals with factors which he thinks render orthodox commentaries on rhetoric unsatisfactory today.

Not long ago, after the New Orleans Conference, Carroll Arnold observed: "One hears much talk about rhetorical theories and communication theories," and asked, "Are there really any bodies of data deserving such grand titles?" Perhaps, he suggested, we are only talking about "eclectic collections of maxims and information 'bits' *about* rhetoric and general communication."[1] If Arnold was right, and I suspect he was, the alternate question posed to the participants, "what problems or topics must contemporary rhetorical scholarship pursue in order to develop a theory of public discourse suitable to our time?" seems a more manageable assignment, and indeed this is the question to which several of our writers direct their attention.

Professor Johnstone proposes to describe the view from his editorial chair, inferring from the flow of articles across his desk some of the problems which rhetorical scholars will or should pursue in the near future. His chair proves to be an excellent vantage point, for he touches upon most of the topics developed by other participants—analysis of the rhetoric of the New Left; relationships between rhetoric and ethics, rhetoric and dialectic, rhetoric and communication theory; an extension and modernization of the *topics*; rhetoric and the mass media; and so forth.

Johnstone's assertion that such tactics of the New Left as shouts, obscenities, and interruptions of lectures cannot properly be dismissed as uses of violence seems to me questionable. The users of these tactics, he says, are not usually violent people; they do not employ the familiar forms of violence; they do not crack skulls. But why, one is prompted to ask, do they refrain from cracking skulls? May it not be because they have learned that certain types of violence bring immediate reprisal, whereas other tactics may be used with relative impunity? Is it less a violent denial of a man's freedom of speech forcibly to silence him by concerted boos, obscenities shouted through a bull-horn, and eggs hurled toward the platform, than by cracking his skull? The fact that most of us would prefer to be struck by an oath or an egg than by a club does not alter the point. When a man is prevented *by force* from expressing his opinion, when he is effectively deprived of his right to be heard—is this not a clear case of violent action designed to block discussion?

Professor Johnstone calls for a new criterion of the distinction between rhetoric and violence. "There is," he says, "the violence of nightsticks and the quite different violence of words." If there is an implication that in making such a distinction we mean to condemn the one and justify the other, it should be noted that the two have at least this in common: both must escalate to achieve continuing effectiveness. The time soon comes when the breaking of windows and the overturning of automobiles will no longer suffice and must give way to still greater violence. Similarly with the use of language: once we turn to obscenity and epithet as weapons, we must continually seek new and stronger words to shock.

Johnstone's comments on rhetoric and ethics are particularly thought provoking. Most of us have been troubled, as he is, by the tendency to assess the goodness or badness of a speaker's rhetoric (in the sense of practical *discourse*) by making an ethical judgment about the ends he seeks. To do this, as Johnstone points out, is to make rhetoric "no more than the means used to achieve an end nonrhetorically certified as good. But once this position is taken . . . it becomes impossible to say why rhetoric rather than some other means—perhaps a more effective means—should be used."

Turning next to the common attempt to distinguish between effective and ineffective rhetoric, Johnstone alludes to the old problem of Hitler's speaking; authors of essays on "The Moral Measure in Rhetoric," he says, in order to make their case must show that Hitler's rhetoric was in some way ineffective. One might object here that writers would be more likely to claim that it was morally indefensible than that it was ineffective, but let us pass this by. Johnstone's central point is that writers turn to "a standard of rhetoric *outside* rhetoric."

There can be no doubt of the truth of this allegation, but it should be noted that there are those who have recognized the problem and are addressing themselves to it. My colleague, Professor Thomas Nilsen, has for some time been engaged in trying to develop a "Moral Measure in Rhetoric" *inside* rhetoric. In "Free Speech, Persuasion, and the Democratic Process" he takes up the problem of ends and means, observing that persuasive techniques are too often regarded as ethically neutral means to some end which may be good or bad. He rejects the familiar analogy of the scalpel, which can be used for good or evil, to take or save life.[2] Persuasive methods, says Nilsen, "influence behavior apart from and in addition to the particular end they seek. When being persuaded, a man is not only influenced directly or indirectly in his choice of a course of action, he is influenced in his method of making the choice."[3] Subsequently, in his little book on the *Ethics of Speech Communication*,[4] Nilsen develops this idea further:

> The moral rightness of our speech turns in large part on the kind of choice making our speech fosters. Here we are not thinking of the end result of the choosing . . . but of the attitudes and judgmental processes that go

into the decision. . . . We are concerned whether the choice-making process we help create is consistent with the nature of the human personality we respect and seek to develop.

Karl Wallace appears to be moving in the same direction when he asserts that ethical criteria govern the rhetor's choice of "means, methods, strategies, and tactics for the realization of purposes," as well as his "degree of respect for conventional forms of presentation."

Professor Becker's paper raises, obliquely and without contentiousness, a question which is certain to receive attention at the rhetoric conference: the relationships between behavioral science and historical-critical approaches to communicative situations. As one unfamiliar with the methods of the experimental or behavioral scholar, I have found much in this stimulating paper with which I can agree, much with which I cannot imagine anyone seriously *dis*agreeing. We have, says Becker, a plethora of communication problems, for some of which new conceptions of rhetoric are needed. We must stop treating message and communication in over-simplistic ways. Messages are diffused over space and time; we learn from a great number and variety of media and from a great number and variety of people. Messages are diffused with amazing rapidity. The transmitting medium can modify the message. The context against which a message bit is sensed affects its perception.

His review of studies supporting and illustrating some of these propositions is interesting and instructive. Although I am not motivated to attempt such studies myself, and lack the competence to do so, I can occasionally glimpse the relevance of their findings to the kind of studies I might like to do. This paper, more than anything I have recently read, persuades me that the behavioral scientist may supply valuable data on the rhetorical situation—data which, as Becker says, "affect the many and varied processes of communication preceding and following the formal speech."

I am not persuaded, however, that the critics have been as naive as he depicts them, or that they are inclined to ignore or deny his principal assertions regarding communication. I know of no competent critics, for example, who would regard a speech as the *only* source of relevant information, the sole determinant of variance in human behavior. Indeed, their acute awareness of the existence of multiple stimuli and of the difficulty, if not impossibility, of ascribing direct cause and effect relationships between a speech and subsequent behavior of members of the audience has made them increasingly wary of judgments concerning the impact or "success" of a given speech. Moreover, Becker's charge that criticism has been excessively preoccupied with persuasion, together with his proposals for alternate emphases, seem to imply a limited conception of "persuasion." It is not clear to me why discourse which operates to prevent rather than bring about change, to restore rather than upset equilibrium, to express values, to convey information, or to give structure to an individual's universe, cannot be regarded as persuasive discourse.

At several points in his paper, Professor Becker poses a set of implied alternatives, accompanied by a clear statement of preference. For example:

> . . . we need criticism or public address studies which depart more sharply from literary criticism or internal criticism where the major purpose is to "explain" the way in which a message "works."

> The emphasis of rhetorical studies should probably remain upon the message, but we must define message in a more fruitful way, in a way that is more descriptive of what man as receiver is exposed to, rather than what man as source creates.

> I am calling for a message-audience centered rhetoric, as opposed to the source-message one which has dominated our field to too great an extent in the past.

> Too many scholars of rhetoric and public address have been concerned only with the discourse of the past. . . .

Now if these are to be interpreted as expressions of personal preference, no rejoinder is called for; I have no desire to substitute my preferences for those of the writer. But it does not seem unreasonable to resist the implication (not nearly so strong in Becker's paper as in much current public discussion) that in one direction lies progress, and in the other (usually labelled "traditional"), fatuity and futility. I think it perfectly conceivable that some of us may wish to engage in internal criticism with the purpose of explaining the way in which a message works. I think some may have a primary interest in "what man as source creates"—or, for that matter, in what man as *receiver* creates out of what he is exposed to. The receiver is not a passive object barraged by multitudinous stimuli, but a purposive, acting agent who can will what he wants to be and where he intends to go. I think, moreover, that there may be profit in studying discourse of the past; one may conceivably conduct such research for reasons other than testing experimentally the relationships among variables in the communicative process. I would, finally, reject the implication (not made by Becker, but occasionally encountered) that the term "research" is applicable only to certain kinds of scientific or quasi-scientific investigation and experimentation—to what the behavioral scientists are doing.

Professor Becker performs a valuable service in proposing new ways of looking at a speech or other communicative event. The more ways we have of regarding the central objects of our inquiry the better. I simply seek to make a modest proposal that the newest ways are not the *only*— and not, necessarily, the *best*—ways in all situations and for the answering of all significant questions.

Professor Wallace's paper provides a corrective, or at least a supplement, to Becker's. Becker is interested in the mechanics of transmitting a message or message "bits" to a receiver. He seeks *testable* hypotheses about how such bits are received, and about factors which impede or facilitate transmittal or reception. Wallace is more concerned about what is transmitted, what ought to be transmitted, and to what end. He is dismayed at the separation of rhetorical discourse from its subject matter and the reduction of rhetoric to a merely methodological art. I. A. Richards once objected to the label "communication" on the ground that it was "likely to leave out just what is of most value in the ideal rhetoric, the judgment of what is communicated."[5] Wallace's paper in this volume suggests that the label "rhetoric" is endangered by the same omission. "The great task of rhetoricians in the generation ahead," he says, "is to reinstate the study of the materials of public argument." Toward this end he proposes compilation of a set or sets of modern rhetorical *topoi*, and calls for an ethic and a logic of public discourse.

In this paper Professor Wallace continues a crusade extending over many years to demonstrate the relationship of rhetorical study to politics, to ethics, and to that now almost forgotten ideal, a liberal education. He evokes once again the image of the rhetorician as generalizer and synthesizer, one who makes use of the studies of linguist, speech scientist, philosopher, psychologist, and historian in describing and evaluating what happens when human beings communicate with other human beings about significant subjects. It may be too much to hope as general education steadily retreats before the advances of special education, as traditional bastions like the Cornell tradition disappear, that the Wallace view can long maintain itself against the specialists with their communication models borrowed from electronics engineers. But Wallace's claim that the study of rhetoric can offer the undergraduate an opportunity to see "what unity there may still be among the studies of his higher education" continues to hold a certain attractiveness for some of us in the over-fifty crowd.

Twenty years ago Dean Hunt called attention to the remarkable similarity between the aims of general education as set forth in the then current Harvard Report and the aims of rhetorical training. The four "traits of mind," for example, listed in the report as fostered by a liberal education (to think effectively, to communicate thought, to make relevant judgments, to discriminate among values) are goals also of the best rhetorical training. Of writers on general education Hunt said: "They seem to be groping toward some new synthesis which has been there all the time, if they would only recognize it."[6] Professor McKeon seems to take a similar position in presenting rhetoric as an architectonic productive art—"an art in which what any one says to be the case, judges to be good or evil, connects in relations, and establishes with some show of system and principles, is relevant as subject-matter, content, and product."

It would not appear that large numbers of educators are today groping in the direction indicated by Professor Hunt, but as Wallace and McKeon make clear, the synthesis is available if anyone is interested.

Each day it becomes more difficult to talk even with one another (to say nothing of the generality of mankind, or specialists in other areas) about "rhetoric." Different groups use the same terms to designate different concepts; new terms are coined for old concepts; familiar terms we thought had been clarified to everyone's satisfaction turn up in unfamiliar contexts. As Professor McKeon says of rhetoric's ambiguous history, "continuing terms assume new meanings in their new applications, and the innovations are seldom guided by knowledge of how renewed terms were used in earlier traditions." In light of such confusion, it seems remarkable that the writers of these position papers devote so little attention to problems of definition. Professor Becker's hope "that we will not be too concerned with the trivial question of what is or is not 'rhetoric'" is amply realized, for the subject is seldom raised.

In 1953, when called upon to delineate the functions and scope of rhetoric,[7] Donald Bryant found it necessary to devote several pages to reviewing the many usages of the term before formulating a working definition of his own. We have had since then sixteen additional years of innovation and confusion in terminology. James Murphy in a review of five recent books on rhetoric notes that whether or not there has been a knowledge explosion, there has certainly been a "category explosion" or a "vocabulary explosion." The term "rhetoric," he says, is being stretched almost beyond endurance; its future usefulness is doubtful if it continues to be broadened.[8]

Perhaps Becker is right, and further disputes concerning what rhetoric is or is not can lead only to increased frustration. But Becker himself later expresses concern about what kinds of data are to be included under the rubric of rhetoric. "What is and is not to be included in our theories?" he asks. "Perhaps we need to ask what is to be excluded." The problem of limitation of boundaries is certainly relevant to the deliberations of those in search of a satisfactory contemporary theory of rhetoric.

In the article previously alluded to, Bryant saw fit to exclude certain means of persuasion from the scope of rhetoric. He eliminated gold and guns as belonging to commerce or coercion, not to rhetoric. He acknowledged the persuasive force of certain kind of symbols, like fog horns, fire alarms, and traffic lights, but declined to regard them as rhetorical devices. Some limits must be imposed, he argued, lest nearly all interhuman activity be admitted to the field of rhetoric. Consequently he assumed the traditional limitation to *discourse*, oral or written.[9] The charge issued by the Planning Committee seems to accept Bryant's limitation, for in the questions assigned for response the phrase "a theory of public discourse" in the first question is apparently intended to be taken as synonymous with "a conception of rhetoric" in the second. Professor Wallace, also, in his initial paragraph defines rhetoric as an art of discourse. Still, there is an almost irresistible tendency to expand the term. The last few years have seen the development of more and more means of influencing thought and behavior—some peaceful, some coercive and violent. Each has been christened as a new brand of rhetoric. Thus we have the rhetoric of massed bodies, the rhetoric of silent sit-ins and protest marches; we may expect to hear soon of the rhetoric of the night-stick and the Molotov cocktail.

As new devices are added to, or substituted for discourse in an attempt to influence public policy it may be useful to think of them as *non-rhetorical* elements in the "rhetorical situation" described by Lloyd Bitzer —symbols or symbolic action introduced into the situation in lieu of or in addition to discourse, for the purpose of modifying the exigence. We may be forced to the position that such persuasive (sometimes coercive) devices, though important subjects for study, though relevant to the rhetorician, are not his central concern and cannot be embraced by the suitable conception of rhetoric which we have been asked to outline and amplify. I am fully aware that such an arbitrary exclusion by definition may be of no help at all. It may successfully be argued that such a position makes it impossible to adjust rhetorical theory "to twentieth-century concepts, learning, and needs," that it would place rhetorical theorists outside the mainstream of present day communicative processes. I am ready to admit that the problem of defining boundaries is a difficult—perhaps an insoluble—one. But I do not see how it can be ignored by participants in the present enterprise.

I should like at this point to turn away from the position papers and respond to the invitation to record some "concerns" of my own. It may be that the apprehensions I am about to express are without substantial foundation. I rather hope they are. But conversations with colleagues lead me to believe that they are not entirely traceable to personal idiosyncracy.

The charge to participants in this conference speaks of "a satisfactory *contemporary* theory of rhetoric," and "a theory of public discourse suitable to our time." The justification of the project submitted to the National Endowment For the Humanities notes "insistent questions concerning the relevance of traditional assumptions about rhetoric and persuasion to contemporary social processes." Implicit in these and other statements about a "new" rhetoric is the conviction that "old" rhetorics are in need of overhaul and modification. With such an implication no sensible person need disagree. I doubt, however, that those who planned this conference seriously considered the possibility that in developing outlines of the new, we should begin with a repudiation of the basic values of the old. Yet unless I misunderstand what I hear at our conferences and read in our journals, there are those among us who would do just that. "Traditional" has become an opprobrious term. The old ways will no longer do. Courtesy, dignity, reasonableness, once regarded as marks of the liberally educated, humane man, are now middle-class values, and hence, apparently, reprehensible. Increasing numbers of people, we are told, reject discussion and the ballot-box as the best means of effecting change—the implication being that these institutions have thereby been rendered undesirable or obsolete. Let me reiterate that I speak now not of the position papers, but of what seems to me an alarming tendency in much writing and speaking about contemporary communicative behavior.

Until quite recently one would have found in our ranks almost universal assent to the familiar statements of Jefferson, Mill, and Lippmann concerning the necessity for open competition of ideas in the marketplace. We once quoted with approval Everett Hunt's definition of rhetoric as "the study of men persuading men to make free choices," and Karl Wallace's: "the art of finding and effectively presenting good reasons." We accepted Sidney Hook's admonition that "the cardinal sin, when we are looking for truth of fact or wisdom of policy is refusal to discuss, or action which blocks discussion."

But suddenly we are not so sure. The streets echo the angry voices of those who would usher in a new order by destroying the old, and some rhetoricians—rightfully indignant at the enormity of past injustices, warmed by sympathy for the goals proclaimed—jettison the old axioms and scramble to rationalize the new reality. Have not the old rhetorics become instruments for perpetuating a corrupt establishment? Have not "reasonable" approaches brought us to the present chaos? Are not civility and rationality masks for preserving injustice? Away, then, with the hypocrisy of prating these middle-class values.

I do not wish to be unfair. With Professor Johnstone I see the need for understanding the rhetoric of the New Left and for analysing the rhetorical effects of shouts, obscenities, and the like. Such analyses are already being made, and I am sure that some of our colleagues who are dealing with these subjects are in patient, kindly quest of understanding. But the evidence seems too clear to be ignored that others have identified understanding with approval, and are rapidly moving beyond approval to implicit or explicit justification. There is a danger, it seems to me, that one may begin by trying to understand: Why do some people resort to violence, why are people often uncivil and brutish, why are demands issued in language unworthy of civilized human beings? and proceed to justification ("I'd do the same thing if I were in their place"). What is, is right—because we can explain how it came about, and because we sympathize with the ultimate goals.

I find, or fancy I find, signs of willingness among students of rhetoric to declare a moratorium on traditionally established values for the duration of the emergency. I am impressed, for example, in reading the proceedings of a recent symposium on issues in public communication,[10] by the tacit assumption by some participants that although *theoretically* we place our faith in reasoned discourse as the best way of resolving difficulties, *in practice, at the present time*, we have our doubts about its wisdom or effectiveness. After one speaker had posited a series of ground rules for controversy in a democracy, the response was: Such rules are fine, but "we find that we've been talking about an ideal."[11] When the old ways don't work (that is, when they fail to achieve goals certified as "good"), we have to find new ways that *will* work.

Another speaker, having declared the indefensibility of overgeneralizations, oversimplifications, and polarization of issues, "by any *ideal* standards," and after paying tribute to "the only universally negotiable coinage I know of—the language of reason," turns to defenses of the new rhetoric. He concludes by saying:

> The times are clearly out of joint, and to expect that the art of persuasion which characterizes these times should be any more orderly is surely to expect the impossible.

This, to be sure, does not constitute endorsement of the innovative "rhetoric" which he has described. But he speaks elsewhere of the possibility of "a rather lengthy moratorium" on rational discourse, and one finds no clear indication that the prospect dismays him.[12] Certainly he does not go out of his way to denounce, or even to deplore it.

One is moved to ask with Professor Johnstone, what is becoming of the concept of reason? Noting that shouts, obscenities, non-negotiable demands, and a refusal to argue seem to be rejections of reason, he suggests that the New Left's refusal to argue may be based on the presumption that to argue is to place one's self on the side of the establishment. A supplementary explanation may lie in the enviable self-assurance, the monumental rectitude which characterizes some elements of the New Left. When one knows the truth and is determined to act upon it "by all means necessary," there is no need for dialectic as a method of inquiry nor of rhetoric as a means of providing good reasons for securing willing assent. Professor Wallace reminds us that "good reasons" are statements in support of an ought proposition. But when *ought* propositions are discarded in favor of *must* propositions, no need is felt for reasons—good or bad. The time for argument, we are repeatedly told, is past. The time for non-negotiable demands and appropriate sanctions has come.

In asserting the superiority of reason over unreason, emotional harangue, or violence in our teaching and writing for half a century we have indeed (to quote our symposium speaker) "been talking about an ideal." One would hope, however, that the ideal is not too fragile to stand the stresses of the stormy present, that it need not be laid away for use in some more tranquil future. One would think, rather, that when reason and civility are threatened, then is the time to defend, not defer them.

Students of rhetoric and public address are of course not alone in wrestling with problems of this kind. Attention has recently been called to increasing criticism by journalists of the concept of objectivity. Herbert Brucker, writing in *Saturday Review*,[13] reports that "objective news has become anathema to young activists in journalism, to some of the rising generation of university intellectuals, and to others who also should know better." Objective news, he says, is viewed as an obsolete convention that blocks progress toward a better world, a device invented by the Establishment to preserve a status quo that should be destroyed. Brucker acknowledges the problem raised in the 1950's by reporting Senator Joseph McCarthy's accusations "objectively," but he goes on to distinguish between "surface" news which presents surface facts without context or perspective (the visible part of the iceberg), and "interpretative" news, relevant facts presented honestly against a background of knowledge (reporting that may be equally "objective"). In a passage which I find particularly apposite to our own situation, he says:

> All attacks on objective news begin with the fact that there is no such thing as perfect objectivity. Granted. But should our answer therefore be, "Why bother even trying?" Or should we redouble our efforts to be as fair as we can?

Similarly, all attacks on rational discourse begin by saying that man is *not* a rational animal—that is, he does not always act rationally. Granted. And is the answer therefore to accept or justify irrationality, or to redouble our efforts to be as rational as we can?

If there is any foundation to my uneasy feeling that some rhetorical theorists, like some social activists, have manifested a willingness to abandon what is established and start all over again, there may be merit in the following suggestion: In attempting "to develop a theory of public discourse suitable to our time" the participants in this and subsequent conferences might well begin by affirming faith in reasoned discourse, not merely as an "ideal" for quiet times, but as an eminently real necessity for the preservation of the values of democratic society—values to which members of the Speech Communication Association are presumably still committed. Democracy, as Nilsen has well said, "is at once a pattern of procedures and a pattern of values; the values must influence the procedures, and the procedures must continuously recreate the values, if democracy is to perpetuate itself."[14]

If I may be permitted the expression of one final concern, I should like to say that I detect in the multifarious outpourings on the subject of "rhetoric" the unmistakable beginnings of a cult of unintelligibility. Perhaps it is traceable to our longing for greater respectability in the academy. Perhaps it comes from the increasing tendency of members of our guild to attach themselves more closely to other disciplines—to philosophy, to social psychology, to literary criticism—and to snarl their terminologies with our own. Professor Everett Hunt observed recently in a convention paper that "The new rhetoric sometimes seems to me to be concerned with producing specialists who do not speak to the public or to each other. And yet the hope of these men seems to be that by producing more specialized research they can inspire the professional respect of other specialists, who probably do not talk their language, nor care what they are doing." Might it not be possible, he asks, to reverse the trend and appeal, not to other specialists for our prestige, but to an intelligent public?[15]

Many years ago, in an article which I hope has not been totally rejected on the ground that it is "traditional," Herbert Wichelns asserted that "The rhetorician's art . . . is to be thought of as the art of popularization. Its practitioners are the Huxleys, not the Darwins, of science; the Jeffersons, not the Lockes and the Rousseaus, of politics." And he went on to say that those "who would tame Leviathan to the end that he shall not threaten civilization must examine more thoroughly than they as yet have done the interactions of the inventive genius, the popularizing talent, and the public mind."

Perhaps Wichelns' words apply to the theorists and critics as well as the practitioners of rhetoric. Perhaps we have almost reached the point at which we might profitably pause in the effort to formulate ever more sophisticated models and systems and analogues, described in increasingly recondite terminology, and attempt to simplify—to take stock of what it is we are trying to do—as for example Donald Bryant did some years ago when he redefined rhetoric as the rationale of informative and suasory discourse and asserted its function to be that of adjusting ideas to people and people to ideas. If it is communication we are interested in, surely there is merit in trying to say something communicable about communication.

Apparently similar uneasiness is being felt among the speech communication scientists. At the 1968 New Orleans Conference, Gary Cronkhite in an attempt to coax his colleagues "Out of the Ivory Palaces," proclaimed the need for two types of persons: those who *translate* and those who *apply* the findings of research. We in rhetoric have our translators (those who can speak meaningfully to both specialist and non-specialist); the fact that the Bryant essay has been reprinted more than a half-dozen times testifies to its utility and catholicity. But as our inquiries become more technical and our jargon more esoteric the need for translators and generalizers will undoubtedly exceed the limited supply.

Those persons who *apply* the findings of research in rhetoric are, I presume, the teachers and the critics. Here the lack is even more poignantly felt. I shall not add here to the abuse of rhetorical critics; they have suffered enough wounds already—many of them self-inflicted. Those who fancy themselves critics have joined with the communicologists in heaping obloquy upon their own heads. They deplore the shortcomings of something called "traditional" criticism, and herald with joy the advent of a "new" criticism which will turn its back on Aristotle and all his ilk. I have not seen many examples of this amazing new criticism, nor have I read much in the last few years that can match in wisdom and insight and illumination the "traditional" essays of Carroll Arnold on George William Curtis or Wichelns on Emerson, or, for that matter, Goodrich on British orators.

That we have not achieved the excellence we seek is evident to everyone. But I doubt that the reason for this is that we have relied on "traditional" methods or that we lack for new patterns of criticism. One can scarcely pick up an issue of our regional or national journals for the past five years without coming upon a suggestion for a new "approach" to the criticism of discourse. We should, we are told, examine the rhetoric of alienation, or black power, or obscenity. We should examine didactic plays and develop a poetics of didactic drama; we should take a fresh look at figurative language, especially metaphors. We should adopt a culture-related methodology, or engage in "existential, phenomenological criticism," or analyse "the components of the listeners' perceptual or cognitive reality." We should apply the insights and methods of Burke or Richards or Wittgenstein.

Now I do not deprecate such suggestions, nor discourage more of the same. I have earlier affirmed my belief that the more "approaches," the more ways of looking at a speech event, the better. Indeed, one of the purposes of this conference is to propose research directions which may disclose new ways of describing, analysing, and evaluating not only a speech, but the communication process itself. But I speak at the moment of the critical act, the application of theory to practice, and I am suggesting that our scholarly efforts in rhetoric and public address have got out of balance because for the past ten years prescription has outrun performance.

There are, perhaps, recent signs that the situation is improving, and that we may yet produce criticism worthy of our theoretical formulations. Yet even in criticism one sees the beginnings of the same cultivated unintelligibility of which I have spoken. Presumably the essential purpose of criticism is not merely to illustrate or exemplify some critical "approach" or theory. Upon the question of what *the* purpose of criticism is, we have not yet reached agreement, and perhaps we never shall. One might hope that we could secure general assent to the proposition that the rhetorical critic's obligation is to try to say something sensible and illuminating about speeches and speaking—as Walter Kerr, for example, has for many years tried to speak sensibly about drama and dramatists, or Walter Lippmann about statesmanship and statesmen. To say something, moreover, that will provide the national audience with valuable and relevant insights. These insights may be imparted by explaining how some element of a message "works" (so Bryant); or by analysing how an orator imparts his ideas to his hearers (so Wichelns); or by showing what kind of medicine a medicine man has concocted (so Burke on Hitler); or by revealing what speeches can tell us about the times out of which they grew and the audiences to which they were addressed (so Wrage). The potentialities of this last approach, incidentally, have not yet been disclosed. Wrage's thesis that the speech critic can contribute to the history of ideas by regarding speeches as *mirrors* as well as *instruments* or *engines* has has been inadequately exploited. It might provide a satisfactory alternative to those who object that criticism has placed undue emphasis upon persuasion or effect or influence upon history.

Some will recall still another proposition advanced by Ernest Wrage. "The ideal critic," he said, "is concerned with ventilating and improving our public talk." This means, as the speech-communication scholars continue to remind us, that we must study the talk of the present as well as the past. If the student of speech (or if you prefer, of "spoken symbolic interaction") cannot find better ways to ventilate and improve our public (and private) talk, to whom shall we turn?

To perform this function, which should be uniquely our own, we must as Everett Hunt proposes address ourselves to an intelligent public, and not merely to other specialists. Among the notes left at his death by Professor Wrage I find this provocative fragment: "Oratory is geared to immediacy—the elucidation of points, the stirring of emotions, and so forth.

To elucidate what is presumptively intelligible by the density of unintelligibility is really the height of preposterous investment of time and energy." It would be a pity if we were to talk in such a learned fashion about talk that no one would understand what we were talking about.

Sometimes I fancy I see a gleam of light on the path ahead. A colleague of mine recently submitted an essay in practical criticism to one of our national journals which evoked from one of the editors this comment: "An exciting study. . . . It is a contribution to the 'new scholarship' in rhetoric, in that it contributes not simply to rhetorical knowledge but to general knowledge as well." If this be the direction of new scholarship in our field, all cannot be lost.

FOOTNOTES

1. Robert J. Kibler, and Larry L. Barker, eds., *Conceptual Frontiers in Speech-Communication* (New York, Speech Communication Association, 1969), p. 187.
2. Cf. Wallace's position paper: ". . . speech is not a lifeless thing to a speaker, external to him, and instrumental like a hammer. Speaking is man's distinctive mode of acting, reflecting his whole being and every dimension of it."
3. *Quarterly Journal of Speech*, XLIV (October 1958), 242–43.
4. (Indianapolis; Bobbs-Merrill, 1956), p. 37.
5. "A Symposium in Rhetoric and General Education," *Quarterly Journal of Speech*, XXXV (December 1949), 423.
6. "Rhetoric and General Education," *Quarterly Journal of Speech*, XXXV (October 1949), 275–79.
7. "Rhetoric: Its Functions and Its Scope," *Quarterly Journal of Speech*, XXXIX (December 1953), 401–24.
8. "Today's Rhetoric—The Searches for Analogy," *Quarterly Journal of Speech*, LIV (April 1968), 164–65; 169.
9. "Rhetoric: Its Functions and Its Scope," pp. 404–05.
10. *The Ethics of Controversy: Politics and Protest.* Proceedings of the First Annual Symposium on Issues in Public Communication, University of Kansas, June 27–28, 1968.
11. *Ibid.*, pp. 72–73.
12. *Ibid.*, pp. 123–42.
13. "What's Wrong With Objectivity?" (October 11, 1969), pp. 77–79.
14. "Free Speech, Persuasion, and the Democratic Process," *Quarterly Journal of Speech*, XLIV (October 1958), 236.
15. "Classical Rhetoric and Modern Communicology," Western Speech Association, Salt Lake City, 1968. James Murphy's review of a portion of the literature convinces him of "a growing lack of communication between communication experts" ("Today's Rhetoric—The Searches for Analogy"). If experts are unable or unwilling to communicate with each other, how much greater must be their inability to reach the "common man."

11 / RHETORIC
IN SEARCH OF
A PAST, PRESENT,
AND FUTURE

EDWARD P. J. CORBETT
Ohio State University

As far as I have been able to determine, this is the first national conference on rhetoric involving participants from such varied academic disciplines as Speech, Communication, Philosophy, English, and Sociology. If we had followed the lead of Kenneth Burke in making use of a number of disciplines for the development of a modern rhetoric, we might have added scholars from Linguistics, Psychology, and Anthropology. But although we are small in number, there are still represented here more disciplines than have ever been gathered together at one time to discuss rhetoric. Until now, those of us interested in rhetoric have met and talked only with colleagues in our discipline, like a seance of Baker Street Irregulars. Panels and symposia on rhetoric have been features of the national conventions of the Speech Association of America for many years. Since about 1963, panels, seminars, and invitational workshops have been part of the program at the national conventions of the Modern Language Association, the National Council of Teachers of English, and the Conference on College Composition and Communication. Recently, however, there have been encouraging signs of cross-fertilization. There were, for instance, the two conferences involving mainly people from Speech and Communication held at the University of Wisconsin in Milwaukee and at the University of Minnesota. I do not know whether people from English have participated in the programs at the national meetings of the SAA, but I do know that at least since 1965 people from Speech have figured in the programs at the national meetings of the MLA, the NCTE, and the CCCC. And the roster of members published in the latest issue of the Rhetoric Society's Newsletter reveals a representation from a broad spectrum of academic disciplines.

Rhetoric is the common interest that has drawn us together. Perhaps the Humanities is the only other aegis under which one could imagine a convention of scholars from so many different departments. And given the mechanism of departmental travel budgets, perhaps only funding by some national agencies could make possible an interdisciplinary conference like this. It will be interesting to see whether this cross-fertilization bears fruit. If it does not, the deliberations of this conference may come to be referred to as Murmurings from the Wax Museum.

What the reading of the position papers convinced me of is that although we share a common interest in rhetoric we do not all have a common vocabulary or a common perspective. One of the consequences of talking about a specialized subject over a long period of time only with one's colleagues is that one loses sight of the fact that even highly literate people outside the clique may not understand what the in-group is talking about. Strange vocabulary of course can mystify an audience, but even familiar vocabulary, if subtly endowed with new meaning, can block communication. But a new point of view, a different angle of approach, a fresh mental-set can also frustrate comprehension. All of us have exposed our thoughts on paper for the others to read before we came to this Conference. One of the objectives of this Conference should be to make sure that even though we may not be able to adopt a common ground for discussing rhetoric we at least come to some understanding of the other fellow's terminology and perspective. If at least that much understanding results, then the real fruits of this Conference may be harvested several years hence, after we have returned to our separate vineyards with fresh insights and liberating points of view.

The task of commenting significantly on the five position papers that were available when I sat down to write this response is indeed a formidable one. It is not only that the papers were long and involved and many-faceted; the task is further complicated for me by the fact that I have read, profited from, and admired the previously published works of all these authors. Awe is not a particularly promising disposition for a critic. Normally, one does not bite the hand that has fed him. I suspect that in my review and assessment of what these authors have said on paper I will often be avoiding comment on those areas that I did not understand or that I did not feel competent to judge. And I will probably be violating frequently one of the cardinal rules of criticism: I will be criticizing the authors, not so much for what they said as for what they did not say.

A good starting point might be to designate the focus of discussion in the five papers. Karl Wallace's intention is "to remark upon the basis for a theory of rhetoric and then concentrate on the subject matter of rhetoric and rhetorical discourse, proceeding later to deal briefly with the ethics and logic of discourse." Richard McKeon's purpose is to suggest guidelines "for the construction of an architectonic productive art of rhetoric and philosophy which can be used to create a method productive of the arts and a subject-matter substantive to the problems of an age of technology." The main question that L. W. Rosenfield deals with is "what intellectual factors have caused orthodox commentaries on rhetoric to become unsatisfactory for contemporary thought." In proposing a conception of rhetoric that will serve the needs of our time, Samuel L. Becker argues that "we need theories which explain the complex web of interactions among ideas, messages, and men, and which are *testable*." Henry W. Johnstone chooses to discuss "the signs I have seen of developments that may take place in rhetorical theory over a certain period in the future."

What is clear from these statements of purpose is that each of the authors has taken seriously the charge set for them by the original statement of objectives of this National Developmental Project on Rhetoric: "What is the essential outline of a conception of rhetoric useful in the second half of the twentieth century?" or "what problems or topics must contemporary rhetorical scholarship pursue in order to develop a theory of public discourse suitable for our time?" Just as Aristotle used a time scheme as one way of differentiating the three modes of persuasive discourse, I find that the five authors have adopted, perhaps unconsciously, a temporal orientation in their approach to the charge. With their pursuit of historical developments, Wallace, McKeon, and Rosenfield might be said to be primarily interested in the *past* as it bears upon rhetorical developments in the present and future; Becker focuses primarily on the *present*; and Johnstone is primarily concerned with the *future*. Before I received the papers, I was fearful that in the concern for the future of rhetoric we might neglect to explore its rich tradition. As it turned out, that fear was groundless, for three of the authors have chosen to give us a historical perspective on the questions that concern this Conference. Yet there is danger too in a preoccupation with the past: a reverence for traditions might indispose us to break the molds and cast new models. But the discussions of Becker and Johnstone prevented that danger.

I found it interesting that only Karl Wallace felt the need to offer a formal definition of *rhetoric* (see the first paragraph of his paper). It would be possible to abstract a definition of rhetoric from what the other

four authors said in their papers, but none of these four presented in cap-
sule form a definition of the term that appeared in the titles of all of their
papers. Perhaps they are just manifesting what good rhetoricians they are.
Knowing that their immediate audience would be made up of people vi-
tally interested in rhetoric, they did not feel that it was necessary to define the term. But perhaps when these papers are published for a wider,
more heterogeneous audience, it might be advisable, perhaps in the Fore-
word, to offer a working definition of the term—a definition that the members of this first Conference might themselves have formulated. Anyone
who has glibly used the word *rhetoric* in formal or informal discussions
knows how often one of the uninitiated has stopped him and asked, "what
do you mean by *rhetoric?"*

Despite the diversity of interests and perspectives in the papers, I
looked to see whether some common ideas or themes occurred. I did perceive that there was general agreement among the authors that rhetoric
must undergo some kind of rejuvenation, some kind of accretion to its
present stock of doctrines and techniques, if it is to be useful and usable
in the modern world. I certainly agree with that thesis, but I kept looking
for one of the authors to make the point that not all the doctrines and
techniques of a discipline as hoary as rhetoric have lost their pertinence
and vitality. Maybe I have misread the papers, but I detected in all of
them at least the implicit notion that the ancient tradition of rhetoric is
mortified and that if we are to get on with the development of a new rhetoric we will have to wipe the slate clean and start all over again. The notion is strongest in Rosenfield's article, prefigured by the word *autopsy* in
his title, but I find it latent in all the papers.

Regardless of what some idolators have said about Aristotle's contributions to rhetorical theory, I would be the first to admit that he did not
formulate the perfect theory of rhetoric. Our knowledge about the speaker,
the message, and the audience in the rhetorical triad has been immeasur-
ably enhanced not only by later rhetoricians but by scholars in such other
fields as psychology, sociology, and communication theory. But as I study
the so-called "new rhetoric," I am simply amazed at how much that is
proposed as new is just Aristotle in new trappings or new terminology.
The limitations of Aristotle's rhetoric are due not to any fundamental my-
opia on his part but to his restricted purview and to the primitiveness of
his research tools. Aristotle's *Rhetoric* did indeed concentrate on a single
mode of discourse, persuasion, but that concentration was the result of
choice not blindness, just as in the text of the *Poetics* that has survived,
Aristotle chose to concentrate on just two of the mimetic genres, tragedy
and epic. Admittedly, Aristotle's treatment of the emotions in the second
book of his *Rhetoric* is primitive and inchoate, but given the fact that he
lacked the apparatus of modern psychology for probing the human psyche,

his rudimentary analysis of the emotions is remarkably perceptive and accurate.

The soundness and continuing pertinence of the classical doctrines are even more apparent in the more thoroughly developed treatises of Cicero and Quintilian. I have often found it to be the case that those who complain about the irrelevancy of classical rhetoric for modern times have not read the primary texts of Cicero and Quintilian, have read only snippets, or have read about them only in secondary sources. If I had only one recommendation to make as my part in this Conference, I would suggest that in our quest for a relevant rhetoric for the modern age we take a firsthand look at the classical rhetoricians, see which of their doctrines still have something pertinent and valuable to say about the arts of discourse, and discover which of those doctrines are the underpinnings of modern rhetorical theory. This is not to recommend an interest in and a respect for the ancient merely because it is old; rather it is to encourage the exploration of the old for its possible bearing on the new.

Another common concern was the reason for the decline of rhetoric. One of the causes proposed by all the authors was the split that developed between matter and form, between thought and expression. The authors spoke about this divorce in different terms, but obviously they were all talking about the same phenomenon. Wallace put it this way: rhetoric "was persuaded it had no proper responsibility for the materials, substance, and content of discourse and devoted its attention to the forms, structure, style, and expression of language as written and spoken." Remarking that invention had always been an important part of rhetoric, McKeon recommended the rejoining of eloquence and wisdom, of rhetoric and philosophy, because when "a productive inventive art deals with content as well as form, it is an art of active modification, rather than of passive reception, of the data of existence." In his autopsy on the rhetorical corpus, Rosenfield views the matter in terms of the increasing isolation between Man Thinking and Man Acting, the disjunction of *being* and *appearance*. Becker concedes that the emphasis in rhetorical studies should remain on the message but would like to see a shift in emphasis from the source-message relationship to the message-audience relationship. In *Philosophy, Rhetoric, and Argumentation*, the collection of essays that Johnstone put together in 1965 with his colleague Maurice Natanson, the lament about the divorce between rhetoric and dialectic was more pronounced than in Johnstone's present paper, but in his remarks about the slippage in the function of the places of argument (the topics) he does suggest, in a rhetorical question, that rhetoric declined because of the loss of concern for content: "Can the shift in the status of rhetoric between Aristotle's time and the Seventeenth Century be accounted for, at least in part, by this loosening and relativization of the idea of place?"

It was heartening to find all five authors lamenting the divorce between form and content and recommending, implicitly if not explicitly, a remarriage. If rhetoric is to become again something more than just a formal or methodological art, if it is to become a substantive art which can contribute, as Wallace and McKeon claim it can, to the general education of modern man, it must be as much concerned about the substance of discourse as with the form.

Most of the authors dealt with the problem that Professor Becker posed in the introduction of his paper: the units of discourse that we need to study. In the past and for a long time, rhetorical analysis concentrated on those oral discourses and, after the invention of printing, on those written discourses whose primary purpose was persuasion. But in the course of time, as the purposes and the media of communication expanded, rhetoric was looked to for guidance in the construction and analysis of many other modes of discourse. Most of our authors are calling for a shift in, or an expansion of, the rhetorical purview. Some of them, like Wallace and McKeon, outline the province in rather general terms. Wallace advocates more attention being paid to "popular discourse"—"the experience of men in their public characters in the roles they take when they are not experts communicating with experts"; "what do people speak about and discuss when they are not specialists talking to specialists?" McKeon recommends that rhetoric should be an art "in which what anyone says to be the case, judges to be good or evil, connects in relations, and establishes with some show of system and principles is relevant as subject-matter, content, and product." Becker and Johnstone are more specific in designating the modes and media of discourse that we need to be concerned with. Becker says that we have concentrated too exclusively on the major speakers and writers of the past and that we should turn our attention to all those contemporary modes and media of discourse which constantly bombard modern man—the newspaper stories, the radio and television broadcasts, the Xerox machine, the "body rhetoric" of mass demonstrations, the complex web of interpersonal communication. Johnstone also recommends that we not limit our attention to formal speeches, to the rhetoric of the legislative chamber and the courtroom but that we study the rhetoric of everyday life. So he would have us direct our attention to the rhetorical strategies of the New Left, with its shouts, obscenities, and sit-ins and to the rhetoric of the mass-media that McLuhan has been preaching.

I agree that one of the ways in which rhetoric will be revitalized is by expanding its purview to include all those modes of discourse which dispense information, influence attitudes, and prompt or prevent action. In the past, rhetoric has focused its attention on the monologue forms of discourse, those forms in which a single man held forth for an allotted time or space, articulating his message in a structure with a beginning, a middle, and an end. But today a good deal of the information-dispensing, attitude-forming, policy-making discourse takes the form of the fragmentary, give-and-take dialogue. Someone needs to formulate the rhetoric of the interview, the talk-show, the panel discussion, the symposium, the brain-storming sessions. I am sure that logical appeals, emotional appeals, and ethical appeals play a part in this kind of stop-and-go discourse, as they did in the monologuist discourse that rhetoric has traditionally been concerned with, but someone needs to explore just *how* those appeals are exerted in the non-linear, often unstructured, modes of discourse. Why, for instance, did Richard Nixon come off second best to John F. Kennedy in the television debates of 1960? Was it that his ethical appeal was weaker than Kennedy's? If so, how or why did Kennedy's ethical appeal come across so much stronger? Was it simply a matter of physical appearance and mannerisms? And if *that* is so, what does that do to Aristotle's notion that the ethical appeal is exerted primarily by what is *said* in the speech? It is questions like those that we need to explore in our study of the dialogue forms of discourse, which more often than not are face-to-face confrontations, and it is questions like those that Henry Johnstone might pursue with his new interest in the role of the person and the self in the rhetorical act.

I was surprised that no one mentioned the relations of rhetoric to the literary modes of discourse—poetry, drama, short stories, novels. Perhaps the authors were conceding that province to Wayne Booth. As a teacher of English, I am naturally interested in the exploration of this relationship, but I detect signs of a growing interest in this relationship even among teachers of Speech. Thomas O. Sloan and Michael Osborn—to name only two speech teachers—have published some very impressive rhetorical analyses of literary texts and of the function of metaphor in literary discourse. In a lecture that he gave at my university in November of 1969, Donald C. Bryant said that if he were now to update his essay "Rhetoric: Its Function and Scope," first published in the *Quarterly Journal of Speech* in 1953, he would devote more attention to the use of rhetoric as a tool for exploring imaginative literature. Professor Bryant made a start in that direction when he served as the chairman of a symposium on rhetoric and poetic at the University of Iowa and as the editor of the collection of talks that were delivered at that symposium (*Rhetoric and Poetic*, 1965).

Although it is possible to regard a literary artifact solely as an object for aesthetic contemplation, it is also possible to view it as a vehicle of communication, as a means of teaching or influencing an audience. Of course some forms of literature have a more overt didactic or corrective design on an audience than others. Satire, for instance, which is almost invariably topical and which is usually addressed to a specific contemporary audience, is as rhetorical in its persuasive purpose as a parliamentary speech. In these rhetorical forms of *belles lettres* there is the same triad of relationships to study—the author, the text, and the audience—as there is in a public oration. In addition, however, one can also analyze the rhetorical transactions going on *within* the literary work—as, for instance, the Duke's subtle manipulation of the emissary in Browning's "My Last Duchess."

I do not mean to make literary critics of us all, but I do advocate that if we are going to turn our attention to the manifold modes of discourse that bombard us constantly in our public and private lives, some of us should turn our attention to those mimetic modes of discourse that have had and continue to have such a profound effect on readers. I for one would like to find some answers to the question of why it is that a theme developed in, say, a novel is often more meaningful, more affective, more dynamic for a group of young people than is the same theme treated in a piece of straight expository prose. The answer cannot be simply that the theme is concretized, "humanized," in the imaginative work. Is the journalistic reporting in works like John Hershey's *Hiroshima* and Truman Capote's *In Cold Blood* rendered memorable simply because the authors employed novelistic techniques?

I think too, along with Becker and Johnstone, that we rhetoricians must turn more of our attention to the study of the many non-verbal media that are having such a profound effect on our lives today. There is no question that music, the most non-verbal of the arts, is the medium that speaks most eloquently to young people today. And it is not just music with an accompaniment of words that appeals to them; pure instrumental music speaks to them too, especially the sounds of stringed instruments and more recently the tones of such gentle wind-instruments as the flute and the recorder. When in the entire history of the world did over 400,-000 people gather together in one place at the same time to listen to a verbal discourse as they did in the summer of 1969 in a pasture in Bethel, New York, to hear three days of folk music? We have always known that music has the power to stir and soothe the emotions. The great attention that the Latin rhetoricians paid to verbal rhythms was an attempt to exploit the emotional effects of sound. I am beginning to wonder now whether music does not also carry some ideational and ethical content that helps to move, to influence, to shape those who listen avidly to it. What is the special charisma that makes such musical groups as the Beatles or such individual performers as Tom Jones or Johnny Cash or Bob Dylan so popular and influential? That may be one of the questions that Henry Johnstone will seek an answer to as he pursues his current interest in the self and the person or that will interest Samuel Becker with his bias for a message-audience rhetoric. As I gaze into my own crystal-ball,

I see a great efflorescence of interest in *ethos*, that element which Aristotle once said was the most influential in the persuasive process.

In the exploration of the *ethos*, someone should investigate the new strategy of ethical appeal adopted by many of the militants. According to traditional theory, a speaker or writer enhanced his persuasive effectiveness if he conciliated his audience. By projecting an image of himself as a man of good sense, good will, and good moral character, he hoped to render his audience attentive, benevolent, and docile. The theory was that an audience was more likely to be persuaded by a speaker or writer if they trusted and admired him. Recently, in much of the rhetoric of confrontation, we have witnessed a radical change in the strategy of the ethical appeal. Many speakers and writers seem to have adopted the deliberate tactic of shocking or infuriating or alienating an audience with obscenities, threats, aspersions. Abrasive language does make an audience attentive, but it is questionable whether such language renders an audience docile and benevolent. And yet "telling it like it is" has had a measure of success in changing attitudes and effecting action. Why is this so? Is it that bully tactics can inspire enough fear in an audience that they are coerced into action or assent, or is there in every man an innate respect for forthrightness, however harsh it may be? This is an interesting question that should be explored. Hostile or rebellious postures seem to be on the increase, on the left and on the right, among the youth certainly but also among the elderly. Maybe the strategy of abrasiveness is a new "available means of persuasion."

I found it rather curious that only one of the five authors even mentioned Marshall McLuhan. By any definition one may choose to propose, McLuhan has to be regarded as a rhetorician, and if McLuhan will learn to sit still long enough to develop some of his theories in depth instead of just darting out a new set of heuristic probes every month and indulging his Joycean delight in puns, he may yet come to be acknowledged as one of the major rhetoricians of this century. I myself have not yet given my full assent to his major thesis that the medium is the message, but I cannot imagine how anyone who has eyes to see and ears to hear could deny his thesis that the electronic media have radically altered the way in which we acquire, structure, and express our knowledge of the world about us. I can understand the resistance of print-oriented English teachers to McLuhan's theories, but I have been rather surprised that teachers of Speech and Communication have not taken up McLuhan more than they have. One of McLuhan's messages has been that we have returned to the audio-visual world in which rhetoric had its beginning. Technology, of course, has made it a *different* audio-visual world from what the Greeks knew, but it is still fundamentally the time-world of sound and icon that the Greeks knew rather than the space-world of graphic symbols that we have been accustomed to ever since Gutenberg invented the printing press. It is true that, except for sporting events and certain talk-shows, the television medium still depends on a *written* script, but the written words acquire a compelling intensity and immediacy when they are translated into the aural and visualist images of the television medium. The TV reporting of President Kennedy's assassination, with its mosaic-like structure, did create a unique kind of "rhetorical situation," which conditioned the kinds of discourse that were composed and delivered during that never-to-be-forgotten weekend in November of 1963. We do indeed have to devise an architectonic art to guide us in the use of and the response to those electronic media of communication which are playing such a crucial role in informing and influencing the international community of men.

Let me comment now briefly on a few of the especially salient ideas presented in the position papers.

I was intrigued by the notion, advanced by both Karl Wallace and Richard McKeon, that rhetoric, if properly reconstituted, can once again become the keystone discipline in the liberal-arts curriculum. As Professor Wallace put it, "To focus on the materials of public discourse is to focus on the substantive equipment of the liberally educated person. . . . I suggest that rhetoricians in the next decade can make their greatest contribution to the general welfare of the free and open society by acting in part as educators essential to the development of the public self of the individual." He sees the study of rhetoric as offering the modern student his only opportunity of perceiving the unity that may still exist in the whole complex of specialized subjects. Richard McKeon contends that rhetoric, if conceived of as an architectonic productive art, can provide "the devices by which to determine the characteristics and problems of our times and to form the art by which to guide actions for the solution of the problems and the improvement of the circumstances," and can suggest the "possible methods of directing and relating knowledge, action, and production." To conceive of the mission of rhetoric in these terms is to give rhetoric a new dignity and a new relevance for our age, and to restore rhetoric to the status of a liberal-arts study that Cicero and Quintilian attempted to give it. It may seem paradoxical to propose that rhetoric, which Aristotle said had no proper subject-matter, become a substantive art. The notion may strike some as being even more paradoxical when it comes from Professor McKeon, who in his paper viewed rhetoric as an art of *doing* and *making*, a conception that would seem to lock rhetoric into the status of a methodological art which it has long held in Speech and English departments. But perhaps it is the very fact that rhetoric is not tied to any particular subject-matter which gives it the potential for being a keystone, a synthesizing art. In any case, this notion of rhetoric's role in the modern world is the one that is most heartening to me. I do not want to relinquish rhetoric's functions as a synthetic art governing the composition of discourse or as an analytic art guiding the criticism of discourse already composed. But I am inspirited by the prospect of rhetoric becoming once again a liberal art which can prepare men to live purposively and harmoniously as social and political beings.

In his historical survey of the fortunes of rhetoric, Professor Rosenfield argued convincingly that the decline of rhetoric was due in large part to the split that developed between the intellectual experience and the political experience or, to use the Emersonian terms, between Man Thinking and Man Acting. This may be another way of saying what Professor Wallace said, that rhetoric suffered when it lost its concern for the content of discourse and concentrated on form and methodology. There seems to be ample evidence in the contemporary world that the split between Man Thinking and Man Acting has not yet been mended. For one thing, we have seen a general avoidance of, even a disdain for, the rational approach in argument; for another, we are witnessing in all disciplines a growing interest in behaviorism. The increasing reliance in the 1960's on "body rhetoric" may be another manifestation of the continuing split. As Professor Becker pointed out, "One has a greater chance of being 'heard' if he *does* something than if he *says* something."

Samuel Becker has made a significant contribution to our understanding of modern communications with his proposal that we consider "the total communication environment and the heterogeneous ways in which people are exposed to messages and the heterogeneous messages to which they are exposed" and with his paradigm of the mosaic cube to help us visualize the "universe of discourse" and the multiple sources of information. After reading his paper, I will never again feel at ease in analyzing the techniques and effects of a single, whole discourse. His cube will be always there to haunt me, to remind me that when I have said all I can say about the potentialities of that single message, I have not said all, and maybe not even the most important things about this particular instance of human communication. And I must say too about Professor Becker's paper that after reading the rather high-level discussions in the other papers, I found it a welcome relief to be presented with several concrete examples from the contemporary scene.

Despite his disclaimer that he is no expert in rhetoric, Henry Johnstone revealed himself to be a discerning observer of the current rhetorical scene and a judicious prophet of things to come. Dealing with the future as he did, he was operating on the most tenuous ground of all. The ground of rhetoric of course has always been the realm of the probable. But in dealing with the past and the present, one can usually establish a higher degree of probability than is possible when dealing with the future. The editor of a journal is perhaps the person best qualified to deal with the theme of *"quo vadimus?"* Confined as we are to our classrooms and the narrow circle of our colleagues, we teachers are often not the most reliable delineators of the "big picture." We can get a sense of what is happening "out there" by attending our national conventions and by reading our professional journals. An editor has those sources of information too, but in addition, he reviews all those dozens of articles that never get into print anywhere. Professor Johnstone spoke about some of the articles on certain themes that the authors were not quite able to bring off, but he read even those unsatisfactory efforts as *signs* of some of the major quests of our time, and he detected in them certain patterns and currents. His professional training as a philosopher also helps to qualify him as a reliable seer. The questing and questioning disposition of the philosopher is the one best calculated to prevent a man from following every will-o'-the-wisp that flickers on the horizon. Perhaps the philosopher is the man best equipped to rise above the particulars and see the roots and relationships of supposedly new ideas and new directions. It helps me to keep my own perspective in focus to be told that the rhetoric of the New Left may have its roots in Wittgenstein's philosophy and that certain other noticeable developments have a local habitation and a name in ontology and phenomenology (even though I do not entirely understand what those branches of philosophy are all about). It shakes up my cozy confidence in traditional logic to be told that, at least for the purposes of rhetorical discourse, we may have to re-examine the concept of formal validity and the notion of logical consistency. It is illuminations and reorientations like these that make me grateful that the first professional journal to be devoted primarily to the concerns of rhetoric should be one bearing the title *Philosophy & Rhetoric.* Of all the alignments of rhetoric with other disciplines, the one that may prove in the long run to be the most fruitful may be the alliance between rhetoric and philosophy.

When I look back over what I have written, I see that, just as I anticipated, I have more often criticized the authors for what they did not say than for what they did say. But maybe this dereliction was just my sneaky way of introducing my own notions about the future of rhetoric. On the positive side, I must concede that the authors have provided us with much fodder for rumination. The discussions at this first Conference may serve to clarify, refine, and amplify the notions advanced in these papers, so that the participants in the second Conference will have firm guidance as they strive to translate these notions into their pedagogical and curricular dimensions. On the negative side, I would have to confess that I did not find any of the essays to be seminal in the way that Herbert Wichelns's "The Literary Criticism of Oratory" or Lloyd Bitzer's "The Rhetorical Situation" were (although Becker's new communication model

12 / WINGSPREAD:
THE FINAL SESSION /
TWO REPORTS

Prior to their final session, participants in the
Wingspread Conference divided themselves into
two committees. One, under the chairmanship
of Samuel L. Becker, was to prepare a summary
statement of the Conference which would be
useful to the participants in the National
Conference on Rhetoric scheduled for the
following May. The other group, under the
chairmanship of Richard McKeon, was to prepare
a summary addressed to the general academic
community. The final session at Wingspread
was devoted mainly to hearing the reports of
Becker and McKeon on behalf of their
respective committees. Presented below is an
abridged version of this final session, held
on January 27, 1970.

ARNOLD: Our immediate business is to hear what the chairmen of these two groups have to say. I gather that the object is not necessarily for us to ratify, but to hear. The audiences being addressed by the two reports are quite different. We'll begin with Sam Becker who reports for the group that addressed itself particularly to the second conference. Then we can turn to the "address to the cosmos."

BECKER: I would remind you of our task which was to bring some topics, questions, problems which we thought might be fruitful for the group of twenty-four to discuss at the second conference. We didn't all agree on all of these but they were things that were at least mentioned.

First of all, it was suggested that it might be important to spend some time trying to identify areas in which classical (if you'll excuse this term) analysis can make a contribution and areas in which other kinds of conceptions are needed for rhetorical studies. We thought it might be worth while for the second conference to discuss the relationship between the work of the rhetorician and the communicaton scientist or behavioral scientist: whether at some points in time they are engaged in the same business or engaged in research which has the same end. We thought it important that in their research, scholars in rhetoric be concerned with how one gets from research to practice either for rhetoricians in other departments, for educated persons in other walks of life, or for our undergraduate students: how the research gets into courses, into textbooks, into other kinds of educational resources. What are the kinds of research (or should we be worrying about the kinds of research?) which can have impact, which do lead to something to say to the undergraduate, which can help bring about educational reform of some kind.

It seemed to us that the second conference might well talk about the immediate implications of these questions for the scholar of rhetoric. For example, someone here mentioned that there is a growing tendency in American society to accept conflict as a normal condition. Well, what kinds of research questions does that tendency imply?

When one thinks about non-verbal as well as verbal discourse, what are the implications of this for research, both for methodology and the kinds of questions one might ask?

Serious thought ought to be given to the development of rigor in critical and historical studies. One might ask, in what senses ought the rhetorician to think about rigor and what ought he to do about it?

We wondered what the differences are in method and approach for rhetorician-as-critic and rhetorician-as-historian. The question was raised, why are students turning away from historical studies? has it something to do with the kinds of history we're doing? There was some concern that people teaching in departments that are concerned with rhetoric ought to think about the relevance of the history of rhetorical discourse (I guess what is often called public address) and the relevance of the history of rhetorical theory to young scholars and other students today. Much of the history of rhetorical discourse is relevant, much of the history of rhetorical theory is relevant, but not always as it is taught or studied in our departments.

It was recognized that an increasing number of rhetoricians are going to want to deal with the data that we get from rhetorical situations in the present day, that is to say, from contemporary situations. We think that timeliness is a good thing, but we ought to reflect on what questions we should be asking of these kinds of data. We need to pursue questions that have some long range value as opposed to questions the answers to which might get into *Time* Magazine. There is a difference in looking at discourse of the past and the present. In dealing with the past, simple description is a scholarly and creative task, but in looking at discourse of the present, description is simply journalism. So what is it that rhetoricians ought to be doing with contemporary discourse in addition to description? What kinds of questions would be relevant in this larger sense?

It was also mentioned as a topic for discussion that research on contemporary problems is not a substitute for some other kind of research. Sometimes people talk about *other* directions for research, but I think at least some of us prefer talking about *additional* directions for research. The question for discussion and thought is how to make history and the theory of rhetoric pertinent to the problems with which students and scholars today are interested.

Another good topic for discussion at the next conference would be the value of studying the primitives: primitive rhetorical theory and such primitive kinds of discourse as children's talk, or breakfast table conversations. Then too there the question of how to grasp and use such materials for the answering of rhetorically interesting questions.

Another question that was raised and that we thought ought to be discussed is, how is logic to be conceived in relation to the rhetorical animal? What is the relationship between rhetorical logic and analytic logic, and what are the implications of this for rhetorical studies? What scruples govern the coming to a belief? Ought we to develop taxonomies and rule systems for describing rational patterns and rhetorical interactions?

We thought that some attention should be given to the uses of various media, various modes of communication, both as tools for study and as objects of study. And to show that we have read McLuhan, we probably ought to consider the nonlinear as well as linear forms and modes of communication. It seemed to us that out of this jumble, there are some questions that could be fruitfully discussed at this next conference. Have my colleagues anything to add or amplify?

BASKERVILLE: No, I think that was a very nice job of making sense out of two hour's talk.

ARNOLD: And often quite heated talk.

CORBETT: That was a fine summary.

ARNOLD: I can think of only one thing to add relative to that last question. It is the problem of how we shall even think about the rhetorical process if we adopt some of the phenomenological and existential observations about the nature of rhetorical "logic" and the mode and methods of observing it. That's where our heat and excitement developed in discussion. So I think this is certainly an especially important issue. It was reported as just one item in the agenda but it occupied our whole last hour of discussion, and it could be the most fruitful of questions.

If there's no further discussion of this report, I turn to Professor Mc-Keon who speaks for the other group addressing the outer audience or the more universal one.

McKEON: Since the difference between the two reports is the difference in the audience addressed, I think it is significant that many of the things that our group discussed appeared also in the Becker report. This proves that departments of speech are with the rest of the cosmos.

We began, since this is a rhetorical approach, by trying to determine whom we were addressing, how, and why. We had been told by our chairmen that we were to talk about that little group of unhappy people who are committed to rhetoric and have no one to talk to. We decided however that they were only part of our audience, that we ought to speak not only to those who knew they were touching on rhetoric and didn't have a means of communicating about it, but also to those, inside and outside of the university, who ought to be doing rhetoric and therefore ought to be concerned about it.

We thought it would be a good idea for someone who knew something about rhetoric to examine some of the texts in which rhetoric was employed: textbooks among them, but also more fundamental research in fields in which communication was employed. For example, Levi-Strauss uses "communications" a great deal and it would be a very good idea to have someone survey the sociological uses of rhetoric.

In the field of law, courses in evidence and pleading are rhetorical. We spoke a little about Wigmore's six volumes on evidence, which are a masterpiece, but we could learn and maybe lawyers too could learn from analyzing this work. I won't go through the list further, but our first main heading would be the examination of texts in which communication, rhetoric, or any equivalents, are already present to a considerable extent.

We secondly thought that we ought to move from the texts—the things already said—to research. What can rhetoric contribute to the guiding of research in other fields especially with respect to the examination of the individual, the examination of society, the examination of the circumstances of times and transactions, the examination of processes? A good deal of what we have been talking about the last two days suggests laying out topics. We kept saying that we were not indicating research programs, but rather rhetorical topics that might suggest lines of research in subject matters, the lines being different from those that are pursued by the experts in the field and being the contribution of rhetoric to these other disciplines.

We thought there was a third field in addition to the use of rhetoric on actual texts and the use of rhetoric in planning new research which would eventually become texts that we could analyze at first hand. This was in the field of teaching. What is it that one would do with teaching?

This inquiry likewise could be generalized so as to have a topical reference that would become particular in each of the departments. It seemed to us, after considering for some time problems of teaching English composition, that there are problems which have had a long history. This history includes teaching the forms of correct composition, which is the way I got it. It includes courses in which you try to stimulate the young writer to bear in mind the examples of various models. But we thought that the rhetorical emphasis would come rather in that reflexive interrelation that we have been talking about so much. The experiments in which the student writes for the student, the student rates his fellow student's compositions, seem to us an incomplete approximation to this. We thought it could be accomplished in a way in which content, form, and the normative would all emerge without being reduced to a simple question of the community serving as judge.

We went on to a fourth level. We had a feeling that in addition to the rhetorical problems of texts that needed interpreting, of problems that needed schematizing for research, of the presentation of education in a form in which it is not a "pouring in" but a "rendering active of the students," there was a special place for creativity: a creativity viewed now within the rhetorical line that we have set up.

Our fifth subject matter was the problem of the educational institution itself, particularly its rhetorical facets. How does one talk to students? How does one perceive the problems that are presented to students? Is there a mode by which the rhetorical approach would take into account what is legitimate in the opposition to the institution, the anti-institutionalism? We thought that much of what we have been saying the last few days has bearing on such questions. But if the assumption is made that what students are saying has a ground—that an asserted fact is a fact and therefore would enter into discussion—in the process of discussion it should be possible to reorient the entire approach to disputes within the universities.

These were our five material heads. We thought then that we ought to turn around and talk about what our rhetorical techniques would be. It would be here that the consideration of communication would come in. What is communication? What are the modes of communication when we bring in the rhetorical element? We thought that a good deal of what we said about the function of criticism—rhetorical criticism—would be the new dimension in the treatment of communication and expression. We thought that the consideration of values or utilities should take the form not of supposing that we can convey values, but of dealing with the way in which argument might lead to the examination and opening up of values. And just as in communication we would not be talking about facts or alleged facts, but the hypotheses that we were working on, so too in the discussion of values, we'd be talking about argument. I think as we went on in the committee, we wanted a broader term. "Discourse" is the good rhetorical term. Discourse would include argument or any other form of sequential narrative, and therefore the use of the discursive analysis would be our supplement to the critical analysis.

Another concern was the very important process of making topics. Even in our talk today, even in some of our papers, the topics were dead topics. They were repeated clichés rather than new arguments. Consequently, we should indicate the need for research in topics that would give an instrumentality for creativity, innovation, and invention.

Our next consideration was of principles. We've gotten into the habit of talking about principles in the nineteenth-century fashion as if they were axioms. Principles are more than that. They are the beginnings. They are the beginnings which stimulate you to activity and a process. They are the beginnings therefore which set up community. They are the beginnings which set the individual into relation with the community. Therefore, moving back from our mathematical axiomatic conception of principles or from our common sense conception of principles in which we say, "In principle I agree with you" (and that usually means we don't agree at all), we could have this rhetorical sense of principle.

Several of the members of the committee said, "We are awfully schematized here. It looks almost as if we're handing out prescriptions. Why don't we compile a series of random suggestions, suggestions through which the inquirer, or the person reading the results of the inquiry, will be betrayed into rhetoric?" These, then, are some of the random suggestions: The Study of Communication among Equals; The New Left: Its Roots, Its Consequences, Its Development; The Ethics of Rhetoric; The Ontological Bases of Rhetoric; The Phenomenology of Rhetoric; Rhetoric and Logic; Rhetoric and Dialectic; Rhetoric and Philosophical Argumentation; Philosophy and Eloquence; Thought and Action; Rhetoric as the Basis of the Liberal Arts; Rhetoric as a Science or as a Humanity; Rhetoric and Legal Procedures; Social Institutions and Structures as Providing a Framework for Communication; Meditation, Speculation and Contemplation in their Rhetorical Aspect; The Rhetoric of Communication with God; How Conflict is Resolved without Violence; What Critical Thought Is; The Rhetoric of Internal Address: The Rhetoric of Internal Deliberation as Opposed to Public Discussion.

What of figures of speech? There was a period in which the Romans had figures of thought; there are at present figures of things.

We thought also of images because an image is what you perceive with the eye. An image is a reflection that you see in the mirror. An image is a figure of speech. An image, we usually think today, is a symbol of status.

We spent some time on history in rhetoric and we decided that it is not merely a question of how much history of rhetoric one considers, but how history is transformed from the rhetorical approach. It is obviously the case that any past event has to be rewritten in every age. We have to redo the Peloponnesian War; it's been done twenty times since Thucydides and it is what has happened since that makes revision possible. If from this large sense of history (and this would be our contribution to the History Department) we move to the history of rhetoric, we see that nineteenth century histories of rhetoric are not good today largely because they do not examine the right things. If someone would go back and reconsider what the Greeks and the Romans did, reconsider the rich rhetoric of the middle ages in terms of problems that we now recognize, this would make the relevance of history to rhetoric greater.

Since we are advocating a normative rhetoric, we thought that there ought to be a consideration of rhetoric as degradations—let's say rhetoric and sophistics, or rhetoric and rhetorics. We thought that once we got into that line, there ought to be an inquiry into rhetoric and dogmatics; and once you got dogmatics, rhetoric and heresies. Etymologically heresy is a very curious thing. A heresy is merely a group that comes together because they are in agreement about a doctrine, and therefore the heretics originally were people who joined together as we have here. And then Christianity came along, and within the confines of this heresy, sub-groups were formed. Since they were deviations from the true doctrine, they were the groups that were formed by adherence to the false doctrines and as a result we think of heretics as being completely wrong. We ought to get a new apologetics for the new heretics.

We thought that testimony ought to be examined, testimony not only in the psychological sense but testimony in the legal sense. And from testimony in the legal sense, what it is that one is a witness to. Consider the martyrs. A martyr was a witness and he was a witness to his faith. That's what martyr means. But what about our witnesses today who stand up, our Kennedys who are obviously making testimony? The important thing is not what they say or what they seem to say, but what they are standing up for. We thought that once we got testimony going, we ought to examine confrontation—a word which has a wide meaning. And if we got confrontation going, we ought to examine distance. Rhetorical distance was an important concept; psychic distance was an important concept, and we're so busy confronting each other, we've forgotten how to get away from each other. This then is the report that we make.

ARNOLD: Are there other members of this group who have comments they would like to make?

JOHNSTONE: I would like to say that is really a masterful presentation of our deliberations and if the presentation is itself rhetorical then we ought to have more rhetoric.

BRYANT: I will say I recognize most of it and admire all of it.

ARNOLD: I am impressed by the degree to which, in two different rooms, we got to the same issues. I have an idea that in both the presentation to the second conference and in the volume this drive toward synthesis of basic considerations which occurred when we were together and when we were apart, ought to be pointed out. It seems to me this testifies to something about the views of this particular conference.

BOOTH: I certainly share the euphoria about this sense of how much we've learned and how much we can do. I do think there is a real danger of imperialism that's likely to result from such euphoria. The twentieth century has seen many panaceas develop and claim for themselves the ability to solve all problems. I think it is in the very spirit of the rhetoric that we have been talking about that we do not do that—that we go out to learn as well as to share what we have. We must be wily as serpents, in a sense, in not saying, "Now here I have rhetoric, and I would like to give it to you." If you do that, you do not have it and you are not doing it. We have to assume that there are many people who are doing a lot of things that we can learn from, and all of us could do better if we were to share what we know.

BROCKREIDE: I think perhaps there is a parallel warning that there is some distance between enumerating the kinds of things that ought to be done and having the energy and creativity to do some of these things ourselves.

BITZER: On behalf of the committee, I want to say thank you to each one of you. The heartening thing throughout this task, since I first wrote invitations to all of you, was the enthusiasm with which you took the charge. The charge was a fantastic one, as Professor McKeon reminded me in the note with which he accepted it. He said it could not be done, but he would do it anyway. You did it with enthusiasm and you did it expertly and we are grateful for your time and your energy and your enthusiasm and your good sense: all of it.

ARNOLD: Another record will be set. This Wingspread conference ended seven minutes early. Thank you all.

PART THREE

NATIONAL
CONFERENCE
ON RHETORIC

St. Charles, Illinois
May 10–15, 1970

13 / OPENING REMARKS TO THE CONFERENCE

DONALD C. BRYANT
President
Speech Communication Association

After officially welcoming the Conference
on behalf of the Speech Communication
Association and wishing it well in its
deliberations, Bryant continued with the
following general remarks:

In the 1920's and 1930's what was needed in the scholarship of public communication was exploration of the potential of a revived Aristotelianism—or at least classicism—in rhetorical studies: redevelopment, after a century or so of obscurity, of interest in the implications of a rhetoric of public address in addition to the familiar rhetoric of poetry—of literature. The new rhetorical studies throve here and there throughout American Academia—at Cornell and Iowa, for example, at Wisconsin and Michigan. A need was satisfied, and a new scholarly venture was created, the monuments of which, though not so numerous as those produced in the older studies, are subjects of rightful pride in our profession. You are familiar with them. I grew up among them.

Along with that development (for our professions have always been first of all teaching professions and only secondarily research professions) new textbooks for the teaching of public speaking were being written on new principles, contemporary psychological principles, just as Winans' and Woolbert's forebears Campbell, Blair, Kames, Priestly, and others had done in the eighteenth century. Only this time it was not the refurbished faculty psychology of Christian Woolf or Hartleyan associationism, but the pragmatic psychology of William James, or Watsonian behaviorism, or Gestalt theory.

Historical-rhetorical studies and scientific psychological borrowing and adaptation in the explication and teaching of communication managed to get along well together, and with psychological-neurological studies in speech correction as well. Perhaps that was because the practitioners were young and innocent or were all outcasts together, but I don't think so. I think that a more fundamental reason for what I remember as mutual support (though it may have been only mutual disregard) is that scientist-pedagogue and historian-critic were both *generating* (and sometimes in the same person) new views of the study of verbal, especially oral, communication, and new insights into the contemporary processes and the historical phenomena.

But new views and new insights become "weary, stale, flat, and unprofitable"—that is, sterile and stereotyped—at a faster and faster pace as time goes on, and methods and modes of approach to the problems of scholarship and teaching tend quickly to turn ritualistic or mechanical through unventuresome, unimaginative use. "Generation" slows up or stops.

During the 1950's and 1960's we have seen widespread weariness and disillusionment (which you may suppose that I do not altogether share) with familiar sorts of rhetorical studies and customary practices in maneuvering students toward intelligent, sensible, orderly, unrepulsive (I am not rash enough to suggest *graceful*) public articulateness. A widespread reaction to the limitations and misapprehensions of customary studies, was enthusiastic resort to immature if not premature behavioral science. The new Aristotelian rhetoric of the 20's and 30's and the new psychological pedagogy of that time, had now to be replaced—both of them—in the opinions of some of our most advanced young thinkers, by behavioral science in communication. Good. "On to Richmond," or whatever the proper saying in this context may be. But let us remember that ritual is ritual, sterility is sterility. Change is opportunity for improvement, but no guarantee of it.

I am no ecumenicist, no notable arbitrator, as everyone knows, or harmonizer of differences, but I would hark back now to what I mentioned lightly in my introduction—the frequent assumption that rhetoric as a scholarly study is preoccupied with hanging onto a fortunately receding past and that behavioral science in communication is the wave of the future.

One would be silly to make believe that there is not a kind of warfare of new and old, of ancient and modern, of "science and religion," among the students of speech communication. When have there not been some good, stimulating quarrels? In my youth they were there; but as I recall, the issues were not whether speech scientists or humanists rode the wave of the future, but whether the future of speech education or scholarship should belong to Wisconsin or Cornell, to LSU or OSU, to Densmore or Mabie. Now the disagreements are more consequential and more serious and call for some mutual illumination among the specialists of both sorts. Something of the sort can be stimulated without anyone's loss of integrity, for example, in the new division of Rhetorical and Communication Theory in the SCA, and in our national conferences on research and development, past, present, and to come.

The Behavioral Conference in New Orleans in 1968, and this Rhetorical Developmental Conference, are major achievements in the professions of speech communication. They were necessities, it seems to me, in our professional progress. Each grows out of the past both positively and negatively, and each looks to the future, the rhetoricians with a little more sense of history and regard for it than the scientists—naturally. The imminent conference on speech development is a similar necessity.

I was about to say that behavioral science in speech had been lustily crying to be born and was weaned at New Orleans, and that rhetoric is being reborn in the aviaries at Wingspread and Pheasant Run. But *birth* won't do for what happened at New Orleans. Too much had been growing vigorously for the previous generation or two. I will keep with the familial metaphor, however, and allege that at New Orleans behavioral science in speech communication made his barmitzvah. Or in the professional jargon he was "legitimized."

That came first, as it should, priority going properly to youth. Now rhetoric is striving for renewal, and I think it will make it. I cannot predict the colors of the plumage which will emerge from Pheasant Run. Nevertheless, the new rhetoric of the seventies, I am sure, will exhibit fresh, contemporary features of countenance and modes of behavior learned from consorting with behavioral science, philosophy, linguistics, and its other friends and neighbors. Its genealogy will still be recognizable, however, and it will not be ashamed of either its ancestors or its new companions.

One of my students last semester produced quite unpretentiously a combined behavioral-rhetorical study which should not have seemed unusual, but it did. In approaching the study of a speech by Enoch Powell, the conservative, anti-black British member of Parliament, she drew from social-behavioral theory principles which could generate hypotheses about what she would be likely to find in a speech presented in such circumstances as Powell was encountering. She then examined the speech much as any rhetorical student would. The difference was that she was asking old questions in a contemporary idiom and in a productive conceptual system which could yield fresh insights. When she found that several of her hypotheses were confirmed, but that one was not, she was stimulated to reexamine the situation to determine what there may have been in the circumstances to account for the failure to confirm the hypothesis. There is nothing amazing about the incident except that it happened—that a good student of rhetoric was impelled to use concepts and methods from behavioral science as part of her critical equipment.

In the same course in public address, one of the best equipped of the behavioral scientists, who is also as learned in rhetoric as most of his colleagues in public address, developed for his major paper of the semester a reformulation, or at least an enlarged interpretation, of certain behavioral principles by bringing to bear historical evidence from the speaking of O'Connell, Cobden, and Bright.

Most of you could cite other examples, which are not so frequent as they can be.

It is no doubt obvious by now that I find no *necessary* conflict between rhetoric and behavioral science nor any *inherent* superiority of the one over the other. In that opinion I know that I depart from some of the professionals in each.

Looked at one way, a way often adopted by humanist-rhetoricians in the past such as Everett Hunt and Hoyt Hudson, rhetoric should be seen as the comprehensive study which shows how the principles established or discovered by the behavioral scientist, as well as those from the social scientist, the historian, the moralist, the ethicist, the literary historian and critic, and the philosopher, may be organized and employed so as to best describe and account for the phenomena and the functioning of the suasory-instructional in discourse. In this sense of rhetoric, behavioral science, like logic, is one of the allies, not competitors of rhetoric. Some behavioral scientists in communication, however, seem to think that *they* investigate, describe, and account for communicative discourse by sound methods in realistic, contemporary terms, whereas rhetoricians look at wrong or fictitious phenomena in antiquated frames of reference with obsolete lenses. Such a position, of course, makes behavioral science in communication a competitor or a necessary substitute for an antique rhetoric.

Touches of presumption, or defensive enthusiasm, in practitioners, however, can easily create barriers between studies where none need arise. The ends of science are theories accounting for phenomena and generating predictions. The ends of behavioral science in communication include theories generating predictions about the functioning of discourse. The behavioral scientist investigates, whenever possible under controlled conditions, the variables which act and interact among source, message, receiver, and context in the communicative situation and process. He seeks knowledge, verifiable knowledge, yielding terms and concepts with which to describe and to account for the phenomena of verbal communication. As scientist he avoids value-judgments.

If these are his achievements—and I am open to correction from my learned young friends, the new men with old backgrounds—then he contributes essentially to the technology, the methodology, the philosophy of rhetoric. And if I am right, the rhetorician has contributed and does contribute to the scientist's view of what he investigates and why it is worth his attention.

If there is or may be verifiable knowledge of human behavior, of the nature and principles of discourse, and of the functioning of discourse in its characteristic contexts and situations; and if from that knowledge may be generated theories or systems of thought which enable us to describe and account for suasory discourse and discourses and to understand them in their relations to the dynamics of society; and if for the moment we may call such systems *rhetoric* (as some very bright men at Wingspread, including a couple of behavioral scientists, were inclined to do); then behavioral science in communication is a member of the rhetorical complex, the partner with the many studies which contribute the knowledge essential in the equipment of the complete rhetorician, or better the theorist-critic of communications.

Finally, before receding into the silence enjoined upon observers by the laws of this conference, may I conclude with a small item of wisdom given me this week by an estimable colleague, Donald K. Darnell. He called it "Thoughts While Walking to Work":

> The next to worst reason for doing anything or doing something in a particular way is, "It's traditional."

> The worst possible justification is, "It's *not* traditional."

> The best justification is a combination of these, "It's novel (so we may learn something from it), and it has logical roots in past experience (so it entails minimal risk)."

14 / REFLECTIONS ON THE WINGSPREAD CONFERENCE

CARROLL C. ARNOLD

My assignment is not to summarize the Wingspread Conference. Materials from that meeting are in your hands. What I shall undertake is to verbalize some major thoughts and presuppositions that emerged during the Wingspread discussions but which, for one reason or another, are not obvious in the records of the conference.

The ideas I am going to discuss were seldom tightly focused on in January and some—especially the presuppositions—were verbalized only briefly or indirectly.

One idea that importantly colored discussions at the Wingspread Conference Center was the conception that "rhetorical studies" and "rhetorical concepts" touch human experience along a far broader intellectual front than traditional rhetorical theory implies. But this thought was not simplistically held. Of course, the conferees recognized that as media for influential communication multiply, rhetoricians must raise their eyes from printed pages and platforms. And, of course, participants saw that the role of nonverbal behavior as influence is unquestionable, hence rhetoricians need to give nonverbal stimuli more attention than heretofore. But the perceptions of the discussants at Wingspread were more penetrating than this. Becker's paper, for example, suggested that the *totality* of people's exposures to information and suasion is a "unit" of rhetoric requiring holistic exploration such as it has not received. Things said in Wayne Booth's paper, and at the end of Richard McKeon's essay, further extended the boundaries of what the conference chose to include within its concept of "rhetoric." Education, itself, was seen as rhetorical experience deserving rhetorical analysis, especially in the humanities and social studies. To this already panoramic view of what rhetoric is and where it occurs, Chaim Perelman added that the very means by which a culture's or a profession's heritage gets handed along to successive generations are *rhetorical* means, whether what is being handed on be law, sociology, historical interpretation, or some other set of ideas. McKeon spoke for all his colleagues, I think, when he asserted that *anytime an affirmation is challenged, that action is rhetorical action* and becomes a legitimate object for rhetorical study. In other words, whenever and wherever claims occur and those claims either are or might be challenged a situation exists which can be fully explained only if *rhetorical* explanation is provided along with any other explanations that may be germane.

I am trying to emphasize that the conferees at Wingspread had in mind a much more sweeping reconceptualization of "the rhetorical" than is conveyed by their specific references to the importance of studying the effects of media and of nonverbal communication. It seemed to me, as an observer, that these scholars were saying that *any* discriminable human experience in which suasion *or the semblance of* suasion occurs is a "unit" of "rhetoric" deserving intensive study by rhetoricians. For these discussants, one does not decide what is rhetorical by looking at the *form* of communication; attempted influence with practical goals in view is rhetorical, no matter what the *form*.

Whether you, at Pheasant Run, will want to accept and recommend upon this sweepingly inclusive vision of what is "rhetorical" awaits your own decision. I only report that this inclusive view of rhetoric was treated by the interdisciplinary conference in Racine as a self-evident definition of what "rhetorical studies" ought properly to treat. Surely their conception will need some consideration by your committee on the scope and place of rhetorical studies in higher education.

Perhaps because they saw rhetorical concerns so broadly, members of the conference at Wingspread were at pains to emphasize that rhetorical scholars need to address themselves energetically to the tasks of conceptualizing rhetorical transactions more precisely and with more philosophical penetration than has been customary. Though their consideration of this matter was discursive, there did evolve across the hours of discussion a set of headings. I presume you will want to make some career assignments under these headings to all of us when you come to say what needs doing in the next decade in order to refine our conceptions of what rhetorical transactions really are and how they may best be interpreted and criticized.

The group at Wingspread seemed agreed that there is special need for very careful formulations describing the relations that rhetors have to audiences and *vice versa*. Among the specific analytical tasks they pointed to were the following:

1. We need clearer explanations of how relations of rhetors and audiences develop and alter through time, for rhetoric *creates* relationships as well as uses them.
2. We need clearer explanations of how relations of rhetors and audiences are constrained by participants' conceptions of subjects and the ways those conceptions change within rhetors and respondents as communication goes on—and afterward.
3. We need more precise explanations of how relations of rhetors and audiences are constrained by participants' identifications with reference groups—as those identifications are perceived by rhetors, by auditors, and as they are projected by one party upon the other.
4. We need fuller explanations of how relations of rhetors and audiences are or may be predetermined by nonadaptive choices which rhetors make as they instigate.
5. We need explanations of how relations of rhetors and audiences are predetermined by the ideational and the linguistic possibilities that inhere in specific subject matters and in the kinds of transactions that are allowable in respect to those subjects.
6. We need more precise explanations of how relations of rhetors and audiences are determined by the general social conditions under which rhetorical transactions occur.

In general, I understand these observations to be calls for philosophical analyses of the myriad relational possibilities that may exist within any class of rhetorical transactions. The issues as discussed were not empirical but philosophical ones. As Henry W. Johnstone, Jr. put it at one point: Rhetorical acts are not sociologically studiable—*as acts*; the acts that transpire must be analyzed philosophically, though the parties to specific rhetorical transactions may be understood sociologically, or psychologically, or both.

I do not think this call for more comprehensive philosophical descriptions of rhetorical transactions needed to be as anti-psychological as discussion at Wingspread sometimes made it seem. What was not said, but might have been, is that before we can empirically describe rhetorical transactions as processes, we must have proved we can conceptualize them as possibilities. In asserting this by implication, most of the Wingspread conferees were making an assignment fairly new to the field of speech. Sociological and psychological study of communicators and audiences is familiar to us, but philosophical analyses of the dimensions of rhetorical acts have only recently begun among us, and have scarcely begun at all in the academic fields of English and the social sciences.

In what I have been saying I have used the phrase "rhetorical transaction" several times. The choice was deliberate, for all who attended the first conference envisaged rhetorical events as dynamic, interactive, constantly changeful predicaments experienced reciprocally by rhetors and respondents. If there was an orthodox stimulus-response adherent at Racine, he held his peace while his psychological conceptions were consigned to the limbo of outmoded ideas. In this conference it was taken as given that rhetorical events are dynamic *transactions*, for the full explication of which we require a fuller accounting than our philosophies of rhetoric and our theories of communication can yet give. Behind all that was said, by the critically, philosophically, or scientifically minded, there seemed to stand a conviction that the relationship of "speaker and audience," so central to traditional rhetorical theory, has to date been superficially conceived by all of us. This conviction was expressed with special sharpness in discussions of the subgroup assigned to address *your* conference directly. There it was generally agreed that of all rhetorical studies in speech and English, the so-called historical-critical studies have been least sophisticated. For the most part, they have not penetrated the dynamism of rhetorical interactions but have explored artifacts without seeking to use historical and critical data to reconstruct the interplays of human experience that were. In a similar vein the same subgroup complained that our course programs in the literature of rhetorical address and in rhetorical theory too often enthrone history and biography while consigning criticism and theory to the intellectual pantry. There was no view in all of this that historical-critical studies are without merit. The judgment was that studies of public address and rhetoric too often presuppose straight, stimulus-response relations between rhetors and respondents and that courses in rhetorical theory are too often courses in history but not in rhetoric. Either failing, it was charged, ignores the intricacies of the transactions that all oral rhetorical engagements are. In a different session, where like themes came under scrutiny, Professor McKeon made the same point in another of his excellent, summative statements: "The 'speaker-audience' is not *one* but *many* relations—as perceptions." That statement epitomized the view of the Wingspread Conference: rhetorical events are *actions*; when communicative, they are *trans*actions. To understand them, we must move beyond simple stimulus-response psychology and communication models derived from the circuitry of thermostats. I believe these judgments—their truth and their implications—deserve the serious consideration of each of your committees.

Another presupposition, used but never verbalized in my hearing at Wingspread, was that we are continually dealing with some sort of reasonableness or rationality when we deal with symbolic interactions properly called rhetorical. Virtually all that was said presupposed that there exists, somewhere, an answer to the question: "How shall we conceptualize 'reason' when we are thinking of the processes associated with rhetorical transactions?" The subgroup assigned to address *you*, directly, had time to direct your attention to but one of the intellectual issues connected with this question. They ask you to consider what implications there are for our research and pedagogy in modern phenomenological and existential conceptions of analysis and evaluation. It seems to me their specific request drives you back to the more fundamental question: how shall we conceive of "reason" and "rationality" in studying communication about matters not decidable on a fact-nonfact basis? Indeed, the more I reflect on what I heard at Wingspread, the more I believe that without ever verbalizing it, this is the root question the "Wingspread Dozen" dropped into your laps: what *is* the "reason," the "rationality," that makes a challenge-situation a "rhetorical transaction" and not a squabble of alley cats? That some factor distinguishes a cat fight from a "rhetorical transaction" was assumed at Wingspread. I do not see how, at Pheasant Run, you are to direct the course of rhetorical studies for the next decade or so without explicating in some degree what "rationale" it is that constrains interaction when it may be plausibly called "rhetorical" rather than "martial." I do not suppose you can settle that matter, but some tentative settlement must surely be implicit in meaningful statements about the scope of rhetoric and the natures of rhetorical invention and criticism.

The distinction between the rational and the not-rational seems crucial because of a fifth, and to me most intriguing, idea developed at Wingspread. The idea was succinctly but somewhat cryptically expressed in the phrase, "Rhetoric is *method*, not merely form and strategy." It was argued that the term "rhetoric" ought not designate just the collection of verbal forms a rhetoric textbook might discuss nor just the strategies of attempted influence a theory of rhetoric might explain—though both of those bodies of ideas are pertinent to "rhetoric." The conferees asserted that, for them, "rhetoric" referred also to *a way of looking at*—a way of interpreting—issues and meanings. It was said that when subjects, data, and their meanings can be interpreted as assented to simply by distinguishing facts from nonfacts the "method of rhetoric" is inapplicable, but issues on which meaning can*not* be determined by fact-nonfact judgments are precisely those on which decisions can be reached only through rhetorical considerations of the *choices* available to men.

You will have noticed that Booth's, McKeon's, Perelman's, Johnstone's and Duncan's papers all assert or imply that much—perhaps most —humanistic and social thinking addresses problems that are *not* open to fact-nonfact determination. These men argue that problems of these kinds must be settled either by force or by conviction through rhetoric; "proof," except in a rhetorical sense, is impossible.

Operating on these premises, a subgroup at Wingspread asked, "what would happen if we were to recognize throughout education—as we seldom do now—that in humanistic and social studies fact-nonfact judgments simply cannot yield final *determinations* for critical questions?" The question was truly rhetorical, for the assumed answer was: "Education might become more honest and disillusionment less common." No one disputed the implied proposition that rendering education "relevant" to "real life" requires the revolutionary step of treating vast areas of thought rhetorically rather than "mathematically" or "scientifically."

The claim that major areas of education require to be seen as inherently dominated by "the rhetorical method" was further enriched by Hugh Duncan's assertion that any rhetorical model appropriate to a democracy must be a *"conflict* model." Duncan argued that, to be democratic, institutions must not only systematically conserve and facilitate, *but also contain conflict.* Elimination of rhetorical conflict would prove an anti-democratic action, he contended. His colleagues seemed to agree, and they interpreted what they called the "open prospect" of "rhetorical method" as the only view of decision-making that acknowledges *both* the propriety of conflict and the necessity of its regulation. It is because your precursors thought in these ways that one of their subgroups asked you directly whether our pedagogies ought not be altered to emphasize to students that their social and rhetorical presuppositions must allow for the proposition that orderly facilitation of conflict is a higher democratic value than "balance" or "equilibrium."

Epitomized, the "Message from Wingspread" runs something like this, I believe. To be comprehensive, rhetorical studies must treat the influential roles of untraditional media and of nonverbal communication. To be incisive, rhetorical studies must probe the various aspects of rhetorical transactions philosophically as well as historically, psychologically, and sociologically. To be penetrating, rhetorical studies must probe rhetorical transactions phenomenologically and existentially, as well as traditionally. To be clear, rhetorical studies must stipulate better than they have how "reason" and the "rational" are understood to exist and function in communications aiming at influencing human choice. Withal, rhetorical studies ought not abandon any linguistic, historical, or analytical prescience developed through past inquiry and experience.

How these tasks may be begun, or even accomplished, during the coming decade or so, it is given to you to suggest. The "Wingspread Dozen" had only to propose; you are asked to dispose—melding their thoughts with your own and recommending to all of us what we need most to learn, what we need most to teach, and what deserve to be our most favored methods—into the 1980's.

15 / MORE REFLECTIONS ON THE WINGSPREAD CONFERENCE

LLOYD F. BITZER

This National Developmental Project on Rhetoric, the first of its kind, has the mission of pointing toward a conception of rhetoric needed in our time. Our task is to pave the way toward this new rhetoric by outlining the needed framework of ideas, research priorities, and educational policies and practices. The Wingspread essays and reports provided rich lines of thought toward a vital conception of rhetoric; thus our Project is half completed. The second half of the Project is for you to accomplish. In your committee deliberations and in general sessions at this conference, you are asked to prepare reports and recommendations that will give valuable guidance to a wide audience of scholars, teachers, students, and administrators who are concerned with communication studies and, in particular, with rhetorical studies. I should like to discuss some leading ideas and themes from the Wingspread Conference, relating them specifically to the work of your committees.

To the Scope and Education Committee, the message from Wingspread begins with the declaration that *this is a rhetorical age*. What does such a declaration mean?—after all, every age is rhetorical in some sense, because people have always addressed one another in order to inform and persuade. Why is this age particularly rhetorical?

First, today there are totally new communication media, new message forms, new orders of outcomes, new types of audiences, new techniques of information and persuasion. Such powerful instruments never

200

before have rested in the hands of communicators and of those who control agencies of communication. Information, arguments, and images never before have influenced so many people in their beliefs, attitudes, and actions. Message creation, transmission, and presentation have become in our own time major industries involving a massive technology and comprising a basic segment of the economy. The point is surely clear: this age is more rhetorical than any previous one because there is a vast quantitative difference in media, channels, messages, message forms, audiences, publics, communicators, techniques, and outcomes—a difference which has occurred largely in the last twenty-five years.

As rhetoricians, we have a tremendous amount of work to do. What are these new forms, audiences, and techniques? How do they work? What are their principal effects and side effects? When we can answer these questions, we will find it possible to incorporate into educational programs information needed by people who encounter communication elements as speakers or as audiences. We need also to assess the new elements and submit them to exacting criticism using criteria beyond mere efficiency. Moreover, through rigorous criticism, we should assist these new forms and techniques struggling to achieve artistic form. For example, during the past few years we have seen a rhetorical form, the demonstration, struggling to become an effective rhetorical genre. It appears to be needed in these times to give voice to persons who cannot find other effective communication forms, but it frequently fails. It needs study and criticism. Just as deliberative oratory once needed to be rendered artistic, the demonstration needs to be brought under the guidance of artistic principles. I mean that this and other forms should be defined and characterized in terms of purposes, uses, misuses, and, above all, methods.

There is a second reason why this is a rhetorical age. The crucial problems of the next decades will be solved, if at all, either by the assistance of campaigns of discourse or by coercion. The great contemporary problems facing rhetorical practice are plain to people of intelligence and humane sense: eliminating war and instruments of war, and developing world community; solving the problems of hunger and poverty; adjusting world populations to the capabilities of our planet and technology; making urban areas not just habitable but desirable; ending the senseless corruption of the environment; assuring human rights to all. I am tempted also to add—eliminating the misuses of communications. These enormous and perplexing problems will serve as fundamental motives of rhetorical practice. Detailed study of these problems, including the technology and resources needed to solve them; campaigns of discourse calculated to develop new publics willing to authorize change; persuasion of audiences whose decision and action can produce needed change—all of these are required. Rhetoricians looking for important applications of their knowledge and skill must lack normal sensitivity and imagination if they fail to see the opportunity before them—the opportunity to conceive the rhetorical campaigns necessary to push these problems toward solution. I am suggesting that we view rhetoric as a discipline and art whose practical mission is realization of the great aspirations of the human community. In this conception, the methods of rhetoric—methods of invention, analysis, judgment, communication—are applied to the vital subject-matter of our times. Taking seriously such a conception would necessitate some changes: for instance, the subject-matter in our basic rhetoric and public speaking courses might be not methods of speaking and writing, but problems related to environmental quality, to which rhetorical methods would be applied; the topics for investigation in doctoral theses might shift away from tedious studies of source credibility (or another study of Milton) and toward investigations of the ways in which communication can help develop world community. Rhetoric as a study and practice is made vital by its relation to vital subject-matter. The question before you becomes, therefore—what steps must we take to effectively engage rhetoric with this subject-matter?

Mention of these great problems leads to another reason why our age is rhetorical. These, and many similar problems, are essentially rhetorical, not scientific; they require rhetorical analysis and resolution. Rhetorical invention—the methods of analysis, discovery, investigation, and judgment—must be returned to a position of primacy in our theory, criticism, and educational programs. Bacon reduced rhetorical invention to the techniques of recollection and transmission; Campbell, Blair, Whately, Spencer, and Bain—men who strongly influenced nineteenth and twentieth century theories—either subordinated the methods of discovery and judgment to scientific method or omitted them altogether. Rhetoric has been in the shadow of empirical science and psychological studies for two hundred years; it must free itself. Numerous papers and discussions at Wingspread call for new studies of discovery and investigation, a new approach to the theory of positions and topics, new studies of the grounds of belief and modes of argument, a reconsideration of the nature of rationality and rational discourse. To paraphrase a line in McKeon's essay, in these times all men need an art of invention, judgment, and action enabling them to understand contemporary problems, to formulate and evaluate positions, and to engage in intelligent dialogue and action.

Finally, rhetorical methods should be regarded as not essentially linked with speeches or with any kind of public or interpersonal messages. It is true that we have been and should continue to be students of messages, which usually involve method. But we should remember that rhetorical method operates in stages prior to the creation and presentation of a message, and frequently it has operated even when no message was generated or uttered. I mean that methods of analysis, information collection, internal deliberation, meditation, and argumentation occur as parts of the rhetorical process—even when the final stage of message creation and presentation is omitted. We must understand also that conventional messages comprise only one of numerous outcomes of rhetorical method. The use of method may terminate in a decision, or an act, or a work of art. One of Professor McKeon's main points is that rhetoric must be expanded to apply to the innovation and judgment of things or products—the objects which distinguish a technological age. Rhetoric as method thus should assist in determining what new technological products are needed and in judging the utility of the things provided by technology.

I turn now to some ideas related to the work of the Committee on Rhetorical Invention—ideas in addition to those just mentioned. Rhetorical invention obviously does not mean sheer creativity or ingenuity in creating messages. What does it mean? We would be hard put to improve upon the classical meaning. Rhetorical invention is the use of concepts and methods which guide and assist the analysis of subject-matter, problems, and situations; the discovery of issues, grounds of agreement, and lines of argument; the assessment of propositions of several kinds; the topics and value terms guiding thought in various types of investigation. It is concerned with analysis, investigation, and proof.

In dealing with *inventio*, we face very difficult problems. The first arises from the fact that this branch of rhetoric has been largely neglected since the eighteenth century, when theorists such as Blair and Campbell, under the influence of the scientific revolution, dismissed *inventio* as trivial on the assumption that there is a single methodology to be used by sensible people in all kinds of investigations and deliberations, namely the methods of empirical science. Subsequent rhetoricians followed their lead, and consequently we have virtually no continuing scholarship on which to build. We are just beginning serious work in the area of invention— and some of you have done it. But it is probably true that the major work recently has been done by philosophers and theorists of law who are dealing with practical reasoning and argumentation and who, like Perelman, have rediscovered the tradition of rhetorical invention. These writers must be studied.

Secondly, we need to clarify the relations between scientific and rhetorical methods—the methods of scientific investigation and proof and the methods of rhetorical investigation and proof. The naive view of eighteenth and nineteenth century rhetoricians and theorists of other disciplines that scientific method is all-sufficient has been widely rejected. The methods of inquiry that are relevant and decisive in handling a problem in experimental physics are not equally relevant and decisive in deliberating whether to commit troops to Cambodia. The fields differ, and the methods must differ. Rhetorical matters, the Romans said, turn upon questions of conjectural fact, upon definitions and hierarchies of conceptions, and upon qualities and values. It is not at all clear to me how to define and characterize a contemporary theory of rhetorical invention, but I am confident it must be autonomous; that is, it must not be reduced to scientific method, or to a branch of psychological studies, or to any other science.

A third perplexing matter is the current dramatic cultural change and diversity. It was one thing to devise a theory of invention for ancient Athens, where the public was very small—a city-state, a community having stability of beliefs and values. Today there are multiple communities marked by swiftly changing populations, conventions, beliefs, and values, but trying to talk with one another and needing desperately to join in wider and more fulfilling communities. Amid such diversity and change, can a theory of invention be devised? Can legitimate grounds of judgment and action be discovered or generated? Can community be formed? Is it true that a workable theory of invention depends on the existence of community? Are we witnessing the breakdown of traditional communities and the transition to something very new—perhaps a universal public, a universal audience? How do the traditions and practices of a particular community or people affect our theory of invention? What do we know about *inventio* in different, particularly nonwestern cultures?

Perhaps the most difficult task is that of elaborating sound procedures of investigation and proof—the methods of certifying positions, of judging that something is true, valuable, proper. What logic of belief and action is suited to the arena of public deliberation and practical action, the arena in which feelings, values, and notions of propriety enter proofs as crucial elements? Do we need a new and expanded conception of rationality which includes feelings, values, and conceptions of good and evil —elements frequently excluded from rational deliberation and proof by rationalistic philosophies and empirical science?

Finally, if we suppose sound answers to these and similar questions and if we suppose success in working out a general theory of rhetorical invention, there remains the problem of giving it a broad application in practical affairs in our culture. How can a new logic of belief and action come to play a vital part in public decision? This depends very heavily on general education. Once a crucial part of liberal education, rhetoric was weakened in the eighteenth and nineteenth centuries when most of its inventional and argumentative procedures were diminished in significance or lost. As a result, there now exists virtually no rhetorical tradition in public education in the United States. Probably every high school graduate has received some systematic training in mathematics, in some set of sciences, and in the concepts and procedures of scientific reasoning. But the types of reasoning necessary in public dialogue and decision, as well as practice in debate and advocacy, are quite incidental. At the college level, courses in English composition tend to emphasize poetry and the literary aspects of prose composition, while in departments of speech the basic courses do not always teach rhetoric or rhetorical invention even when these terms are advertised in course descriptions. I would suggest that the problem of giving a theory of rhetoric, and particularly invention, broad application in our culture is associated with what we may presume to be flaws in educational practice and policy, including the conception of liberal education.

Numerous ideas relating to the work of the Committee on Rhetorical Criticism have been discussed already. I would like to call attention to four particularly important matters.

First, should criticism continue to deal with traditionally conceived messages and contexts, or should it expand to cover new message forms, new techniques, new contexts and forms of interaction between people involved in communication, including non-verbal communication? The advice from Wingspread, and the advice in many of your statements, is "Expand." We must enlarge the field of objects for critical study by first of all keeping speech criticism and rhetorical criticism not separate, but in perspective, for the two are not the same, although they do overlap. More important, we must take account of new forms and techniques—news reporting and broadcasting, advertising, documentary films, drama, music, the novel, non-fiction books, the news conference, and such non-verbal forms as the protest march or demonstration. Furthermore, if we follow McKeon, we need to develop a criticism of things—a criticism of the products of technology ranging from moon vehicles to toothpaste. How do these forms work? What are their dangers? What are their unrealized potentialities? There is a claim in Wayne Booth's paper, which I suspect is true: in our time, the rhetorical uses of such poetic and aesthetic forms as music and film account for more value formation than all the sermons, political speeches, and classroom lectures put together. Criticism should expand in order to examine the processes of interaction that are at work in all these forms; for instance, some processes regard people as objects, or encourage deception, or invite ambiguity, or promote distortion, or imply inequality.

Criticism also should expand in order to examine several levels of critical objects: at the first level, specific techniques, lines of argument, and images; at a broader level, a particular message in its historic situation, or a genre over time or across cultures; at a more general level, studies of campaigns and movements, for they reveal processes and outcomes not present in the lower levels. We need to examine, as the broadest object, systems of communication: for example, the systems of decision making at various political levels; the mechanisms by which news is made, filtered, reported; the ways in which institutions or communities function as speakers and audiences. We should be interested also in knowing what sorts of things are wrong with existing systems which fail to produce sound decision, or fail to engage relevant information, or seem to push people toward expressions of violence, or which are otherwise productive of disvalue.

A second major area of concern involves the question of criteria. How do we assess techniques, messages, campaigns, systems? Many modern rhetoricians and researchers apparently have thought that the single ruling criterion is the efficiency of the instrument. Employing the efficiency criterion, they have inquired in their critical and empirical studies whether a particular element was effective, and have concluded that the audience retained so much information, or moved a certain distance in attitudes, or was convinced or moved to act. Yet there are other important considerations: Was the information worth retaining? Were the beliefs and arguments sound? Was the judgment true or just or expedient? Was the outcome good? Rhetoric as an instrument of technology would not have to consider such questions, but rhetoric as a humane discipline or art surely must consider the moral, aesthetic, and civilizing aspects of communication. Critical grounds, in this case, will lie elsewhere than in the easy principle of efficiency.

Third, there is the problem of developing a sound and influential criticism of contemporary rhetorical practice. The fact is that very little criticism is written, and not much of it deals with contemporary practice; what is written appears in seldom-read journals—we address ourselves—hence, the influence of our criticism is extremely modest. It seems clear that we must find ways to develop contemporary criticism. This means finding and educating promising critics and teachers. What should they know? How can they acquire the needed skills? It means we must find new outlets for criticism—in the national magazines, the daily press, in broadcasting. Should some major departments concentrate on criticism of the public arts of communication? Should we initiate programs of criticism joining departments of speech, English, journalism, philosophy? Should this or that professional organization issue a new journal for the publication of critical articles addressed not to scholars but to the reading public?

Finally, I would remind you of a fact about our most distinguished predecessors in the history of rhetorical theory. They were reformers; they were against the sophistry of their time; they called for major revisions in practical rhetoric, and they provided the theoretical base for revision. How is it possible to call for reform unless one has a view of the better alternatives—unless one has a notion of the ideal? There is much to oppose in the whole range of communication practice in contemporary life, and oppose it we must—if we are rhetoricians in the tradition of our best guides. Our task is to conceive the better alternatives and do the theoretical and empirical work that could make the alternatives operative. Success in this task requires philosophic speculation, scientific research, and moments of vision.

In these reflections on the Wingspread Conference, I have not attempted to include everything that was valuable. There are ideas in the essays and in your rationale statements that ought to supplement or replace the suggestions I have offered. I have sought also to avoid repeating parts of Carroll Arnold's excellent paper. My task was to translate the Wingspread ideas in terms of the work of the three committees at this conference and to urge you to make this conference a turning point in the development of our field.

16 / REPORT OF THE COMMITTEE
ON THE SCOPE OF RHETORIC
AND
THE PLACE
OF RHETORICAL STUDIES
IN HIGHER EDUCATION

DOUGLAS EHNINGER
Chairman
THOMAS W. BENSON
ERNEST E. ETTLICH
WALTER R. FISHER
HARRY P. KERR
RICHARD L. LARSON
RAYMOND E. NADEAU
LYNDREY A. NILES

Rhetorical studies are properly concerned with the process by which symbols and systems of symbols have influence upon beliefs, values, attitudes, and actions, and they embrace all forms of human communication, not exclusively public address nor communication within any one class or cultural group. Such studies are philosophical, historical, critical, empirical, creative, or pedagogical. Their principal goal is to advance the knowledge of human communication in order to apply that knowledge to the practice of rhetoric as a major means of problem-solving.

Rhetorical scholars observe, analyze, and describe human communication not only as it did occur, might have occurred, or ought to occur, but also as it is occurring. They are active observers and evaluators of contemporary society and advisers of those who participate in rhetorical situations. No single scholar can be prepared to work in all areas, but each must be able to evaluate and adopt information from diverse sources for use in his special area. This means that rhetorical scholars must be trained not only to complete original research in a specialized field, but also to communicate with other scholars in rhetoric who have diverse competencies, to consolidate diverse information into systematic works, and to communicate publicly the results of research for general use.

Our comments regarding the future of rhetorical studies must begin with a reference to the social-political conditions in which they will be conducted. At this moment in history, we are compelled to view with great foreboding the character of public communication regarding social and political issues. Institutions in a free society are as good as the rhetorical transactions that maintain them. It is disturbing to note, therefore, the increasing evidence that communication is ever more difficult to achieve and in some cases appears almost impossible. For example, we believe that communication problems to some degree underlie racial conflict, anti-war protest, alienation of the young, attempts to suppress free speech, campus disruptions, and inattention to differing views. Communication problems are obviously present when groups are unable to gain an audience, open lines of communication, establish the possibility of persuasion, and thus alter belief and action related to their interests and welfare.

The pervasive sense of frustration, despair, powerlessness, and alienation present in some groups, and in other groups a disregard for, misunderstanding of, or unwillingness to accept the different images that people have of themselves have produced polarized types of public language in our society: an establishment rhetoric and a rhetoric of revolution. One may become more deeply aware of the divisions present in society and begin to see foreshadowed the type of rhetoric necessary to resolve destructive human differences by contrasting these types of communication as they appear to persons in opposition.

Establishment rhetoric reflects a proprietary view of rationality, narrowly defines acceptable social roles, and projects a stultifying decorum. The establishment sometimes means by "rational," procedures that are in fact *ad hoc* and ideological, and that bend intellection to the service of predetermined conclusions. Most important, one employs establishment rhetoric when one faithfully performs the roles assigned to him by the society; that is, one accepts the identity implicit in the roles one plays. This means that one must communicate in line with what is thought to be reasonable by society, use reasoned discourse, and conduct himself reasonably—that is, know his place in the social-political hierarchy, address the proper authorities when, how, and where they please, and be polite, patient, and non-threatening. This is the style of establishment rhetoric.

The rhetoric of revolution is based on an intuition, apprehension, or assumption of a true belief, a cause, and a faith. Revolutionary rhetoric is meant to induce religious conversion; its expression may be fanatical—certainly in many instances, it is frenetic. Revolutionary rhetoric, when it is not violent, insists, demands, prompts, provokes, or is designed to panic audiences into recognition of truth and justice and action in accordance with a particular moral view of man and society. Its aim is a redefinition of roles, of the identity assigned to those who would not only live but participate wholly in society. So, the black power advocate seeks to create an acceptable image of the black person; the student power advocate seeks to redefine the identity—hence the role and functions—of students; and, the feminist seeks to correct the view of women in society. Current among many revolutionary rhetoricians is the notion that action provides meaning in life; some of them are influenced by existentialism and mysticism.

The most immediate social responsibility of rhetorical scholarship in the United States is to ameliorate, insofar as scholarship can, the diremption that has occurred in our public language, to investigate further the reasons for that fissure and, more challenging still, the prospects for transcending it. We certainly do not hold that rhetorical scholarship should be subordinated solely to immediate social needs; but we do observe that scholarship which does not engage these problems is, to the extent of its disengagement, remote from the rending passions of this country.

Rhetorical studies are not in themselves the solution to social, political, or personal problems. They are, however, by their nature and functions relevant to the tasks of social betterment. Rhetorical studies are humanistic studies. They focus on how and in what ways man uses and is used by symbols of inducement; how man's symbol-using affects and determines personal and social decision-making, what values guide his conduct. Rhetoric is not exclusively a study of public speaking; its concern encompasses symbols of inducement whether they are expressed as speeches, essays, in films, drama, novels, poems, or demonstrations.

We believe that it is an encouraging sign of the viability of rhetoric that so many critics have begun to turn their attention to questions of protest and dissent, and to hitherto neglected media and technologies. It is not enough that rhetoric be based on an analysis of protest demonstrations, however. Rhetoricians began to study the demonstrations when they emerged in the 1960's as an important source of symbolic influence. It was the importance of the demonstrations to society at large which prompted us to study them, and not their inherent relevance to rhetorical theory, though that relevance has now been established beyond question. If and when social unrest finds new symbolic forms, we expect rhetoricians to help account for them.

The study of protest and dissent has revived the interests of rhetoricians in social upheaval, in questions of value in discourse, and in the problems of minority or anti-establishment forces attempting to bring about social renewal. The demonstrations have not only drawn attention to themselves, but have also raised our sights from too exclusive a concern with public speaking, thereby encouraging us to examine other verbal and non-verbal forms that may well be more persuasive and enduring. Applications of rhetorical theory to philosophical dialogue, film, media, technology, and social interaction generally continue to be made, and continue to show promise.

We believe that our system of higher education contributes to the separation of cultures, to the inability of groups within our society to communicate effectively with each other, and to the widespread but unconscious adoption of standardized ways of reacting to problems and provocations. In most institutions of higher learning, the student's experience encourages him to be passive and to comply with the wishes of administrators and faculty, in order to pass his courses (usually isolated from one another), total up the proper number of credits, obtain his degree, get on with the business of earning a living and take his place in a society already established for him. The machinery of higher education conditions the student to accept a conventional niche in a society in which honest communications on fundamental issues is less likely than is acquiescence in what one sees and hears. Conventional curricula and patterns of academic organization are partly to blame for these difficulties.

A most alarming weakness in higher education is its failure to make students sensitive to the ways in which they are using language and other symbols, and the ways in which language and other symbols are being used in dealing with them. There is a paucity of formal instruction designed to develop such sensitivity in the curricula of most colleges. For example, it is common for a student to take a freshman course in English composition, but this course is often designed simply to help him gain some competence in the conventional language forms, or to help him transmit ideas clearly, or—in the hands of some instructors—to help him learn to use words more "imaginatively." Few freshman English courses invite the student to consider what sorts of acts he is performing when he uses language in addressing a reader or listener, or what his instructor is doing when *he* uses language, or what his classmates are doing when *they* use it. Fewer still, we think, invite the student to consider what happens to him when language or symbols are used in the larger world—by his friends, his family, the newspapers, television, and movies. If he chooses to concentrate in English, he studies works of literature to be sure, but the way in which language is selected and ordered by writers and speakers and the ways it may affect his mind or his feelings are rarely discussed in such studies.

It is also common for students to take an introductory course in Speech or Communication, in which they may be exposed to some communication theory, may be taught the discovery and use of arguments, and may be encouraged to give some performances (public talks, readings, and so on). But here too, little attention is given to what happens when the student chooses and uses symbols, or what happens when such symbols are used in addressing him. He is neither helped toward an understanding of his own language nor toward an understanding of the language of others. For the student who elects to concentrate in communication studies, there may be some minimal concern with these subjects later in his college career. For the student concentrating in neither English nor Speech-Communication, the study of what is happening when he talks or listens is rarely available or, when it occurs, is unsystematic and superficial.

This means that the student seldom has a chance to stop and think about very many of the rhetorical events to which he is a party. He goes to lectures, hears some language, but rarely examines it or how it affects him. He reads books, but rarely considers what demands are being made of him, what claims are being asserted, what presuppositions implanted, what values taken for granted—and how he changes as these rhetorical events progress. He participates in class discussion, usually intent on demonstrating his mastery of a subject by advancing the substantive content of the discussion, and neither he nor his instructor pauses to consider the kinds of rhetorical transactions in which members of the class are engaging or the sorts of "reasoning" they are employing. He meets requirements by completing a curriculum that is described in language and based on assumptions that he rarely has a chance to examine. He engages in extra-curricular activities in which (often) winning trophies and getting things done is important, but not the rhetorical transactions of which his acts form a part. He sees films and watches television and listens to music and goes to the theatre, but often without thinking about what is happening to him in the process—how he is being shaped by the language and symbols he experiences.

Increasing a student's awareness of what is happening when he uses symbols and responds to them may be one way to increase his ability to deal with the problems in his society. If this is to happen, we believe that rhetorical studies—whether conceived broadly to include any transaction involving the use of symbols between human beings, or more narrowly to include only those acts of communication where persuasion is attempted or where a challengeable affirmation is made—must assume a more prominent place in college work and in the programs by which we prepare our future college teachers. While it might be presumptuous to suggest that the study of language and other symbols—the means by which rhetoric works—should become the heart of undergraduate college programs, it certainly seems appropriate to invite instructors and students in their college training to become aware of what rhetorical acts they engage in, to examine and discuss those acts and determine on what assumptions they rest, to evaluate their consequences and consider alternative acts and their results. This committee cannot here recommend a course or courses. (Rhetorical studies should include much more than classroom instruction. They might well include filming, videotaping, or recording for study the events happening in the larger community outside the campus, or examining the rhetorical transactions to which a citizen is a passive party on any given day.) We do recommend, however, that the workings of symbols and the kinds of interactions that symbols facilitate be a major focus of all teaching. We also recommend that the ways in which different people use symbols and define themselves by their symbols—minority groups for example—be deliberately considered in social and scientific studies as well as in what are traditionally called the humanities. If human beings by nature respond to symbols, and if man's uniqueness is partly his capacity to symbolize through language, surely the uses made of language and symbols, not just by artists and scientists but by ordinary citizens and by established social institutions, are worth a great deal more attention in higher education than they now get.

If these statements, "rhetorical" by almost any conception of the term admitted at Wingspread, can be accepted even provisionally, some distinctive implications for college teaching seem to follow. First of all, although the primary responsibility for the study of language and symbols may rest with one or two groups of teachers (commonly called "departments"), a concern for how language in particular and symbols in general affect their creators and perceivers should not be narrowly confined, but shared by scholars in whatever fields of learning symbols are prominently employed. If they share this concern, college teachers will see that students begin, early in their college careers, study which will lead to awareness of the processes of human symbolic interaction, so that they will be prepared to understand, evaluate, and use symbols appropriately in all areas of study.

If these changes are to occur, however, other changes in our way of preparing teachers and designing college programs must accompany (or precede) them. Teachers in all symbol-using subjects, for example, will need, as part of their professional training, to develop an awareness of how symbols work and how they affect, simultaneously or successively, their users and their perceivers. To assure teachers of the kinds of preparation they need (and to help them keep up with knowledge of this subject), journals and other media of communication concerned with the subject of symbolic processes should become more flexible in format, more varied in content, and more broadly directed. And customary patterns of academic organization (by departments, disciplines and courses) may need to be modified so that the study of linguistic and other symbols (their effects and the value of these effects) will cross the conventional boundaries of disciplines and of media.

Undergraduate curricula in the liberal arts and sciences perform their mission insofar as they bring students into genuine contact with nontrivial expressions of human thought and feeling, and insofar as they train students in rigorous intellectual procedures. Subsidiary to these two missions, the curriculum should offer training in pure skills or techniques only when they are essential to the accomplishment of the missions themselves, or where such skills obviously and necessarily derive from them.

This conference has recommended a wider definition of rhetoric as a discipline and as a field of human achievement. As a discipline, rhetoric is being taken to include the theories and methods of investigation pertinent to human symbolic inducement. As a field, rhetoric is interested in all symbolic interaction to the extent that it reveals such inducement in either form or function.

What implications for the undergraduate study of speech follow from such a broadening of definitions? Certainly, a continuing enrichment of the methods and materials traditional to the field. But we do not urge that departments abandon theories and genres simply for the novelty of an immersion in popular media. The liberal arts have traditionally provided a base for aspiration and criticism. They should continue to do so, for in their noblest function, they encourage a Socratic undermining of what is untrue, unjust, or ugly from a perspective created out of the interaction of social values, self-knowledge, and intellectual skills.

CONFERENCE RECOMMENDATIONS

The following recommendations, submitted by
the Committee on the Scope of Rhetoric and
the Place of Rhetorical Studies in Higher
Education, were adopted by the Conference.

1. The conferees encourage that the phrase "rhetorical studies" be understood to include any human transaction in which symbols and/or systems of symbols influence values, attitudes, beliefs, and actions; they

encourage individuals and groups to conduct investigations and publish findings dealing with many different kinds of such transactions.

2. The conferees recommend that although the major responsibility for instruction in rhetorical transactions rests with departments of English, Rhetoric, Speech, and Communication, other departments also bear responsibility for increasing awareness of rhetorical transactions.

3. We encourage departments offering undergraduate courses involving rhetoric to experiment with new subject matters and formats which emphasize discovery, participation, and application to the contemporary scene. For example, we suggest:

> a. That courses be developed in which various media—print, group interaction, electronic media, film—are employed as tools of observation and channels of information in the study of human communication.
>
> b. We urge wide acceptance of new means of composition. Students might dictate rather than write their papers, or present their writings in the form of journals, or act as each others' editors.
>
> c. Curricular investigations of cross-cultural, inter-cultural, and intra-cultural communication.
>
> d. Curricular investigations of how linguistic and other media of communication function in various settings, past and present. Such occurrences in political, social, or organizational settings should be observed directly in the field at least part of the time.
>
> e. Courses in decision-making through rhetoric might be organized around problem areas (war, poverty, racism) rather than media (public speaking, written composition, film, group discussion, etc.).
>
> f. Courses or programs investigating the bases of criticism and offering training in the practical criticism of popular arts and public dialogue in all media.
>
> g. The use of written social documents, philosophical dialogue, films, television programs, popular journalism, popular theatre, musical comedy, and similar media that use language and symbols, as subject matter for the study of rhetoric.
>
> h. Courses which investigate dialogue as an informing principle in rhetorical transactions. We mean by this not only face-to-face interaction, but also the idea of dialectic as it is evidenced in single works, in campaigns of instruction or persuasion in social movements and in the creation of proportions among values. Even rhetorical notions of irony and ambiguity are matters relevant to dialogue.

4. The conferees encourage maximum flexibility in instructional materials, design of programs, and assignment of teachers to promote comprehensive examination of rhetorical transactions. The conferees particularly recommend: (a) that colleges and universities not always tie students to the traditional system of courses, hours, and units, but experiment

with granting of credit for periods of full-time independent study, travel, or work, particularly for work in the community that requires the student to develop understandings about communication; (b) that universities offer expanded opportunities for independent study and research by undergraduates; (c) that universities include in undergraduate programs opportunities for students and faculty to collaborate on research projects; (d) that teachers skilled in using one medium (e.g., film-making) be assigned occasionally to the teaching of another medium (e.g., writing, public speaking).

5. The conferees encourage the establishment of experimental baccalaureate programs in which study will center upon (though it would not be limited to) the workings of language in a variety of contexts: in literature, journalism, interpersonal communication, intergroup communication, the classroom, historical writing, philosophical writing, and so forth. The proposed instructional programs would examine these and other contexts in an effort to enlarge students' understanding of the nature of rhetorical transactions, the bases and assumptions on which such transactions are conducted, the difficulties that arise in the conducting of them, and the ways in which language shapes beliefs and understanding of propositions and supposed facts.

6. Recognizing that habits of communication and attitudes toward language, toward symbols, and toward communication are often well established in the student by the time he enters college, the conferees recommend increasing attention to the teaching of communication and rhetoric—broadly and flexibly construed—in elementary and secondary schools, and they further recommend that more training in the use of language and other symbols, and in communication, be offered to prospective secondary and elementary teachers.

7. The conferees urge that in accepting students for graduate study in rhetoric, departments not impose requirements and prerequisites which are peculiarly departmental but not essential as background for advanced study of rhetoric as this conference has defined it.

8. The conferees recommend greater flexibility in the conception and execution of the doctoral dissertation. Traditional conceptions and formats have their place, but we urge that graduate departments encourage and support exploratory, critical, and speculative dissertations as well as new formats appropriate to these modes.

9. To encourage the furtherance of interdisciplinary work in rhetorical studies, the conferees advocate: (a) the support for team-written dissertations by students representing different fields of study; (b) the establishment of special degree programs involving various departments whose faculty members are interested in the study of language and symbols and their effects; and (c) the development of interdepartmental

graduate degrees in rhetorical studies, which would enable students to look at the same rhetorical transaction from different perspectives.

10. In order that graduate students may be better equipped to perform the tasks required of them on leaving the university, the conferees strongly support a requirement that students have practical experience in their field of special interest or future responsibility, that is, teaching positions, internships in communications activities, research assistantships, positions in community agencies as communication consultants, and so forth.

11. The conferees reaffirm the traditional conception of the Ph.D. program as primarily designed to train students to carry on research. Therefore, they support the offering of the Doctor of Arts degree, as defined by the Council of Graduate Schools, for those graduate students who seek positions in which their primary responsibilities will be in teaching rather than in research.

12. The conferees urge that departments develop special programs in rhetorical studies designed to meet the needs of community college teachers.

13. The conferees encourage the expansion of research in the following areas:

a. The theory and practice of forms of communication which have not been investigated as thoroughly as public address. (The conferees were especially interested in the rhetorical nature of such forms as television news and editorial programs, multi-media campaigns, political demonstrations, and teaching in all its variations. The conferees also felt, however, that to neglect public oral discourse would be to invite further debasement of public dialogue. When public talk is not taken seriously, it ceases to be serious. We do not require a proliferation of rules and devices for the management of influence, but we continue to need both academic and popular criticism of public address as a social indicator and social force.)

b. The theory and functioning of language and other symbol systems which influence man. (The conferees were especially interested in how particular uses of language create an image of the user which affects both the user and the respondents in a transaction, and in how assumptions regarding verbal and non-verbal behavior can be exploited for persuasive ends.)

c. The development of new models which more accurately reflect the complex character of the rhetorical transaction. (The conferees were especially interested in models which would reflect the complexity of the behavior of respondents and which would elaborate other elements which are now represented too simplistically.)

d. Intrapersonal rhetoric. (The conferees were especially interested in intrapersonal communication as a vehicle for constitution of self and perception of self, and as a means of gaining further understanding of the effects of participation in rhetorical transactions on both initiators and respondents.)

e. Rhetorics of "outgroup" communication. (The conferees were especially interested in rhetoric which, instead of teaching the techniques of cajoling or persuading those who are like us in background and values, teach us to speak across class, race, age, and cultural lines.)

f. The precursors of contemporary rhetoric and the potential bases for future rhetorical systems. (The conferees were especially interested in identifying and gaining access to related work in such fields as philosophy, linguistics, psychology, and sociology. Our present conception of the history of rhetorical theory encompasses chiefly the works on which the relatively restricted rhetorics of the early twentieth century were based. Fuller identification of sources would enrich our understanding of the present and enhance the development of future rhetorics. Interdisciplinary bibliographic projects are needed.)

g. Evolving patterns of communication within movements. (The conferees were especially interested in the changes in communication and influence which occur when movements face apparently irresolvable conflict, the ways in which conflict has been resolved, and the shifts from nonviolent to violent behavior.)

h. Expectations and potentials regarding rationality in human communication. (The conferees were especially interested in definitions of rationality that might be useful in the teaching and criticism of rhetoric in contemporary contexts.)

i. An ethic for rhetoric and continuing attention to the freedom accorded communication in this country. (The conferees noted that much attention has recently been given to the forms—and the dangers—of dissent. While such research should go forward, they felt that increased attention should be given to the public and governmental response to disagreement, dissent, demonstration, and disruption.)

j. Rhetoric as a means for studying the clustering of social values in various periods and places. (The conferees were especially interested in calling attention to the intimate relationships between rhetoric and values and to the sensitivity of rhetoric as a glass for studying changes in values.)

14. As a means of encouraging speculative, critical, and pedagogical work among faculty members, we recommend that university administrators and personnel committees consider such work favorably when deliberating questions of promotion, tenure, and salary.

15. Recognizing that the recommendations of this conference could and hopefully will result in a substantial increase in the quality, diversity of subject matter, and approaches used in rhetorical studies, the conferees urge the establishment of one or more new journals devoted to publishing not merely articles based on research, but speculative pieces, theoretical explorations, position papers on current issues, papers comparing the rhetorical characteristics of different media, rebuttals and rejoinders to other

published papers, dialogues, symposia, and so on—forms of writing for which there is not now sufficient space, and of which there is thus not sufficient representation, in our journals.

16. In order to provide wider dissemination of new and diverse concepts in rhetoric, at a time when specialists in the field are few, we recommend the exchange of persons among departments by means of visiting professorships, summer appointments, special conferences, and short courses.

17. Rhetorical scholars who, following the suggestions of this conference, expand the scope of their studies and thus enter new or unfamiliar areas, are urged to undertake advanced study under the guidance of specialists. Such study would be facilitated by the creation of institutes, post-doctoral programs, seminars, and workshops.

18. In order to develop in the general public a sensitivity to the workings of rhetorical transactions, the conferees encourage scholars to present their findings, when appropriate, through media which engage the public at large.

19. The conference encourages the Speech Communication Association to explore the feasibility of establishing, or cooperating with other institutions in establishing, an institute for applied rhetoric and communication.

20. The conferees recognize that many of the areas for investigation in rhetorical studies which they have identified, but for want of time could not pursue—particularly the suasory and other effects of language and symbols, the correspondence of symbols to reality, the nature of reality as it is represented in symbols functioning in a rhetorical transaction, the relation of the media to reality, the character of reasoning in rhetorical transactions, the meaning of "to invent" and "to create"—can hardly be discussed without reference to insights of classical and modern philosophy. Accordingly, they support and encourage collaboration between scholars in fields traditionally concerned with rhetoric, such as English and Speech Communication, and scholars in Philosophy for the investigation of these and other fundamental questions. Besides applauding the creation of the journal *Philosophy and Rhetoric*, they urge in particular: (a) the use of joint appointments in Philosophy and English or Speech Communication as a way of allowing qualified scholars to teach at the points of intersection of these fields; (b) the establishment of instructional activities or programs which explore these points of intersection; (c) the support of inquiries into philosophical questions as legitimate areas of research for scholars in English and Speech Communication; (d) the development of additional graduate programs combining work in the three fields; (e) the inviting of philosophers to participate in meetings of professional associations in English and Speech Communication.

17 / REPORT OF THE COMMITTEE ON THE ADVANCEMENT AND REFINEMENT OF RHETORICAL CRITICISM

THOMAS O. SLOAN
Chairman
RICHARD B. GREGG
THOMAS R. NILSEN
IRVING J. REIN
HERBERT W. SIMONS
HERMAN G. STELZNER
DONALD W. ZACHARIAS

THE IDENTITY OF RHETORICAL CRITICISM

Rhetorical criticism is to be identified by the kinds of questions posed by the critic. This position involves a shift in traditional emphases from identifying rhetorical criticism by material studied to identifying it by the nature of the critic's inquiry. Implicit in this shift of emphasis is an expansion of traditional concepts of rhetorical subjects. We shall no longer assume that the subject of rhetorical criticism is only discourse or that any critic studying discourse is *ipso facto* a rhetorical critic. The critic becomes rhetorical to the extent that he studies his subject in terms of its suasory potential or persuasive effect. So identified, rhetorical criticism may be applied to any human act, process, product, or artifact which, in the critic's view, may formulate, sustain, or modify attention, perceptions, attitudes, or behavior.

The effort should be made to expand the scope of rhetorical criticism to include subjects which have not traditionally fallen within the critic's purview: the non-discursive as well as the discursive, the non-verbal as well as the verbal, the event or transaction which is unintentionally as well as intentionally suasive. The rhetorical critic has the freedom to pursue his study of subjects with suasory potential or persuasive effects in whatever setting he may find them, ranging from rock music and put-ons, to architecture and public forums, to ballet and international politics. Though the subjects of his investigations should be expanded, his identity need not be lost.

Regardless of what subject he may be investigating, the rhetorical critic is identifiable by the nature of his inquiry. For example, self-persuasion or meditation, insofar as it is analyzable, is within the purview of the rhetorical critic; however, the construction of psychological theories or generating categories of human behavior are part of his work only to the extent that they assist him in the study of the suasory potential or persuasive effects of any act of self-persuasion or meditation. Both non-verbal and verbal behavior in a student demonstration fall within the rhetorical critic's purview, as well as the actual and potential consequences of the demonstration on the students, the universities, state or national political figures, or institutions; but the historical comparison of the demonstration to similar events or a sociological classification of the demonstration as a type may be involved only as they assist the rhetorical critic in accomplishing his unique task. The impact of a poem on receivers falls within his purview to the extent that he discusses that impact in terms of its suasory potential or persuasive effects; formalistic literary criticism or the description of literary genres are ancillary to his task. Thus, psychologist, historian, sociologist, literary critic, each performs certain types of work that may or may not be relevant to the rhetorical critic's inquiry. We are arguing that any critic, regardless of the subject of his inquiry, becomes a rhetorical critic when his work centers on suasory potential or persuasive effects, their source, nature, operation, and consequences.

SUGGESTED PRIORITIES IN RHETORICAL CRITICISM

The Committee on Rhetorical Criticism in no way wishes to restrict the creative potentials of the readers of this report. At the same time, we believe that some types of rhetorical study have higher priority than others. Specifically, we regard as fundamentally important that rhetorical criticism (1) contribute to rhetorical theory or (2) illumine contemporary rhetorical transactions.

1. Members of the committee are painfully aware of the deficiencies in existing conceptualizations of rhetorical processes and in the ways in which critics have contributed to theory. (What we understand by the term *theory* is well expressed by Becker in his Wingspread paper.)

Rhetorical criticism begins with inquiry. A problem with the present state of criticism is that full-scale inquiry is inhibited by a set of assumptions which frequently prejudge and fail to account for the rhetorical transaction. Much of our theory has presupposed formal platform speaking and has thereby ignored a multitude of presentational and transactional possibilities. This emphasis on discreteness discouraged expansion of theory to encompass a wide variety of presentational forms ranging from 1848 campaign songs to rock and roll light shows. The emphasis on platform public speaking also inhibited the critic's exploration in such obvious rhetorical transactions as small groups and confrontation interchanges. While rhetorical criticism was enriched by contributions from formalistic literary criticism, it nevertheless suffered from the formalist's lack of concern with audiences. This interdisciplinary relationship produced an emphasis on the speaker and his message and as a result there was little sense of a completed rhetorical transaction. What the speaker said and how he said it were seen as the culmination of the critic's study, rather than that lively interplay which is the essence of the rhetorical transaction.

Whether rhetorical criticism *ought* to contribute to theory seems to us to be beyond question. As rhetoricians we have obligations to practitioners of the craft, whether they function as senders or as receivers. Minimally, we must provide them with viable concepts and theorems. Whether rhetorical criticism *can* contribute to theory seems much more in doubt. Certainly, much that we value as criticism is atheoretical; by contrast, much that passes as theoretical involves uncritical applications of categories to cases. We will have more to say about how criticism can contribute to theory in our discussion of methodology.

2. We suggest that critics focus on the contemporary for several reasons.

a. Man is faced today with a number of communication crises which simply demand a major share of our time and energy. We find ourselves in an age of tumultuous conflict. To the extent that some forms of communication can contribute to productive management of that conflict, we feel ethically bound to discover and recommend them; to the extent that some current communication practices unnecessarily exacerbate tension, we feel obligated to expose them.

b. Changes in rhetorical practices have challenged our theoretical conceptions at their very roots. Confrontations, for example, have led us to question time-bound distinctions between coercion and persuasion.

c. The gains in perspective and objectivity enjoyed by critics of the discourse of the past may be more than outweighed by the contemporary critic's access to materials and his awareness of the distinctive nuances of contemporary culture.

METHODOLOGY

The foregoing raises questions about methodology. How can one contribute to theory? How can one illumine contemporary rhetorical transactions?

The terms "critic-scientist" and "critic-artist" signal for us two poles, between which are arrayed a variety of possible methodologies. At one extreme, we envision the critic acting much like the scientist: deriving hypotheses from systematized constructs, controlling extraneous variables, minimizing error variance, operationalizing terms, arriving at low-order inferences about classes of events with a minimum of experimenter bias. At the other extreme, we envision the critic functioning artistically: immersing himself in the particulars of his object of study, searching for the distinctive, illumining with metaphor the rhetorical transaction.

Current philosophical thought on the nature of knowing suggests that the "critic-scientist" and the "critic-artist" are not as far apart as they might appear.

1. The scientist proceeds methodically but not mechanically; he maintains distance from his object of study but does not proceed "objectively." His theories are likely to build on metaphors; the process by which he arrives at hypotheses from theories are likely to be "under-supported" by rules; his operational definitions are likely to reflect less than what he really means by his constructs; his interpretations (if useful) are likely to go well beyond his data.

2. The "critic-artist" may have the same kinds of evidence, but his reports are hardly as unsupportable as is frequently maintained. The "critic-artist" is himself a rhetor who, by taking into account his own audience, phrases his insights, analyses, and judgments in a way that orders or reorders the rhetorical event. Essentially, his transaction with the receiver consists of a set of arguments aimed at compelling acceptance of his case. Admittedly, we are hard pressed to indicate how the arguments are made convincing. One member of the committee talked of "romancing" the reader; another cited examples of the metaphorical prose so often contained in artistic criticism: Mailer's contrast between the wide-nostriled Chicagoans and the narrow-nostriled supporters of Eugene McCarthy;

McGinniss' characterization of Nixon as a man who could depersonalize his political behavior because he had plumbed the depths of hell. Another member offered what he described as an "imperfect metaphor": "We may think of the critic in a sense as a prism: filtering, defining, and analyzing the light shed by a rhetorical event. Not only the light but the prism itself is an object of interest. As the prism turns, different colors and shades are brought to our attention, each having a single source but each so fused in the single source that only the prism may articulate it. On the other hand, the critic is not an inanimate object, like a prism, with only the capacity for passive reflection. The critic's humanity is necessarily inherent in his work. His critical act is constituted of and by his choices and judgments. He chooses an event for study and is guided in that study by his own values and predispositions. He chooses, too, within the framework imposed by the nature of his study, as we have defined it, the extent to which his critical language will be laden with his own values and predispositions."

We believe it is both possible and desirable to join the roles of "critic-scientist" and "critic-artist." It is by means of a rapprochement between the two that the critic may most usefully contribute to theory. An exclusively scientific approach prohibits abstracting from the particulars to some larger class of events or processes. *The scientific and artistic approaches function in complementary fashion when the critic immerses himself in particulars and at the same time stands, psychologically, at a distance from them.* On the one hand, he acts empathetically as a pseudo-participant in the rhetorical event; on the other hand, he acts dispassionately so as to transcend the event. Theory is made richer by the critic's involvement in the events he studies; theory is made clearer by his transcendence of those events.

Although we would be content to see atheoretical contributions which illumine contemporary rhetorical transactions or theoretical contributions which focus on the past, we believe it is possible for critics to focus on the contemporary with theoretical orientations. Here the critic may select a contemporary case, raise theoretical questions about the problem for his study, or generate theoretical issues following upon a more clinical approach to his object of study.

The contribution to theory can take a variety of forms. The critic can show why a theory or theoretical principle or distinction is not applicable to a given set of conditions. He can show why other concepts are needed to understand a phenomenon. He can clarify a distinction or at least show why an accepted distinction is unclear. He can show how a theory may illumine a complex phenomenon. He can speculate about relationships among variables that have not previously been considered. He can provide a comparative test of two competing theories. He can show certain uniformalities or commonalities among cases previously thought to be dissimilar.

IMPLEMENTATIONS

We recognize the scholarly justification of all criticism, whether it be theoretical or atheoretical, historical or contemporary. We have been asked, however, to designate priorities. This committee believes that the following two tasks are of the utmost importance: the illumination of contemporary rhetorical transactions and the development of rhetorical theory. The emphasis on contemporary criticism or on historical studies which can illuminate the contemporary is in no way meant to denigrate historical scholarship which is simply aimed at forming perspectives on the past; rather, it reflects a deep concern for the pressing problems of our time.

The task of rhetorical criticism has always been a complicated one, requiring finely honed judgmental abilities. The task is rendered even more difficult in our contemporary age, as we come to realize that the profusion of media results in a new communication environment, where the quantity and variety of rhetorical transactions have increased. More than ever before, the rhetorical critic must enrich his perspective and analytical approach with the full range of insights, conceptualizations and methodologies being developed by his own and other disciplines. We also realize that the constituent elements which we take to comprise the rhetorical transaction occur in more numerous human behavior contexts than we have heretofore studied systematically.

The imperative we feel to study contemporary rhetorical transactions requires that we revise our present courses in rhetorical criticism, that we build collections of rhetorical materials, and that we generate greater interaction among students and scholars who act as critics.

CONFERENCE RECOMMENDATIONS

The following recommendations, submitted
by the Committee on Criticism, were adopted
by the Conference.

1. Rhetorical criticism must broaden its scope to examine the full range of rhetorical transactions; that is, informal conversations, group settings, public settings, mass media messages, picketing, sloganeering, chanting, singing, marching, gesturing, ritual, institutional and cultural symbols, cross cultural transactions, and so forth.

2. Rhetorical criticism should continue to examine, insofar as it can, contemporary rhetorical movements; that is, the rhetoric of the black power movement, the chicano movement, student protest movements, the women's liberation movement, and so forth.

3. As rhetorical critics we should undertake the examination of the rhetoric of such areas of study as sociology, political science, psychology, anthropology, English, history, education, speech, and so forth. For example, we need to make a rhetorical analysis of values and assumptions underlying theories of language development and behavior.

4. We should encourage team research, both intra-disciplinary and inter-disciplinary in order to provide a more complete rendering of rhetorical transactions.

5. We should encourage field studies where individual analysts or teams of analysts move into an area to gather data and undertake analyses of rhetorical transactions.

6. We should encourage that courses in public discourse center upon genre, problems, issues, and rhetorical functions.

7. Courses in rhetorical criticism should be developed for undergraduate students, especially those who intend to teach speech, English, and drama in secondary schools.

8. More courses should be team-taught with specialists from other disciplines.

9. We should encourage departments to develop a procedure which permits two or more graduate students to undertake a common research project leading to the publication of separate dissertations or of a co-authored dissertation.

10. The Speech Communication Association should take the leadership in encouraging and if possible providing for the common gathering of small groups of speech analysts who are working on similar projects for the exchange of points of view and findings. The association should encourage departments to provide expenses for their faculty members who will participate, attempt to locate and apply for institutional and governmental grants to underwrite such projects and in any other way possible to support such gatherings.

11. The Speech Communication Association should take the leadership in establishing repositories for the collection of contemporary raw data, for example, the video-tapes and tape recordings of contemporary speeches, publications of such groups as the Black Panthers, the John Birch Society, anti-war protest groups, recordings of any reflections of contemporary culture. The most expedient and efficient way to establish such repository centers would be for the association to designate various departments around the country and charge each with the responsibility

of collecting certain kinds of data. Each center should disseminate bibliographies to all interested persons or institutions.

The SCA should encourage public officials to make available their public statements for a national library of such materials. It is imperative to collect press releases and videotaped recordings of all presidential and vice-presidential public statements. The association should urge Congress to collect in videotaped forms all the campaign speeches by presidential candidates during an election year.

The SCA should prepare a guide to the holdings related to rhetorical transactions housed in centers for ethnic studies, folklore, and study of public affairs.

12. Reflections on rhetorical criticism initiated at this conference should be continued at the national conventions. The practice of reading papers on a program should be more extensively supplemented by a series of workshops. Discussions of papers previously submitted or seminars with a limited number of participants should be planned.

13. The SCA should provide funds for sponsoring interdisciplinary research projects as a way of encouraging the recommendations listed here.

14. We endorse the plan of the research board of SCA to establish graduate seminars jointly conducted by several universities and urge that the program be expanded.

15. State, regional, and national organizations should schedule sessions at their next conventions to consider ways of implementing the recommendations of this conference. They may wish to invite members of the conference to act as consultants at these meetings.

16. Critics should be encouraged to develop new ways of disseminating their findings and not feel bound to the writing of journal articles and scholarly books. Multi-media shows and films, for example, may be effective ways of reporting critical insights.

18 / REPORT OF THE COMMITTEE ON THE NATURE OF RHETORICAL INVENTION

ROBERT L. SCOTT
Chairman
JAMES R. ANDREWS
HOWARD H. MARTIN
J. RICHARD McNALLY
WILLIAM F. NELSON
MICHAEL M. OSBORN
ARTHUR L. SMITH
HAROLD ZYSKIND

MAN'S RHETORICAL ENVIRONMENT

We begin with the assumption that a vital aspect of man's experience is rhetorical. By this we mean that every man will find himself in circumstances in which he cannot act alone, in which he must seek to act cooperatively with others, or in which others will seek to make him act cooperatively.

From his interactions with others, man finds that his ability to share symbols gives him the power to meet his rhetorical needs with rhetorical materials. Because of compelling social realities man's consciousness of his rhetorical environment is expanding. The technological revolution in media and in traditional forms of persuasion have significantly extended man's inventive needs and potentialities. These changes are critical to his ability to share and perceive symbols.

In the pages that follow, we understand that the old concepts of *speaker* and *audience* or the newer concepts of *source* and *receiver* only point vaguely to the varied nature of the roles of interacting communicators. Likewise, the old term *message* is scarcely adequate to contain the shifting reality of current discourse and of non-discursive forms.

THE GENERAL NATURE OF
RHETORICAL INVENTION

Rhetoric's traditional involvement with persuasion about probabilities links it inevitably with invention. The subjects about which men persuade do not by themselves mandate an order to discourses. Invention, in sum, is not a product of necessity. It depends on an action of the mind. In more limited terms, so far as rhetoric is an art of communication among people, rhetorical invention is that aspect of the art which constructs its subject matter. It is important, in an age in which fixed forms—whether in metaphysics, art, politics, cultural patterns, and so forth—are under attack, to look at the world from the perspective of invention, taken as the generation of something new. In this sense discovery, invention, creativity are overlapping processes, or aspects of the process of generating the new. Invention (used now as the generic term) becomes in this context a productive human thrust into the unknown.

This view requires an expansion of most conventional treatments of rhetorical invention. Conventionally it has to do with the making of arguments by a speaker for an audience for the purpose of gaining assent to a predetermined proposition. The major shortcomings of this approach to invention are three: (1) It tends to rob the inventional process of its dynamic character and to substitute a static relationship among the fixed entities of source, facts, receiver, and goal; (2) it tends to describe the inventional process as though its energies were expended by a single unit, the speaker, in a single direction, the hearer's psyche; (3) and finally, it tends to assume that the inventional process is more the recovery of already existing facts than the actual discovery of facts and creative solutions.

In the conventional view the process of invention comes into play only after the speaker has decided upon the proposition he will advocate. He makes that prior decision on the basis of ethical values and ratiocination; *then* he invents arguments to make it appealing to the audience.

What is recognized in the revitalized conception we seek is the fact that even the ethical values and logic, which the speaker employs prior to "normal" invention, were themselves once discovered. All concepts and even all things in man's world were once—were first—discoveries. Thereafter they move towards the status of tradition. In any event, they continue to exist and exert influence in man's world only so far as men's minds and beliefs sustain them. From this perspective the core social process turns on the coming-to-be, the nourishment, and the evolution or replacement of inventions. Life may thus be looked at in terms of the processes of change and habituation which constitute it.

To create a description of the process of rhetorical invention consonant with this perspective, we need to ask ourselves the crucial question: What is required to explain the coming-to-be of the novel, the new, the "invented," and to explain it in such fashion as to aid one not only in understanding but also in participating in the process?

In the tradition of rhetoric we seek a perspective, overview, or promptuary scheme with which to examine this process. It should serve as a generative theory of rhetoric. The development of such a scheme is in fact a primary task of rhetoric today. We suggest two such schemes below. They are offered as suggestive. More important, we indicate here the criteria to be satisfied by them. First, the scheme should be such as to provide a place for—indeed to invite—not only specific topics but whole systems of invention. Second, the scheme should itself accommodate the interplay among systems of invention. It ought to provide a basis for communication among them. Third, it would even allow for—indeed provide intellectual space for—their respective efforts at self-aggrandizement—that is, efforts to take over the field. The scheme should provide a marketplace of ideas in competition, in accordance with the honored practice in rhetoric of determining outcomes in fair and free contests to win the assent of men. Finally, the scheme should treat its systems from the standpoint of their instrumental or other value in the processes of invention—that is, as invention-functional.

One such scheme offered as satisfying these criteria has three descriptions: (a) *formally*, as a kind of process; (b) *conceptually*, as an orientation or point of view; and (c) *analytically*, as involving separate constituents of invention.

(a) As a kind of process, invention takes place in a field of persons interacting, each necessarily from his own perspective at any moment, by communications. What agent or speaker or audience or subject matter or other terms mean is derived from their roles and interactions in this process. This conception borders the generative explanation not only of particular communications addressed to immediate practical issues; it explains general theories as well. Indeed, in its frame a general theory is also a particular—for even such a theory can emerge in the communication process as something discovered by an individual, from his own perspective, and "transmitted" to others in a particular context at a given moment.

Moreover, we should especially note that the rigidity of the distinction between speaker and audience loses its sacredness. Not only does the feedback process undermine this distinction, but also the interplay of various points of view is often more generative than a single person's efforts. Even when that is not the case—even in conventional speaker-audience situations—the "acceptance" by the audience of a proposition must often depend on the audience's reinventing the communication for itself, however subvocally. The distinction between the audience as active and as passive acquires a profound meaning when thus conceived as a distinction between the process of reinventing and the process of merely "soaking up" a communication; and it becomes significant also for learning theory. Being an audience—not just being a speaker—is also involved in the process of generating and regenerating one's self, one's beliefs, and one's actional stances.

(b) The world comprehended from the viewpoint of this process consists of: whatever creations from the past are influencing the present moment, that moment itself as the field of co-existing cultures and power, and the future as projectible and inventible. What we are suggesting here is a rhetorical way of looking at history—rhetorical insofar as the past exists for us only in its vital influences upon us. The past exists through the action of minds interpreting, applying, or rebelling against live reinventions of historical records and remains.

Ortega's concept of "the generation" is useful here in describing the "world" of rhetoric. Indeed, the very ambiguousness of the term "generation" is suggestive in considering the process of invention. Ortega conceived of each generation as an intersection of past and future, and as unique in its traditions and its purposes. Although different generations may possess many of the same ideas or symbol systems, the earlier generations possessed as innovations what later generations possess as traditions. The difference is crucial, not only psychologically, but also to the very meaning and force of the idea or symbol. The rhetorical world is just such a dynamic stream of influence in constant interplay and reformation, and accordingly inventional theory would have to comport with this dynamic quality. To adopt a determinant and structured theory would be arbitrarily to exclude too much, to be false to history, and to cut ourselves off from the infinite potentialities latent in the world of rhetoric.

(c) Having treated the generative framework formally as a process and conceptually as a viewpoint, we may now consider it analytically as a set of fundamental frames. The constituents of invention are: social conditions and resources, perspectives on facts, persons, deep structures, and presentational forms.

(1) The social reality of the present moment may be viewed in terms of the resources for innovation or the defense of tradition. One can explain the coming-to-be of a new event or object, whether a speech, a new model of automobile, or a decision to expand a war in Asia, by con-

sidering the creation in terms of the question: what are the social conditions and resources available to the inventing person? For example, what uses are automobiles put to in society, what conventions govern the uttering of messages, what understandings does a nation have about the character of Asians or the events of war and peace?

(2) A second set of questions: What are the materials and perspectives upon facts out of which invention may be fashioned? What technologies may be harnessed in making a car, what facts or interpretations of facts may be spoken, what political or military conditions may be used to ground or justify the invasion decision?

The levels of generality here are not restricted. At one extreme we would note the way in which a traditionalist and a revolutionary perspective would determine the configurations in which whole social "movements" appear. For them perspectives need not always be value-laden, even in normally rhetorical terms. They may rather be such as to make facts appear determinate and necessary or contingent and optional.

(3) What about the *persons* who will participate in the innovation—and the drives which make them vital or retarding factors in the process? Who will make, sell, use the car; create, challenge, assent to the speech; announce, administer, implement the invasion? Questions of such specificity may be broadened to consideration of such creative emotions as Bergson describes by which some persons generate fundamental insights into the nature of man.

(4) What is the *deep-structure* of the invention? What are the underlying relationships between motor, transmission, steering, and so forth, of the car? How are the parts, conceptions, and relations embodied in the speech? What are the reasons, methods, and results of the invasion decision?

(5) Finally, what *presentational form* is adopted for the thing invented? What stylistic features shall the car exhibit? How shall the speech be arranged, phrased, transmitted? In what manner will the decision be offered to those affected? One feature of this topic is that it views "style" as itself inventive. But "style" should not be taken narrowly. The relation between this traditional rhetorical rubric and today's "life style" must be considered. What happens to the concept of life when it is viewed under such rubric? The critical point about this rubric is that it sees what is invented as a manifest object which can pass concretely in fact or appearance from one person to another. Finally, symbolic systems *as* symbolic (e.g., Burke's logology) would fall under this topic, since the relevant characteristic of a symbol in communication is that it is the object which actually passes between the parties.

These five aspects may be considered as a generative frame, an ordering of all the relevant aspects of any invented, innovative, or novel creation. As such they provide a place of places, a frame of frames, an account of the origin or creation of all things novel, including rhetorical artifacts.

A major advantage and value of this scheme is that, while it is at a level of reflection above the construction of, say, a communication on a political policy, yet it does not put us as theorists in a different world looking out on the world of rhetoric as different from that in which we view it. The use of the frame of frames, or even thought about it, is "rhetorical." It treats each of the constituents in the form they have *as* influences in the process of invention and it uses them to find places for systems as well as for particulars.

In brief we have here a set of topics comprehensive and neutral enough to qualify as the place of places for a generative rhetoric.

A WAY OF CONCEPTUALIZING A DYNAMIC NOTION OF INVENTION

Let us consider now another overview of invention which we believe helpful. Undoubtedly it is not the only way of conceptualizing invention consistent with our desire for a dynamic, open view.

Let us conceive of a universe of arguments and persuasive tactics, and of galaxies within the universe which are formed by relationships and clusterings among the rhetorical materials. These galaxies have centers, which may be called world-views or stances or originating positions. One such galaxy may center about the Burkeian notion of root metaphor; for example, "Man is a brick," "Man is a machine," "Man is an animal," "Man is the Son of God." Another may concern the individual's perceived relationship with the social, economic, political world about him: "Others are trying to destroy our world" (conformity and identification) or "The world is trying to destroy me" (alienation). Still another may center in a political system's view of the individual: "Government is the servant of the individual" or "Government is the master of the individual." And so on. There is no effort here to chart all the galaxies within the universe of rhetorical possibilities.

The point and the assumption of this perspective is that inventional resources may vary radically from one galaxy to another. There may also be important elements of commonality or similarity, such as recurrent patterns of reasoning and symbolizing. These resources will include: (1) alternatives for symbolic roles for communicators, (2) alternatives for forming or transforming an audience role, (3) a broad spectrum of verbal and non-verbal tactics (including premises for reasoned argument, ritualized gestures, God and Devil symbols and so on), all intended for maintaining and stabilizing the world view and audience-rhetor roles within that view, or for courting and proselytizing adherents. The "age" of the galaxy will be an essential shaping factor: whether the world view is coming to birth, is developing in popularity, is dominating its population, is decaying in influence, and so on.

The discussion thus far may raise the question of the relation of this kind of overview and the frame of frames. For one answer, the following might be considered.

A man with a system of organizing frames, operating within a galaxy, will undoubtedly have strong commitments. From his world view the fundamental frames become instruments for rhetorical invention. The question arises, however, how do galaxies shift? How do new centers of commitment come into being? The frame of frames may provide a focus beyond existing galaxies, helping to bring new world views into being. Conversely in the perspective of a world view, the frame of frames may be treated as partial and, therefore, censurable. The critical point is the peculiar function and power of each. A world view is something lived in and by; the other frame is (ideally) a comprehensive set of neutral instruments or checkpoints for invention.

The point of departure herein discussed obviously does not provide an inventional system. What it should provide are "places for the places" in a kind of organizing or at least encompassing and perhaps even generating view. Inventional systems as such will result only from programs of research which will examine and illuminate the rhetorical resources peculiar to and common to world views. We anticipate that the procedures of both criticism and experimentation may prove useful within these programs.

We ought to recognize that the universe-galaxy metaphor can carry us only so far. Given the flexibility of view which we hope would be suggested by the figure, a person may "join" and "withdraw" from various conceptual frames during the course of a lifetime, and may "belong" to various world views simultaneously without contradiction. In each, however, insofar as he has a consequential commitment to its perspective, he may profit from an inventory of the basic rhetorical resources available to it.

Insofar as we are dealing with an infinite and "expanding" universe, and galaxies beyond enumeration at this Conference, our research must be selective and continuing. We must ask, just what are the most fundamental ways of looking at human experience, commitment to which results in significant variation in life style and social organization.

If a revitalized conception of rhetorical invention takes on form and substance, its pedagogical impact and its promise for instructional improvement should prove considerable. It should open perspectives on the rhetorical dynamic operating not simply in public address, but in history, literature, philosophy, and other disciplines. It should sensitize the critic to the rhetorical presence within these dimensions, and sharpen his perceptions and evaluations of such presence.

CONFERENCE RECOMMENDATIONS

The following recommendations, submitted by the Committee on the Nature of Rhetorical Invention, were adopted by the Conference. These should be regarded as proposals for inquiry rather than as "action recommendations" in the usual sense. They indicate lines of research and frameworks in terms of which valuable scholarship in inventional theory might be pursued.

1. That research be undertaken on the nature of invention in nonwestern cultures; and, further, that the interactions between cultures and inventional processes be explored.

2. That the parameters, levels, and functions of diverse topical schemes be investigated with a view toward finding an architectonic overview—a place of places—and that the concept of an architectonic overview itself be investigated; that the parameters, levels, and functions of diverse topical schemes be investigated with a view toward finding their generative potentialities.

3. The study of classical schemes of invention and the study of historical movements with a focus on inventional forces accompanying innovation and change should be re-examined in terms of the dynamic conception of rhetoric as discussed in the report of the Committee on Rhetorical Invention.

4. That inquiry be made into the problem of "producing" rather than "discovering" the universal audience or audiences.

Perelman's concept of a universal audience is obviously important in the search for rapport or at least operational agreement among diverse groups. However, efforts directed to finding this audience or to describing it fail to take account of the pervasive importance of invention. Rather, (a) audiences are made, not given; (b) there is no *a priori* reason that there may not be many universal audiences, although not in a single situation; and (c) most important, the task is not, as often assumed, to address *either* a particular audience or a universal audience, but in the process of persuasion to adjust to and then to transform the particularities of an audience into universal dimensions.

5. That research be encouraged on the inventional role of language in the process of transforming world views into argument.

The choice of language may be to a significant extent determined by the world view of the communication source and, further, may reflect the source's conception of the world view of the receiver. Language choices, accordingly, may be one indicator of the congruity or lack of congruity between the world views of participating members.

6. That the relationships between rhetorical and aesthetic invention be explored; that, further, those who wish to develop rhetoric's function as an architectonic art explore the modes of discovery in all areas, taking upon themselves the task of systematizing these modes, their respective values, and their transferability from one area to another.

7. That programs of research be encouraged which will examine the rhetorical resources peculiar to and common to world views. Priority should be assigned to investigating the connection between different life styles and social organizations on the one hand, and different world views on the other.

8. We endorse the concept of further interdisciplinary conferences exploring such relationships as those between rhetoric and philosophy, rhetoric and literature, and rhetoric and film, journalism and television. Further, we urge that the Speech Communication Association and regional associations sponsor periodically joint discussions between scholars whose work employs chiefly experimental methodologies and scholars whose work employs chiefly critical methodologies on theoretical issues common to the disciplines of rhetoric and speech communication.

9. That research efforts be devoted to the development of a theory of the structures of inquiring, deciding, and choosing.

10. That departments be encouraged to develop courses embodying a revitalized concept of invention as described in the report of the Committee on Rhetorical Invention.

Such courses will confront students at a time when they are most eager to establish identities and are perhaps most vulnerable to the blandishments of competing world views which offer identity as a concomitant of commitment. The courses should assist students in decisions to embrace or to reject world views; once commitments are made, such courses should assist students in relating to and becoming effective rhetorical participants within the styles of life implied by variant views. The courses should confront students with the implications of their choices and should make choice more responsible. Insofar as commonality exists among world views, such courses should assist students in understanding and tolerating other life styles, in identifying to the extent possible with the humanity shared by all men.

11. That we re-examine the relationship between "rhetorical invention" and "creativity."

CONCLUSION

After the National Conference on Rhetoric, the
planning committee prepared a final report of
the National Developmental Project on Rhetoric,
and submitted it to the National Endowment
for the Humanities on December 10, 1970.
Sections of interest found in the report
comprise this conclusion.

RESULTS OF THE PROJECT

The ruling objective of the Project was to develop an outlined conception of rhetoric applicable to our own time. We conceived of rhetoric in the classical, and richest, sense—as the theory of investigation, decision, and communication concerned particularly with practical, especially civic, affairs. Our central aims, then, were to revitalize a humanistic discipline whose theory and literature are exceptionally rich, and to attempt redefinition and perfection of that discipline as a modern method of problem-solving and decision-making. The eleven scholars who wrote essays and participated in the Wingspread Conference dealt with this ruling objective directly despite the variety of traditional academic disciplines from which they came.

The twenty-three conferees of the second conference were concerned mainly with the subordinate objectives: to discover implications for educational programs; to lay out directions and priorities for research; to identify, clarify, and amplify central theoretical and social issues especially requiring solution through better understanding of rhetoric and rhetorical processes; and to reassess and redefine the relationships between rhetoric and cognate subjects of study. Since the participants in the two conferences were not instructed to avoid each other's provinces, there was considerable overlapping of themes and recommendations. In the following paragraphs we attempt to summarize the most prominent contributions of the essays, deliberations, reports, and recommendations.

From the discussions and documents of the project, there emerges a set of basic themes and statements regarding the outline of a satisfactory contemporary theory of rhetoric. This represents a consensus judgment which may be understood as the Project's answer to the basic question: What conception of rhetoric is needed in our time?—or, what are the primary dimensions, terms, and problems involved in elaborating a new rhetoric?

1. The technology of the twentieth century has created so many new channels and techniques of communication, and the problems confronting contemporary societies are so related to communicative methods and contents that *it is imperative that rhetorical studies be broadened to explore communicative procedures and practices not traditionally covered*. At the second conference the committee on criticism declared in its final report:

> The effort should be made to expand the scope of rhetorical criticism to include subjects which have not traditionally fallen within the critic's purview: the non-discursive as well as the discursive, the non-verbal as well as the verbal, the event or transaction which is unintentionally as well as intentionally suasive.

This means that critical understanding and assessment should be brought to bear upon such objects as contemporary popular music which is helping to educate or otherwise shape the understandings of a generation of young Americans, news reporting and interpretation which are principal sources of public information about civic matters to be understood and judged, and poetic and dramatistic forms—film, drama, the novel, the poem—which increasingly influence attitudes bearing social consequences.

2. *Our recognition of the scope of rhetorical theory and practice should be greatly widened.* Rhetoric at one time in history was a method for investigating subjects and creating speeches or formal essays; in the Renaissance, rhetoric expanded to apply to the conception and explication of artistic creations. Today, in a technological age, rhetorical analyses should be applied even to things—the products of science and technology. Men need to understand and use the arts of investigation, judgment, and communication to help decide what new products are needed and to determine the real utility of products for individuals and society. They need to communicate their reasons and judgments to others by means of shared meanings, shared reasons, and justified conclusions. In civilized communities, the conferees said, such deliberations and communications are no longer merely scientific and private: they engage probabilities as well as certainties, values as well as facts; at every stage they are complexly public; they are therefore essentially rhetorical.

3. At the same time, *a clarified and expanded concept of reason and*

rational decision must be worked out. Some widely held conceptions of rational behavior have associated rationality with scientific procedure and certainty, or with tautological reasoning. As a consequence, that great area of discussion and deliberation invested with value and uncertainty has become regarded as an area of mere emotional commitment, or of whimsy and chance. It is precisely this area of the contingent, the relatively uncertain, in which rhetoric has had its primary application, and it is this same area that is the locus of most issues and discussions having public consequence. Rationality applicable to procedures of investigation and judgment must be devised and widely taught, so that rational decision marks our choices in the area of the contingent. Thus Henry Johnstone's Wingspread essay suggested that we consider "what is becoming of the concept of reason. Shouts and obscenities seem to be a rejection of reason. So do the non-negotiable demands, and refusals to consider proffered compromises." Johnstone saw in these and similar events a tendency toward non-rational immediacy. This same tendency prompted Barnet Baskerville to suggest that one of education's first declarations might well be a reaffirmation of the primacy of reason and reasoned discourse. In our attempt to perfect theory, he said, we "might well begin by affirming faith in reasoned discourse, not merely as an 'ideal' for quiet times, but as an eminently real necessity for the preservation of the values of democratic society—values to which members of our Association are presumably still committed."

4. *Rhetorical invention should be restored to a position of centrality in theory and practice.* In the major classical theories, invention meant the use of concepts and methods which guide and assist the analysis of subject matter, problems, and situations; the discovery of issues, grounds of agreement, and lines of argument; the assessment of propositions of several kinds; the topics and value terms guiding thought in various types of investigation. Invention was concerned chiefly with analysis, investigation, and proof. This branch of rhetoric has been largely neglected since the eighteenth century when theorists influenced by revolutions in science and philosophy dismissed *inventio* as trivial on the assumption that a single methodology—namely the new science—should be used by sensible people in all kinds of investigations and deliberations. It seems clear to us that methods of discovery and proof far wider than empirical methods need to be elaborated, taught, and widely used. Only a small fraction of the problems and issues encountered at all levels by people in their personal and public roles admit of scientific analysis and resolution. Most of our problems, including the great social and political issues, are moral, or humane; the analysis and resolution of humane problems requires the application of methods to uncover facts, to be sure, but also to determine

relevant criteria, to form new definitions, to critique values and hierarchies of value, to bring sentiments and feelings into relation with thoughts. These functions have always belonged to the art of rhetorical invention. This art has not been taught seriously and widely for at least two hundred years.

These four themes, summarized above, are fundamental. A rhetoric reconstituted along these lines will not be a technique for adding flourish to prose, nor will it be a pejorative quality in public messages. It will be an art of inquiry and communication, seeking to generate agreements among people and cultures on probable matters. It is founded on a recognition of man's rhetorical aspect—the need to find agreements through communication—and on the fact that experience presents issues and problems which are essentially rhetorical. While this art regards rational deliberation and judgment as the mode of agreement, it sees the necessity of engaging sentiment, value, and conceptions of reality as crucial elements in reasoned discourse. As an art of inquiry and communication, rhetoric is prescriptive in the sense that it studies the forms and methods which ought to guide human discourse: it therefore identifies and labels various degradations of thought and language; it examines and criticizes communication practices for their quality—ultimately in terms of their contribution to the aspirations of the human community. Indeed, the methods of rhetoric allow us to judge and order competing conceptions of "the aspirations of the human community."

SUGGESTIONS FOR FUTURE PROJECTS

1. The National Developmental Project on Rhetoric was suggested in 1968 as an analogue to the Speech Association of America-U.S. Office of Education Conference on Research and Instructional Development in Speech-Communication (Contract 4–7–070193–3157, Arts and Humanities Branch), carried out in 1968. At that conference, participants urged their colleagues in rhetoric "to undertake a program of formally defining the outlines of speech-communication theories" which, by that conference's definitions, include all phenomena associated with the notion of rhetoric. The Rhetoric Project has accomplished this purpose.

The completion of these two projects naturally suggests a third which would have as its central object synthesizing speech communication theory and research. Such theory-building and research have tended to be frustrated by a confusion of behavioral terminology and concepts and humanistic terms and doctrines. For example, scientists studying communication have developed a rich literature in a branch of study called "conflict resolution." It turns out that this material overlaps rhetoricians' discussions of argumentation and controversy. At this and at many other points the scientific and humanistic "cultures" need to talk with one another, develop common language, and contribute *jointly* to men's understanding of investigation, decision-making, and communication. We suggest, therefore, that an appropriate committee of scholars develop a plan for a series of conferences and other developmental activities leading to programs of research and joint humanistic-scientific efforts in stylistics, controversy and conflict resolution, assessment of varying effects of communicative environments, communication among sub-cultures, the rhetoric of confrontation, and the like.

2. While very large sums of money have been granted to institutions and agencies conducting research in the sciences, relatively little has been channeled into critical and humanistic enterprises. Yet daily events dramatize the fact that a high proportion of the problems in our culture are humane, not scientific. They involve judgment, conceptions of value, balancing of conflicting interests, and public communication of the merits and demerits of competing plans for social change. Inevitably, communicative practices and media are involved; not infrequently they are parts of the problem in question.

We urge that appropriate federal and private agencies consider favorably proposals to establish institutes which would conduct research relating to the qualities of deliberation, decision-making, and communication in such enterprises related to the public interest as news reporting, legislative deliberation, entertainment presented by the media of mass communication, and mass demonstrations used for purposes of social and political influence. To speak specifically, such institutes could train ten times as many expert analysts of rhetorical behavior as we train at present. There are literary critics in abundance. But there are very few critics trained to analyze and assess, for the public or for specialists, those communications and transactions that are essentially rhetorical. Such institutes also could undertake to assess the quality of the "communication environment," which is as readily polluted as the natural environment.

3. It is clear that the public schools offer very little systematic instruction in methods of rhetorical inquiry and communication, even though the normal high school graduate's most important decisions in public and private life are those we have characterized as rhetorical. Influenced by the scientific revolution and impressed by the advances of science and technology, we have stressed in public education the methods of mathematics and empirical science; indeed in the average school system, the typical graduate has acquired, through levels of courses, the elements of "scientific" reasoning. We do not propose to abandon such training. We do recommend that persons involved in educational policy and teaching recognize that the student's ability to engage intelligently and

responsibly in rhetorical inquiry, deliberation, and communication is essential to his adult participation in crucial decision-making situations. Yet a systematic unfolding of rhetorical concepts and methods is virtually unknown in the public schools.

It is proposed, therefore, that we examine anew the curricular objectives and materials in the language arts, and perhaps also the social studies, in the primary and secondary schools. It would be important to know whether suitable rhetorical methods and concepts are acquired by students in the public schools. We strongly believe they are not. We are inclined to agree with the frequently expressed conviction that our nation's schools have largely ignored the development of students' creative and critical skills related to intelligent participation in rhetorical encounters. Surely we ought to commence studies designed to find out what the needs are and how the needs can be satisfied.

4. Rhetorical discourse implies the existence of some agreements, and it seeks to generate additional agreements while recognizing the inevitability of differing views. Both the condition in which rhetoric is possible and the objective rhetoric seeks to realize point toward the importance of community. We need to know a great deal more about the nature of communities, particularly of publics, than we know at present. What is the role of communication in the formation of publics—from local ones to international ones, from specialized communities of persons sharing a special interest to a universal community united by overriding universal interests? In the past, government and its leaders, the church and its spokesmen, and cultural traditions played very important roles in determining the nature of publics and assuring their stability while providing room for open disagreement. But in the contemporary world, the influence of these factors has changed. The institutions which furnished our chief forums in the past have themselves altered. Other agencies have risen in competition.

Clearly, the United States "public" is difficult to identify. There are competing publics; there are cultures in opposition to one another; there are swiftly changing groups of many kinds. How can we identify the public(s) which should authorize public policy? What are its marks? How can it be formed? How should it be judged, encouraged, or deterred? What is the role of communication—of broadcasting, of political debate, of public ceremony, of presidential address, and of art—in the formation and stabilizing of the public? What, indeed, is the "public interest"? What is the public interest in relation to the "state's" interest?

We propose that the National Endowment for the Humanities support a project designed to examine the arts of communication for their service to and impairment of community; to consider the communicative practices of government and its leaders in relation to the communicative practices of other centers of influence; and to determine, if possible, the nature of the public and what is meant by the public interest.

THE PROJECT IN RELATION
TO THE PUBLIC INTEREST

The National Developmental Project on Rhetoric was concerned with problems and issues that are, by their very nature, related to the interests of the American people, both individually and collectively. The Project's central problem—the nature of probable knowledge and its communication—is a major problem wherever human choice is at issue and especially where deliberation on public policy and development of support for policies occur. Everyone associated with the Project was concerned of necessity with methods of decision and communication employed by people to decide and act on questions of practical import in which wisdom and value, rather than demonstrable fact and scientific truth, are decisive.

The scholars and teachers at both conferences were especially concerned with the relations of education to social forces. Both conferences addressed themselves to a question of grave import to education at all levels: does education unwarrantably represent social and humanistic subjects as amenable to analytic reasoning and apodictic proof rather than as subjects only amenable to practical assessments on the basis of values and preferences humanly held? Reports of both conferences answer this question affirmatively. Issues in the arts, in politics, in social organization, are not apodictically resolvable and the pretense that they are is a major cause of contemporary social and educational unrest. It was argued, especially at the Wingspread Conference, that to encourage expectations of "scientific" or apodictic determinations in problem areas where such determinations are by nature unattainable will foster disillusionment and distrust of the institutions encouraging so unattainable a hope. Participants in both conferences emphasized the need to treat such subject matters as topics which only allow conclusions found through choosing from among alternatives—all rationally defensible but engendering different human values from among which men must choose according to their own hierarchies of value. To approach in this way social issues, political issues, cultural problems, as well as artistic problems, would be to apply in these areas of thought the principles of *rhetorical* invention and of *rhetorical* communication in the classic sense. At its fullest, rhetorical analysis is simply investigation to discover the relative *values* of alternatives; and at its best, rhetorical communication is the presentation of the human worth discernible in any answer to any practical question.

Were the judgments of our conferences accepted, sweeping changes would be necessary throughout the educational establishment of the nation. In the humanities and in the several fields of social inquiry especially, "scientific models" would be relegated in application to those matters of detail in which "fact-nonfact" judgments are possible, and a "rhetorical model" specifying that human valuation is all that men can attain would control the analysis and presentation of most major data and issues in these branches of learning. To adopt such emphases in research, teaching, and public affairs would be revolutionary and would require ways of thinking, communicating, and evaluating scarcely noticed in Anglo-American thought since the so-called "Age of Enlightenment."

Calls for adoption of "the rhetorical stance" throughout the "soft sciences" and the humanities have implications of such magnitude that it is possible only to hint at the results of accepting conference urgings. Much literature would be newly seen as strategic address to evaluating audiences. Social organization would be viewed as a way of encouraging or discouraging conflicting interpretations, in one degree or another; implicit in the view would be the presupposition that humane values are best served by abetting conflict at ideational levels while constraining conflictive action. Politics would be seen as instrumentation for change rather than as "science" for determination or as activity in pursuit of fixed goals. And pragmatic communication would be seen as proffered interpretation rather than as fiat or definition. In short, to replace the "scientific stance" and the "analytic stance" with a "rhetorical stance" in humanistic and social affairs would be to effect a major cultural change. The fact that scarcely any among our thirty-five carefully selected experts dissented from the Project's call for this cultural shift is itself remarkable.

The Rhetoric Project has, then, produced a call for cultural change that deserves notice at the highest levels of educational and governmental policy making. The issue becomes: shall there be concerted action to "rhetoricize" rather than "scientize" social and humanistic study and action? Our conferences have suggested that intolerance of differences, exacerbation of disagreement, and distrust of the content of modern education are at least in part the consequences of educational and other public policies which imply that objective, depersonalized conclusions or "truths" are or should be possible, though indeed no such possibilities do or can exist. In the tons of print and hours of sound expended upon "the cause of the present malaise," one finds almost no attention given to the fact that decision-making in a vast array of problem areas has been culturally misrepresented (as scientific) to several generations. One does not see it noted that a possible result may be today's mounting frustrations. Our conferences asserted that cultural and educational aspirations have been for the impossible—"certainty" and "adjustment" in realms of experience always uncertain because value-laden and never adjusted because resolvable only by temporizing human choice. Our planning committee finds much "sense" in these conclusions by our conferences, much that is fresh and unhackneyed, and much that deserves prompt attention by statesmen and scholars.